GOOD CHILDREN OF THE FLOWER

For my daughter, Sybil

MAIN CHARACTERS

Immediate Family

Father: born in Zhejiang, sailor on the Yangtze River. Half-blind, he spent many years at home.

Mother: born in Zhongxian County, Sichuan, a shipyard laborer. Her first husband was a mob boss; her second husband was a sailor.

Elder Sister: daughter of the mob boss and Mother's first child. Sent down to the countryside on leaving school, she returned to the city many years later.

Elder Brother-in-Law: Elder Sister's third husband, a worker.

Second Sister: daughter of the sailor and Mother's second child; a primary-school teacher.

Second Brother-in Law: Second Sister's husband, a worker.

Third Brother: son of the sailor and Mother's third child. Sent to the countryside on leaving school. Inherited his father's job after coming back to the city.

Third Sister-in-Law: Third Brother's wife, a worker.

Fourth Sister: daughter of the sailor and Mother's fourth child. Sent to the countryside on leaving school. Once a worker, but now living in London working as a waitress. Married and divorced. Lover of Tang.

Fifth Brother: son of the sailor and Mother's fifth child, a worker.

Fifth Sister-in-Law: Fifth Brother's wife, a housewife.

Sixth Sister, known as Little Six: Mother's illegitimate daughter. Ran away from home in the 1980s and became a writer. Moved to England, where she married a professor. She later divorced and returned to Beijing.

Others (in order of main appearance)

Potbellied Cat: a neighbor, funeral organizer.

Spectacles Wang: a neighbor, former head of the neighborhood committee. Mother's enemy since before the Cultural Revolution.

Auntie Ma: neighbor, owner of a small grocery shop.

Tang: university professor and lover of Fourth Sister.

Xiaomi: Elder Sister's second daughter, a hairdresser.

Shouli: Mother's godson, a driver.

Uncle Jian: sailor on the Yangtze River. Mother's good friend during the Cultural Revolution.

Auntie Wang Guixiang: Mother's good friend, her shoulder-pole partner at the shipyard.

P: famous historian and professor at a British University, lover of Little Six.

Cousin Chun: another of Mother's friends from shipyard days, now a businesswoman.

Yueyun: Mother's roommate at the shipyard. A group leader in one of the rebel factions at the shipyard during the Cultural Revolution.

Auntie Mo: Mother's good friend, an old woman living in the countryside.

W: English, tall, in his fifties, novelist and CEO. Born in Hong Kong.

CHAPTER 1

I

Have you ever seen a weeping datura? We Chinese call this mysterious Indian flower a mandala, after the kaleidoscopic patterns used in Buddhist meditation. It has a sharp spine within trumpet-like petals and leaves that bleed toxic tears.

It doesn't matter if you haven't seen it. Just look at me. My mother said that I must have learned some strange tongue like Sanskrit while I wandered around Java or another exotic land in a previous life. She said I was both good and evil, both cure and poison. My mother also told me, "Now that you've come to me in this lifetime, my little sixth child, you no longer need the sharp thorns that grew over your body in those wild countries. But keep one sharp blade ready so that, when I am gone, you can face the world that scares you so."

Tenderness and ferocity are essential for a woman journeying far from home.

I have a passion for mandala flowers, especially when they're bloodred. The God of Flowers just passed by my window, mandala petals falling from his head like raindrops. My forehead suddenly felt burning hot. I heard my mother's voice but couldn't understand a word she said.

She was beckoning to me from a courtyard entrance, waving to me just as she had in the past. I walked over, and she took me by the hand. We were going to pay respects to our neighbor's grandmother, whom we all called "Grandma." Her body was laid out on a wooden board in front of the door and covered with a white cloth. Silken funeral banners were hung about her like sheets, while dozens of people gathered around. A lady all in black parted the crowd, threw herself down on her knees before the body, and began to bawl violently. Her body shaking with grief, she reached out to lift the white cloth as she wept.

Caressing Grandma's face and hair, she chanted rhythmically in a hoarse voice, "Grandma, take care on your way to the underworld. Don't exhaust yourself on your journey. Please accept my apologies and forgive my mistakes. Some rich people have come, and we're running around nonstop, slaughtering ducks and chickens in your honor. All a poor person like me from the younger generation can do is to set aside an inch of cloth every day to make you a humble suit of clothing. All a poor person like me can do is to set aside three bowls of rice every day to make Grandma happy in the next life!"

The crowd was moved by her words, and Grandma's family was particularly touched. The two families had long ago fallen out over some trivial matter, and the lady in black and Grandma hadn't spoken in years. It was generous of the lady to rise above the feud and travel such a long way to pay her last respects.

Mother, however, looked grim. She waited till we were on our way home to explain.

"That terrible woman smeared paraffin on her hands before touching Grandma's face so that Grandma won't be reincarnated as a human being in her next life. Now Grandma will be trapped in the underworld forever."

It was the most terrifying thing I'd ever heard.

This all took place right before I turned four years old, or maybe just after. I had long forgotten that scene, but it suddenly came back to me very clearly this afternoon. The image of the body shrouded in white was so vivid I thought it must be a bad omen. I never expected it to be a message from my mother.

2

In a room halfway up the hill near the south bank of the Yangtze River in Chongqing, Mother lay in bed gasping for breath as Yama chased her along the path to the underworld. Fifth Sister-in-Law knocked on the door without getting an answer, but she assumed that Mother was just sleeping. Later, Fifth Sister-in-Law called out to Mother and received no reply. Only then did she enter the room. Mother's face was ashen, and her lips were turning blue. Hurriedly, Fifth Sister-in-Law telephoned my sisters and brothers. Mother was staring fixedly at the clock on the wall. The hour hand was on three, and the minute hand on twelve. It was as if time itself stopped at 3:12 p.m., Wednesday, October 25, 2006.

3

My phone call reached me while I was working on my computer. It was Fourth Sister.

"Little Six! Something is wrong with Ma!"

I gasped. No wonder I'd had that burning feeling and heard my mother's voice. Fourth Sister was at my mother's bedside with Second Sister and Third Brother. Fourth Sister said that Mother would vehemently shake her head any time anyone mentioned the word "doctor."

I wanted to cry. My nose stung.

Putting down the phone, I glanced at my watch. It was 4:15 p.m.

I hurriedly stuffed some clothes into a backpack and headed to the airport.

Boarding had already started by the time I found my gate, but I decided to try calling Fourth Sister. She and Second Sister were each holding one of Mother's hands tightly, calling to her over and over again, while Mother looked around as if searching for something. She struggled to keep her eyes open. Her lips were blue and her chest sagging with pain. Second Sister tried to give Mother some water, but Mother shook her head.

"Mom's waiting for you, Little Six. Where are you? Do you have your ticket yet?" Fourth Sister asked desperately.

I asked her to put the phone to my mother's ear and said, "Mom, I'm just getting on the plane. Wait for me!" I could make out the sound of Fourth Sister sobbing in the background, and I could hear her whispering to Ma. I said, "Mom, do you hear me? Don't go—hang on!" I began to shout. "Mom, you have to wait for me. Just another two and a half hours, and I'll be by your side!"

The flight attendant and the other passengers were staring at me, but I didn't care. "Oh, Mom," I continued, "promise you'll wait for me!"

The plane had already begun to taxi. The flight attendant asked me to sit down and fasten my seat belt. I did as she said, exhorting my mother one last tearful time to wait. "Wait for me, Ma! You have to wait for me!" Finally, I turned off the phone.

The plane soared a thousand feet into the sky, passing through the clouds as it climbed. My eyes filled with tears.

I looked up and rubbed my eyes. My mother was advancing slowly down the aisle toward me. Then she was standing by my side, gazing at me with an expression I'd never seen before. She reached out her hand to touch my tear-soaked face. I held my arms out to embrace her, but an unfathomable force pulled us apart. As if in agony, she stepped back and receded out of sight.

"Mom, please don't go!" I cried. "I don't want you to go!"

"Please calm down, ma'am," the flight attendant said icily as she proceeded down the aisle, a tray of hot towels in one hand and tongs in the other.

At half past ten, my flight arrived at Chongqing Jiangbei Airport, and I caught a cab for the five-mile drive to the South Bank. The highway was dimly lit, and the traffic sparse. From time to time, the mountains would appear reflected in the river and the city lights would suddenly spring to life, twinkling in the distance with renewed intensity.

The taxi crossed the Yangtze Bridge and merged onto South Bank Road. Before long, I caught sight of the cigarette factory near my old home. No more than ten minutes later, I paid the driver and began making my way gingerly up the precipitous hill in the dark.

The area was a slum without a single streetlight to penetrate the darkness, and I could only just make out my surroundings. Filthy water ran through the open sewers, while almost all the old houses had been knocked down. Mounds of broken tiles and reeking garbage covered the original stone paths. Long, wild weeds rustled from time to time as furtive rats darted through them, the only disturbance in the otherwise dead silence.

I had to hold my nose to endure the stench. The hill left me breathless and exhausted, but a flight of stone steps rose ahead of me. I finally reached the top and made my way around the dark ruins of houses, panting heavily as I went. When I caught sight of white lightbulbs shining high above Compound No. 6 and a tent set up below, my heart sank. Almost involuntarily, I cried out, "Oh, God. I'm too late!"

I tore through the courtyard entrance to find a dozen people seated in front of a coffin that rested on a bed of white flowers. A large black-and-white photo of my mother stared back at me from an embossed frame wrapped with black cloth.

I froze.

Two men dressed in black shot out of the doorway, holding long strings of firecrackers, the red paper casings scattering amid deafening explosions.

4

"What are you waiting for? Kneel down and pay your respects to Mom," Third Brother hissed.

I knelt as fast as I could. Someone handed me a bundle of incense sticks and said, "Kowtow. Quickly now."

I kowtowed over and over. I recognized the voice behind me as that of Elder Sister.

"What are you doing holding that incense in your left hand? Put it in your right hand!"

When the incense burned down, I asked for six more sticks, carefully separating them into two bundles and explaining to my mother in a whisper that each stick was for blessing someone dearest to me.

"Heavens. Do you have to burn so much incense?" A coarse and reproachful voice came from behind me.

I turned around and saw that almost all of our relatives had come. There were even a few people from branches of the family so distant I wasn't sure how we were related. They sat at tables drinking tea and cracking open sunflower seeds with their teeth. I couldn't tell who was who, but every face looked familiar.

The hastily assembled group overseeing the formalities consisted of Third Brother, Fifth Brother, and Potbellied Cat, who made a living arranging funerals. My elder sisters had deferred to the men, not wanting to stir up trouble with their sisters-in-law. Third Brother said that Potbellied Cat offered comprehensive service that included setting up the marquee, renting floral wreaths, arranging musicians and singers, and holding the funeral procession. Potbellied Cat, who lived on Middle School Street, had heard about my mother's condition and made his way over even before she'd drawn her last breath. While my elder sisters were holding Mother's hands as she struggled to breathe, Potbellied Cat insisted they move her to a bamboo board in an outer room. He was concerned that Mother would die right there on the bed, which would be inauspicious for her descendants. Dying in bed was a taboo that absolutely could not be broken.

As soon as Mother was lifted onto the bamboo board, he began to change her into white hemp clothes and shoes for the funeral and asked Second Sister to wash her body with clean water.

Potbellied Cat and his two assistants helped Third Brother put up the funeral marquee and write the memorial tablet. They used a clay bowl filled with millet for the ritual rice, standing a pair of bamboo chopsticks in the millet and placing the bowl in front of the tablet. Potbellied Cat instructed Third Brother to offer starch paste to the Earth God at the local temple three times a day. Preparing the paste and paper horses and carts would have been very time consuming, but fortunately, Potbellied Cat offered a range of ready-made items that would save everyone a lot of trouble. He even had dog biscuits and club-shaped loaves, just in case, on her long journey west, Mother found her path blocked by vicious hellhounds.

He also had Third Brother stand on a stool with a pole balanced on his shoulder. Third Brother then had to face west and call out four times, "Ma, take the Great Westward Road to Buddha!"

It fell to Fifth Brother to burn the paper horses and carts to help hasten Mother's westward journey.

Only when this was done did Potbellied Cat let Third Brother and Fifth Brother place yellow incense papers and mats at the bottom of the ice-cooled coffin, and Fourth Sister and Second Sister cleansed Mother's face with cotton dipped in alcohol. Finally, they laid her down in the coffin. They surrounded her with yellow paper, plant ashes, and the statuette of Guanyin, the Goddess of Mercy, to whom Mother had always prayed, and then closed the lid. They draped a cloth of yellow velvet over the coffin and covered it with flowers.

Potbellied Cat looked to be in his early fifties. He was balding on top with a long, thin neck and a bulging belly. His eyes were narrow, but with his other features, they gave him the look of an honest and considerate man. Spotting me, he asked in a kind voice, "You're Little Six, aren't you? Would you like to see your Ma now?"

I nodded.

Potbellied Cat walked over to the coffin and removed the bunches of flowers and the yellow velvet. I stood behind him, my heart racing. He lifted the lid, and there she was. She'd lost quite a bit of weight and her face was drawn tight, but she looked peaceful enough. She wore a black cap like a Taoist nun. Her torso seemed disproportionately small, and her bony arms and legs only heightened the impression that her whole body had somehow shrunk. Even the black shoes with their white trim looked too big for her. Her hands were covered with age spots, her fingers knotted with bulging blue veins. I went to take her hand, but Potbellied Cat was quicker than I was. He grabbed my hand and said, "Don't, Little Six."

I shook my hand free and held my Mother's ice-cold hand in mine. "Ma, Ma, how could you go like that? You didn't wait for me. When I was at the airport, I asked you to wait for me, but you didn't. Ma, I was too late—*too late*. I hate myself for it!" I struggled to hold back the tears that were beginning to run down my face, and in a faltering voice, I sobbed, "I wish you would just wake up. You told me once that a person without a mother is the most pitiful thing on earth. Now I'm that person. Why did you leave me, Ma?" I began to see stars whirling around me and felt unsteady on my feet. The next thing I knew, everything was dark, and I started falling to the floor, limp as a rag.

Third Brother caught me just in time.

5

After I regained my composure, I found that the frosty expressions of my brothers and sisters had thawed a little. Fifth Brother brought me a cup of tea.

Second Sister told me that Mother had drawn her last breath and closed her eyes soon after she'd heard my voice. "As soon as you said you were getting on the plane, she stopped squeezing my hand."

So I'd been late by a whole two and a half hours. I'd missed the chance to say good-bye to my mother. She had warned me long ago, "Never cry when you are separated from your family, or you won't get to see them when it's their time to die." *I couldn't hold back my tears when I was away from you, and now your words have proven prophetic.*

My relatives sat around the table, describing the scene. Ma had died with her eyes and mouth shut tight. Her face had not twisted out of shape, nor had her limbs gone limp. These were all auspicious signs for her descendants. They said Mother had been close to her sons and that she was blessed to have had both of them at her side. They said Mother had made peace with everything that had happened in her life, and she'd had no regrets—or at least none she'd indicated on her deathbed. They said Mother had been considerate to her children by not hanging on and subjecting them to an exhausting ordeal. Some old people ended up paralyzed or in a vegetative state, or were stricken with cancer or some other awful disease, putting their families through financial and emotional hell for years. Not Mother. She'd just gotten up, brushed the dust off her backside, and walked on without a care.

They droned on and on like flies buzzing in my ear.

"Second Sister's right. As soon as Little Six said she was coming, Mother's chest started to droop." Fourth Sister's voice was a little hoarse as she spoke. "Mother should have been looking forward to her coming. Why didn't she fight off Yama for a little longer? I don't get it. And there's something else that's strange."

"What's that?" Elder Sister asked.

"Mother chose her funeral portrait years ago," Fourth Sister said, "as if she didn't trust us to do it properly ourselves—us, her own sons and daughters! I mean, I know none of us are half as conscientious as Ma, but what was she doing making arrangements for her own funeral?"

"Ma always liked to look her best. She'd only have been happy with a photo she chose herself," I said without even thinking.

In the funeral portrait, my mother's hair was short, falling just down to her ears. She was wearing the most ordinary of gray jackets over a white blouse, the buttons of which had been fastened with great care. She looked around forty. Her eyes were bright and pretty, and a faint smile played on her lips. She appeared calm and collected, but there was something about her that betrayed a stubborn refusal to accept her fate—a slight air of defiance. The photo must have been taken while she was working at the shipyard as a carrier and furnace stoker.

"No, that's not it at all. You need to hear the truth, Little Six. Don't get upset, but Ma didn't want you there to pay your last respects." Elder Sister looked at me matter-of-factly. "Because whichever way you look at it, you're not really a part of this family."

"Mother wouldn't spurn me," I said, brushing her off. "And of course I'm part of the family."

But the doubts in my mind were less easily dismissed. Why hadn't Mother waited for me? And why hadn't she let me say good-bye before she left? Elder Sister had touched a nerve. I had been able to see Mother on the plane because my keen mind had carried me through a tunnel of light to Chongqing. At that moment, she was already on her way to the underworld, but the heavens had taken pity on me and allowed me one last glimpse.

The sight of Mother lying in the coffin stayed with me. She may have looked peaceful, but she was thin as a matchstick, and her ill-fitting false teeth meant that her mouth wouldn't quite close. There was something about this excessive serenity that made me feel uneasy. My mind wouldn't let the image go, and I couldn't stop wondering how she'd come to be in such a sad state.

Why would Mother prepare her own funeral portrait in advance? What had been going through her mind as she took the negative to the photo shop? What had befallen her in the period leading up to her death?

Thinking of all this, I grew inconsolably sad.

Potbellied Cat, with his beatific, almost Buddha-like face, should have allowed me to see my mother alive one last time. What was he in such a rush for? We all die at our appointed time, but after a lifetime of suffering, are we really in such a hurry to go that we couldn't spare another hour or two?

Mother, don't be dead. You can't be. I was already alone in the world. If you leave me, I'll be even lonelier. I already have so few people to rely on. With you gone, I'll be completely on my own.

But Mother was dead, and without her, my world had fallen to pieces. How could I possibly survive?

Elder Sister reached out her hand and touched my arm from across the table. "Don't worry, Little Six. Because we don't have the same father as them, in their eyes, I'm not part of this family either. You know, of all of us, I lived the closest to Mother's place, but they still didn't manage to call me in time. By the time I got here, Mother had breathed her last and Potbellied Cat was setting off the first round of firecrackers to announce the death to the neighbors. They planned it that way among themselves!" She began to cry as she turned away from me to face the coffin. "Oh, Ma, you saw it all, didn't you? They kept your favorite eldest daughter away from you. What kind of a family does that? I loved Ma the most, but she never saw it."

"Elder Sister, let's get one thing straight. You were the first person I tried to call, but I couldn't get ahold of you." Fourth Sister was about to go on, but Second Sister cut her off with a sharp look.

"A saint to your face and a devil behind your back." Elder Sister took out a handkerchief to dry her eyes.

Suddenly recalling Mother's shoes, I asked Second Sister, "Ma's shoes should be size 37, but they were 38s when I looked just now—"

Second Sister interrupted me. "You think we gave her oversized shoes, don't you? Small shoes would be a mistake, but big shoes would be even worse. I'll tell you something, Little Six. You're not as smart as you think. And don't presume you can catch us out. We're your elder sisters. When someone dies, they have to wear bigger shoes. Otherwise, when they reach the underworld, they can't take big strides to get away from the demons." Second Sister looked at me with utter contempt. "You think you know it all just because you're some big writer! Well, let me tell you, if you don't even know something as simple as this, then you need to learn some life lessons from your big sisters. We should charge tuition."

How could I argue with them at a time like this? I couldn't when I was little, and things were no different now that I was grown up. Besides, I didn't want the least bit of tension between us while we stood by our mother's coffin. I pretended I hadn't heard what Second Sister said.

Seeing someone chatting with Younger Uncle, I walked off toward him.

CHAPTER 2

I

There was an empty lot at No. 6 where the old house had stood. All that remained was a section of wall with a doorway. The rest had long since fallen into ruin and had been supplanted by a white, six-story condo building thirteen years ago. Compound No. 6, along with No. 7, No. 8, and some cobbled-together single-story buildings, made up the bulk of the street known as Alley Cat Lane. The eye-catching condos had been even more incongruous amid the tumbledown, blackened remains of stilt houses, mud-brick buildings, and wooden structures that still populated the slum district back then.

My father was still alive at that time. The original residents had all managed to move away, but my parents insisted they were too old to go through the ordeal of getting used to a new place, so they rented a room at No.7. Wanting to do my duty as a daughter, when the new building was finished, I bought them a condo on the fifth floor overlooking the river. It had two bedrooms, a living room, kitchen, and bathroom. The old neighborhood's original residents were offered steep discounts on the new units, but their meager salaries meant that most of them still couldn't afford one. Left with little choice, every other household but two moved away: Baldy Cheng and the son of Mother Zhang the prostitute. In the case of the former, his sons and daughters had scraped together their savings, while the latter's son had taken out a bank loan. The other residents, new faces back then, had become old friends after thirteen years of living together.

I took Younger Uncle's hand in greeting. In the few years since we had last seen each other, his hair had turned almost completely white. He had come across the river with his three children as soon as he got the call. He said that, considering he only had one older sister, he and his whole family would of course attend the wake. He looked heartbroken, his eyes red and swollen from crying.

"Younger Uncle, you're the senior family member here," I told him. "Be sure to let us know if we've overlooked anything."

"That Third Brother of yours is very capable, he's done a good job setting up the hall for the wake," he replied.

It was only then that I looked at it more closely. A floral banner more than twelve feet long hung on the outer wall of the old courtyard, its dark-green background complemented by patterns of yellow blossoms, while a scroll painted with flying cranes hung nearby, symbolizing Mother being carried to the western paradise. Directly in front of the floral display stood the coffin, behind which her funeral photograph hung in the center of the wall, bound up with black cloth and adorned with a border of white and yellow flowers. Scrolls bearing lines of elegiac poetry were suspended from the walls, and floral wreaths lay on either side of the courtyard.

The coffin was wrapped in white silk with white flowers. There were baskets of white calla lilies set off by sprays of gypsophila, and dozens of white roses, mingled with lilies and white chrysanthemums, stood in plastic vases full of water to keep them fresh.

"All her life Mother loved fresh flowers. That was very thoughtful of Third Brother," I said, echoing Younger Uncle's sentiment.

"As if he would spend that sort of money. I had them delivered from a florist in the city center," Fourth Sister said with disdain.

She poured us each a cup of tea and sat down across from us.

Third Sister-in-Law dragged Younger Uncle away to the mah-jongg table. With him, they would have a full table of four players.

I wished I could ask Younger Uncle about why Mother had prepared her own funeral photograph, but even though they'd been very close, I knew I was unlikely to find out anything useful from him. Mother had understood that her younger brother was an honest man, but no good with conflict. She wouldn't have wanted to cause him any trouble.

Now, instead of sitting at the table with us, Mother was laid out in an ice-filled casket. In days gone by, Mother would often interject a few comments of her own, making me laugh out loud. She'd had a great sense of humor and a wonderful way with words. By omitting a syllable here, adding a pause there, raising or lowering her voice, she could create a great range of different effects, parodying any political slogan. Mother had been a true artist when it came to language, a talented performer, skilled at mimicry, and always vividly descriptive. But now Mother was dead. She couldn't breathe, couldn't hear, couldn't speak to me. She would never again take my hand. If I smiled lovingly at her, she'd never know. She'd disappeared in a flash, like a thief, hiding herself away in a place I could never reach. No matter how much I missed her, she wasn't coming back. I'd touched her hand and still felt a little of the coldness of her skin lingering on mine. I had to accept the fact that she really was gone.

But I couldn't. How could Mother just leave me to fend for myself? In those days when gossip could literally prove deadly, she'd had the audacity to give birth to me out of wedlock. She'd dared to bring me up, silently enduring humiliation and disgrace. A mother like that wouldn't leave without saying good-bye to her child.

Of course Mother wouldn't leave me! I was like some two-headed mythological beast, one head understanding Mother's death, the other refusing to accept it. The two heads fought so viciously that it was impossible to tell who was winning.

From the murky depths of my memory rose an image of Mother squatting down to wash my clothes. As the recollection grew more distinct, I realized it came from before I started primary school. We had just finished dinner on the eve of Chinese New Year, and Mother had to go back to White Sand Dune Shipyard, as the transportation team was working overtime for New Year's Day. I clung to her legs and refused to let go until she agreed to take me with her. There were no boats, so we had to take the path through the mountains. As we walked, thunder rumbled in the distance and rain began to fall.

I held tight to Mother's hand, afraid of slipping down the steep mountainside. "You're such a pain," she grumbled to herself. I dropped her hand and got no more than five steps before I fell, covering myself head to toe in mud. Mother tried to pull me to my feet, but I pushed her away and got up myself, almost immediately falling back down again.

Mother grabbed me firmly with one hand and sighed. "You always were a stubborn little thing!"

It was the first time I felt close to my Mother. We trudged on through the rain, and I lost track of time. She took me to the dormitory halfway down the mountain. The compound consisted of half a dozen three- or four-story buildings, all built in the simple, red-brick style that was ubiquitous in the fifties. We entered the third building. The windows and doors were in a state of disrepair, and whitewash was peeling off the walls, revealing layer upon layer of uneven, patchy paint, new slogans daubed clumsily over the old ones. We climbed the dusty staircase to the second floor, whereupon Mother pulled out a key and opened a door to a small room. Inside, against the bare left wall, stood two single wooden beds covered with mosquito nets made of coarse, yellowing cloth. The room also contained an old trunk and a small table draped with a plastic cloth and covered with an assortment of cups, chopsticks, and dishes. A few towels and damp clothes were drying on a line. Mother's bed was by the window, her quilt neatly folded on top of it. I opened my eyes wide and looked around, wanting to memorize every detail of the room where my mother slept when she was away from home. She poured out some hot water from her thermos and scrubbed me clean from head to foot. Next, she changed me into one of her clean shirts and tucked me in under the quilt, switching off the uncomfortably bright fluorescent light overhead. Then she put my dirty clothes into a basin, squatted on the ground, and began to wash them. In the light from the street lamp outside, Mother looked very beautiful, very gentle.

I fell asleep right away.

I dreamt that I woke up, and my mother wasn't there in the bed. I searched all over the shipyard, but there was no trace of her. I began to sob and cry out. When I woke and realized I'd been dreaming, my mother was indeed no longer in the room. The moon was just visible through a mass of dark clouds, its wan light seeping in through the window and bathing the little room in an eerie glow. Terrified, I lay on my mother's bed, drawing the mosquito net tightly around me and not daring to turn on a light or call out. The other bed was also shrouded in netting, but no movement disturbed it. Before long, Mother came in carrying two thermoses of hot water. She walked over, looked into my eyes, and wiped away my tears with her hand. Reassured, I went straight back to sleep.

Had it really been her, or was I still dreaming? My mother had always been short-tempered with me, and could be so extraordinarily cold it felt like a curtain of icicles separated us. She was like a stepmother, never doting on me the way other mothers did on their children, never making any of those little gestures that express a mother's affection for her child.

Sure enough, the next morning she had resumed her usual icy demeanor. She dropped the dry clothes in front of me, complaining, "You wouldn't have a stitch to wear if I hadn't taken your clothes to the boiler room to dry. You cause your mother nothing but trouble!" She seemed like she might lose her patience at any moment.

I told myself that even if it was only a dream, I should remember it always and feel content.

2

Now I sat in the courtyard to keep vigil for my mother.

Outside the courtyard, not a soul passed by. The night sky was a deep, purplish blue. No stars were visible, and the moon was nowhere to be seen. Thick clouds rolled in, growing darker and more menacing by the minute. I said, "I hope it doesn't rain. The marquee might leak."

Potbellied Cat told me he would go and take a look.

Suddenly, a shady figure paused by the doorway for a moment before vanishing again.

My nerves on edge, I pulled myself up and ran to get a better look. It was Spectacles Wang, my mother's elderly neighbor. She was fatter than I remembered, but her back was straight as a board as she struggled down the stone steps. She must have been at least seventy by now.

What was she doing here?

Spectacles Wang lived at Compound No. 8 on the same street. During the famine years, she had been responsible for the factory's scales. She'd picked on Mother ruthlessly, deliberately pouring out the river sand my mother carried and crushing her baskets—even refusing to accept her temporary worker's permit. Spectacles Wang was finally reassigned to a position as director of the local neighborhood committee, where she continued to denounce Mother as a "morally degenerate element."

For making things as difficult as she could for Ma, Spectacles Wang was rewarded every year with "progressive worker" status. The very sight of her was enough to intimidate everyone in our family. We took long detours to avoid running into her on our way home, always fearing that she would find some new excuse to haul Mother in front of the neighborhood committee and the police to memorize and recite whole books of political texts, write self-criticisms, and undergo round after round of reprimands.

Out of all of her tormentors, Mother was most afraid of the young policeman in charge of household registration. He singled her out for special punishments, filing reports against her and having the leader of her work unit assign her endless "thought reform" work. Mother was transferred out of several jobs because of him.

Spectacles Wang had often appeared in my childhood nightmares, and even when I grew up, I still dreamt about her making me stand in the rain until my teeth chattered. Whenever I came back to China to visit my mother, Spectacles Wang would hurl the same old abuse at me from Compound No. 8. "Whore! You child of a slut! You might be a writer, but that doesn't give you the right to look so pleased with yourself." At the end of each string of curses, she would spit on the floor.

Once, a foreign TV crew came to film a special about me coming home to see my family and wanted to get shots of the entire street. Spectacles Wang was eating her lunch on a low wooden stool in Compound No. 8. Spotting us, she unleashed her huge yellow dog, urging him to bite us and interrupt the filming. The director went over to complain and was struck on the head by her bowl of rice congee.

In a stern and self-righteous tone, she proclaimed, "The lessons of history should be learned. It's the east wind that prevails over the west wind, not the other way around. Bring as many Western hotshots as you like. I, Madam Wang, won't be taken in!"

The final cut of the TV show includes a shot of Spectacles Wang with her brown plastic glasses and white hair, gesturing contemptuously with her chopsticks. A smile plays across her lips as she speaks. "Go on, film then, you son of a bitch. I'm not falling for your nonsense. You might think she's made something of herself, but she's still the same in the eyes of the revolutionary masses!"

She was right. I am the same.

That day during the shoot, I told the interviewer that, whenever I pick up my pen to write, I am always that little girl from the slums on the south bank of the Yangtze River. How many viewers knew what I was even talking about? And who among them could really comprehend what it meant?

My mother understood. Every year without fail, she would go to the temple. She would light a seven-star lamp, kneel down piously on the prayer mat, and chant: "Bodhisattva, bless Little Six. Give her lilies and mandalas. Give her the power of the Yangtze River. Give her the clouds and mists of Wushan Mountain. Give her my heart, my life. May her misfortunes turn into blessings. May a hundred paths be opened to her wherever she goes, and let her continue unhindered in whatever she does."

Wreaths piled up on either side of the courtyard entrance until there was nowhere left to put them, and then they began to amass along the wall. The names on the wreaths seemed unfamiliar at first glance, but then memories began to surface. Mother had hardly had any friends while she was alive, so I was surprised to find so many coming out of the woodwork now that she was dead. I ran my eyes over the dedications on the wreaths. All six of us children had lain a wreath, as had most of our friends and family. Many of the unfamiliar names seemed to be my mother's fellow workers from her days at the shipyard. The neighbors had also sent a wreath, a big one, upon which a long list of names was intricately inscribed with a fine calligraphy brush. Oddly enough, Spectacles Wang's name was among them.

Auntie Ma, one of the neighbors, happened to be nearby, so I asked her about it. Seeing the perplexed look on my face, she said, "It was just two yuan from each person on the street. Who would go to the hassle of trying to get out of it? Even if they had, I'd have insisted they cough up their share."

After the Gang of Four fell from power in 1976, Communist Party policy began to change every few years. A few families on our street made a small fortune by opening hot pot restaurants, although once they'd made their money, they moved out of the slums as fast as they could. Others became regular blood donors, making ends meet by tightening their belts. Still others left to start small businesses in other parts of the country, wanting nothing more to do with the old place. Quite a few girls left for Shenzhen or Hainan. The ones that did well came home decked out in gold and jade, buying black-and-white TV sets for their parents. The ones that didn't simply disappeared.

Auntie Ma had lived in our compound for a long time. Though blind in one eye since birth, she worked as a porter in a plastics factory, while her husband worked on the boats. Her son earned a little money and bought them a small, two-story house. It sat at the end of Middle School Street, a prime location, so Auntie Ma opened a little store, installed a pay phone, and business was soon booming.

In those days, nobody had anything but praise for Deng Xiaoping. With people's sights set firmly on making money, there was a lot less political antagonism. You rarely heard about trouble, and saw even less. Times were peaceful. Spectacles Wang's power waned.

Back then, when the original Compound No. 6 was still standing, Spectacles Wang's husband and three of her sons began to have debilitating muscle spasms. One after the other, they started walking around with their fists clenched and their necks twisted sideways, their eyes frozen into a terrifying mask, until finally their throats clamped shut and they suffocated. The youngest son had better luck. By the age of fifteen, he still showed no signs of having inherited his father's illness. He ran away, never to return, as if fleeing the God of Pestilence himself.

Left alone, Spectacles Wang moved in with Auntie Shi, whose husband had died from a cerebral hemorrhage. Auntie Shi's home consisted of a single room at the far end of a shared kitchen. Its west-facing windows allowed a distant view of the ferries on the Yangtze at Turtle Rock and Marble Rock.

Spectacles Wang and Auntie Shi were like two peas in a pod. Every day they'd invite people over to gamble and curse men. They were reasonably lucky, usually winning enough to cover their daily expenses. When they lost, as happened from time to time, they would drink herbal wine, and strains of Sichuan opera would waft from their little room by the river. Spectacles Wang would sing the part of the young nun. *"His eyes watching me, my eyes peeking at him. Him and me, me and him. It all began in that one little moment."*

Auntie Shi would join in at a higher register. *"You fool! How could that marriage ever be? We'll die in front of Yama's palace! Let him crush us in a mortar. Let him go to work with his saw. Let him grind us on a millstone. Let him fry us in a cauldron of boiling oil!"*

Finally, they would belt out in unison, *"Alas, let him go! Alas, let him go!"*

But before long, they began to argue, and Auntie Shi kicked Spectacles Wang out. Spectacles Wang scooped up her bedroll in her arms and stormed out with her head held high. Everyone in the shared kitchen could hear Auntie Shi crying to herself, "This is my fate, to be treated like dirt! Chickens in the stew pot have better prospects!" When she had worked herself up into a real state, she began to wail that her son and his wife were coming back to live with her. She should be happy, she said, but she just couldn't muster any enthusiasm. It was such a shitty little room, she howled. In winter, you froze. In summer, you felt like you'd been hung out in the sun like a dead tiger. There was just no end in sight.

When my mother heard Auntie Shi, tears welled up and streamed down her face. One of the coal briquettes she'd been feeding into the stove tumbled out of her hands and shattered on the floor, followed closely by another.

"Here you go, Ma," I said, handing her a handkerchief.

"Look at your hopeless ma. What am I crying for? I won't cry." She took the handkerchief, but her tears flowed all the more profusely.

My mother didn't even like the old hag, and yet she had cried for her. Why? The eighteen-year-old girl I was spent her days thinking of nothing but getting into college and moving far away. She couldn't be bothered to find out what her mother was feeling.

3

I went up to the fifth floor by myself.

I was out of breath and pushed the door open. The guests' coats were piled haphazardly in the living room, but no one was there. I nudged open the first door on the right and walked in.

It was my mother's bedroom. On the right was an imposing wardrobe with three doors, and on the left an old-fashioned dresser with five drawers, on top of which perched an eighteen-inch television draped with a blue cloth. Beside the dresser were two stools my father had made, and on top sat three old wooden chests partially hidden by a sheet of red sackcloth. The double bed facing the door had a shiny black, heart-shaped headboard, the luster of which seemed particularly pronounced against the white wall. The old wicker chair by the bed was stacked high with quilts and sheets. My mother used to sit there waiting for me, staring at the door. Every time she saw me come in, she'd say, "Oh, my Little Six has come back! Be a good girl and come sit with your mother."

I would let my suitcase drop to the floor and walk over, a smile spreading across my face.

My mother wasn't there now.

I moved the quilts into the wardrobe and sat on the edge of the bed. My mother looked at me sadly from the wicker chair, too tired to fully open her eyes. I reached out to her, but my hand met with empty space. I got up to touch the chair. Its yellowing bamboo wicker was worn and split in several places, but still remarkably strong, just like my mother's hand. It even seemed to retain some of her warmth. I took a deep breath. The room was full of her smell, her voice, the sound of her rare laughter and equally rare crying—the latter so uncommon I'd hardly ever heard it. I felt enveloped by it all. There was the smell of death too, of course, hanging heavy in the air. I stood up, drinking in every detail around me. Right there, out on the balcony, Death floated on the wind, rattled the door.

I walked over, and Death moved swiftly aside. The rain blew sideways into the room in fine threads. A quilt and some sheets had been left in a ball. They were damp in places, presumably from where my mother had wet herself as the end came. Her clothes were there too, lying wrinkled on the floor—a floral cotton top and navy-blue, calf-length trousers, faded from many washings. I held them close to me for comfort. After a couple of minutes, I neatly folded the clothes and sheets, then rolled the quilt up and wrapped it in a plastic sheet. I placed it all carefully in the corner of the balcony.

The thunder began to rumble loudly, and lightning flashed in the distance. My mother would always say, "I hope it rains hard. Heavy rain's better than light rain. Once it's finished, that's it. I hate when it drizzles for days on end." She would lie in bed, looking out at the sky through the window, and when I left, she would make sure I took an umbrella. But my mother was no longer there.

Father's funeral portrait still hung above the top left corner of the headboard, his eyes gazing fixedly into the distance. If a child without a father goes through life blind, then a child without a mother must go through life in despair, twice as blind.

I felt as if my father were slowly turning toward me—like he had something to say. As I stepped closer to the portrait, a cold wind gusted in, the curtains fluttering. I rushed over to shut the balcony door, then turned back to my father. He was no longer looking at me.

4

Out in the corridor, I leaned over the railing to check on the courtyard below. The clear plastic marquee was securely fastened from top to bottom, holding out against the rain. The guests were still sitting there playing mah-jongg.

The air felt much clearer now, but sweat still clung to my skin. I brought my own towel and soap into the bathroom, turned on the water heater, and took a quick shower. From the bathroom window, I could see the houses dotted across the mountainside that sloped down to the river. Their bright lights huddled together in some areas but were more scattered in others. I'd known this place since I was a child, but now, with my mother gone, it looked somehow different, foreign. The tears began to fall once more. I dried my body and eyes with my towel and quickly dressed.

Just as I went back into Mother's bedroom, Fourth Sister strode in. She wore a wide-brimmed black hat, a black blouse, and a tweed skirt. She was tall to begin with, but the outfit made her look even taller. I wondered what she—the great beauty in the family—was doing dressed up at this late hour. She looked surprised and more than a little puzzled to see me.

"Where are you sleeping?" she asked.

"I'm going to sleep in Ma's bed."

She knitted her brow.

"The bedding's all been changed, hasn't it?"

"Yes, but aren't you afraid?"

"Afraid of Ma?" I asked.

Embarrassed, Fourth Sister changed the subject. She said that she had accidentally let her tears fall on Mother in her last moments and now she wouldn't be able to dream of her. Not being able to dream of Mother made her feel like there was a rock in her heart. She was furious with herself and exhausted from desperate kowtowing to a multitude of spirits and bodhisattvas. Was there to be no release for her?

Fourth Sister began to talk about old Auntie Chen, the lady who'd lived across from us in the compound where we grew up. When Auntie Chen died, her son, a model of filial piety, also got his tears on the burial robes. They said that even if he had the power to move mountains, he'd still never be able to see his mother again. "Little Six, you didn't get any tears on Ma when they opened her coffin, did you? If you get so much as half a teardrop on the coffin, you'll lose the chance to see Ma again too."

I said I didn't think I had.

I opened Mother's wardrobe to look for something to wear to bed, but all I could find was one of my mother's old undershirts. I changed into one before turning back around.

Having removed her hat, Fourth Sister was peering at her face in the mirror, examining some unsightly dark patches on her cheeks. She headed off my question by explaining that she'd been undergoing laser treatment for freckles since her return from London a few weeks prior. She had also been using some kind of Chinese herbal cream. The treatments were expensive, but the doctor promised he'd keep at it until the blemishes were gone.

I looked at the outline of Fourth Sister's back. A figure-hugging black sweater and tweed skirt wrapped around her girlish figure, accentuating her waist. Her stylish outfit was completed by a pair of knee-high, black leather boots.

I got into bed, making myself comfortable on the right side.

Whenever I stayed at the house on my visits to Chongqing, I always slept on my mother's right. Tonight I would do the same. Once Fourth

Sister had finished getting ready for bed, she took the left side and turned out the light.

The rain had stopped. The water that had accumulated in the plastic awning over the balcony fell drop by drop over the edge with a loud splashing sound. The fluorescent light from the living room shone in through the cracks around the door, and lights from the middle school on the mountainside seeped in through the curtains, faintly illuminating every corner of Mother's room. The old, yellowing New Year picture fixed to the back of the door caught my eye. In it, a pair of chubby-faced children, a boy and a girl, held aloft a vase of flowers and a colored lantern, offering wishes for a bountiful year. One year, my mother had told me over the phone that she'd bought a very festive poster and stuck it up on the door. "You can see it when you come back for New Year, my little daughter."

Which year it was I couldn't recall, but I was certain I hadn't come home for the holiday. How many years had it been since I last came home for New Year? Ten? Twenty? Maybe more. Mother must have longed to see me every time it came around. She must have stood on that balcony, watching for my distant figure on the long flight of sloping stone steps. She must have been so disappointed not to see me, yet she never once complained.

Just then, Fourth Sister nudged my shoulder, "You're in touch with him, aren't you? We need to talk about how that jerk has been treating me . . ."

I pushed her hand away, but she was insistent.

"Come on! Just for a few minutes."

I shook my head to say I didn't feel like talking.

5

Two more tables of mah-jongg players had joined the throng in the courtyard below. Others sat around offering advice, crowding the tables, which were covered with one-, two-, and half-yuan notes, the lateness of the hour apparently doing nothing to deter the competitive spirit of the assembled relatives. Some of the lightbulbs that had been hung in strings from the building had gone out, but the remaining ones were more than enough to keep the place brightly lit.

Potbellied Cat was nothing if not conscientious. He came upstairs to inspect the rainwater that had accumulated on the plastic awning. He used a bamboo pole to give the awning a good shove and let the water run off, reducing the weight on the thin plastic sheet.

The white building they'd constructed on the ruins of Compound No. 6 had never found its way into my dreams. In fact, 90 percent of my dreams seemed to be about old Compound No. 6. My sleeping mind is sharply honed, deftly penetrating the earth from some other point in space and time, seeking out and sinking into Compound No. 6, the place that is gone, never to return. Each time, I pause before the heavy double doors and push on them with the strength of a baby suckling at its mother's breast. The doors creak as they swing open.

The courtyard is overgrown with moss, on top of which are arranged a number of wooden buckets and flowerpots. Laundry hangs overhead on bamboo poles. Noise spills out of kitchens large and small, the families all busy washing rice and vegetables for dinner. An old woman with bound feet sits in the main hall, her eyes half-closed as she knits. A little girl with my face climbs up a narrow wooden ladder. Her blind father cocks an ear in concern.

"Get down off there, you little scamp," Third Brother shouts from his spot feeding pigeons on the roof.

The child continues to climb.

"You looking for trouble?" Third Brother hurls a steel chisel at the girl.

The girl dodges successfully, but the chisel makes a big hole in the roof, and the crash scares her so much she slips. The girl cries out at the top of her voice, "Ma, Ma!" as a woman charges toward the ladder in a desperate attempt to catch her.

"Little Six, stop shouting!" Fourth Sister shook me awake.

"Fourth Sister! You disturbed my dream!" I said unhappily.

If Fourth Sister hadn't interrupted, maybe I would have seen my mother racing to catch me. But even though I hadn't seen her, I could somehow tell that she looked young and agile as she ran over. She seemed to be wearing a purple silk cheongsam.

In reality, I had never seen my mother wearing a cheongsam. I remembered seeing one or two in a wooden chest when I was little, but not since then. My mother had probably destroyed the traditional dresses to avoid trouble during Mao's Cultural Revolution—unless Elder Sister had stolen them before then. She was taller than Mother and they wouldn't have fit her, but she might have given them away to ingratiate herself with her classmates. Among the few black-and-white photographs still in the house, there was a shot of Mother in a cheongsam and high heels with her hair permed. She looks lovely in the yellowing photo, her high forehead giving her an air of elegant yet melancholy serenity, and a hint of a smile on her lips. Her eyes are gazing intently at something out of the frame, and while they don't necessarily look happy, there's a brightness in them that seems fresh and alive. Not many people could resist that kind of beauty.

No one had ever called me or my sisters ugly, but we'd been blessed with only a shadow of our mother's looks. We couldn't hold a candle to her.

Fourth Sister propped herself up in bed with a pillow and took my arm anxiously. "Little Six, we have to talk about that man. The way he's treated us is unconscionable."

There was something menacing in her plaintive tone. I took a deep breath of the cold air and started to sit up, but I thought better of it and lay back down. "I don't want to hear a word about it. At least not at the moment."

Her expression darkened.

"Fourth Sister, we came home because our mother has passed on. This is not the time to discuss other matters. Leave it alone."

"But Little Six, we never get to see each other," Fourth Sister pleaded.

"I don't want to get into this," I said. "You'll go on about it for hours."

"You can't sleep anyway," she countered.

But I'd made up my mind, so I went into the next room. Second Sister, Third Sister-in-Law, and Elder Sister's grandson were already sprawled across the bed. I squeezed into the space next to Second Sister and fell asleep, my feet hanging off the edge of the bed.

6

Second Sister slept with her hands under her head. She wore a thin cotton top, her newly permed hair making her look a bit like Marge Simpson. Her face was pale and sickly, and even her lips were completely devoid of color.

The old-fashioned clock on the wall said it was 1:55 in the morning. The temperature had fallen by at least five or six degrees following the rain, and it was as cold as early winter. I pulled a corner of the quilt over my stomach and drifted back into a fitful sleep.

My slumber was plagued by dreams. In one of them, a sailor on a ferry blew a whistle, the crew hauled up the anchor, and the boat began to move away. The bank of the river drifted in and out of view behind patches of ghostly fog. I stood on top of the cliff, covering my eyes in fear, but peeping through the gaps between my fingers. The ferry suddenly tipped, capsizing, and the river bobbed with people's heads like a sea of soccer balls.

My father sighed heavily and pulled me away toward home. The stone steps were flanked on either side by golden hemlock, and the edges of each step overgrown with moss.

Spring is the dangerous season when the river spirit carries people's souls away. At least, that's what the old people say. It's when disaster lies in wait all around us, like the rose balsam flower—which we

Chinese call "little peach red" and foreigners call "touch-me-not"—which is believed to be stained crimson with human blood. In spring, they believe, whether Fortune spares or rewards you depends on the goodness of your heart.

In the spring of 1953, my maternal grandmother fell seriously ill. Her sons carried her here on a bamboo stretcher all the way from deep in the Zhongxian County countryside. Grandma's disease was the result of hunger. Her stomach filled with gas until it ballooned bigger than the belly of a woman about to give birth, her insides crawling with horrible bugs. Our shared kitchen filled with the stench of herbal medicine, which soon had the neighbors up in arms. When Grandma drank the medicine, she passed an endless stream of white worms, long and flat like ticker tape, some still alive and wriggling. Grandma lay in bed, crying in agony and complaining bitterly as my mother rubbed her stomach.

"You abandoned me, Little Rose Balsam. You left me in Guankouzhai Village to face the shame. Even if I were the thickest-skinned woman in the world, what sort of a life could I have after what you did? Little Rose Balsam, your father died young, and you haven't done right by your ma. How could I have given birth to such a spiteful, ungrateful, disloyal creature?"

Grandma certainly had her reasons for finding fault with my mother. Grandma loathed the big city, but my mother loved it. My mother was willful from a very early age. Before she was as tall as the dinner table, she already refused to have her feet bound. They made her kneel on the scrubbing board and make hemp rope until her fingers bled. They starved her until she fainted, but still she wouldn't give in. In her heart, Mother was sensitive and cautious, but if pushed, she could be feisty and wild. Grandma always said she was like an untamable horse.

The family was poor, so Grandma had no choice but to sell my mother to a rich family, whose son she was to marry when she reached the appropriate age. But my mother declared that she wasn't going to marry this man she'd never even seen, and she was locked in her room for her defiance. When night fell, she opened the window with trembling hands. It wasn't too high, but she'd have to be careful climbing down, because Grandma had sharp ears. Only when she was already outside did my mother realize she'd taken nothing with her. She had no choice but to risk going back in. There was nothing of value in the house, but she found the mosquito net Grandma had prepared for her dowry. She tucked it into her waistband and climbed out again. This time, she twisted her ankle as she hit the ground. Clutching the mosquito net as she fought back the pain, Mother followed the mountain road to the nearest town. Once she got there, she instinctively made for the riverside, where there were steamboats that could carry her far away. She stepped resolutely onto the gangplank and, at just fifteen, talked her way onto a ferry bound for the bustling city of Chongqing.

For years, Grandma assumed her daughter was dead. However, my mother loved Grandma, and once her life was settled, she managed to save a little money here and there to send back to the countryside. When Grandma arrived in such a terrible state, Mother poured herself into the old woman's care, racking her brains for a cure.

"Forgive me, Ma," my mother said to Grandma, knowing she should have written all those years ago to let Grandma know she was alive. She bowed down with her hands outstretched, begging for Grandma's forgiveness.

"Forgive you? Hah! After you let me assume you'd drowned! Not a chance. You can get that idea out of your head right now."

Mother dropped to her knees in front of Grandma's bed. "Forgive me, Ma. It was my fault. I should have brought you to the city earlier.

If you had come, then you wouldn't have gotten so sick. I truly am a disloyal daughter!"

But Grandma turned her face away. Until the day she died, Grandma never uttered a word of forgiveness, no matter how Mother begged.

Before Grandma breathed her last, though, she at least stopped cursing her daughter. As she gasped for air, she haltingly asked to be buried in Guankouzhai Village.

And so, my mother saw to it that Grandma's body was transported back to her hometown and buried beside Grandfather on the mountain behind the village. Grandfather's grave was surrounded by rose balsam bushes, which had grown from the seeds Grandma had sown when Mother fled the arranged marriage. Each year, the whole mountainside would be awash with rose balsam blossoms. Grandma would walk around the grave, talking to Grandfather.

Tears streaming down her face, Mother led Elder Sister over to kneel before the grave, a few rose balsam blossoms cupped in her hands. "Little Rose Balsam," Mother told Elder Sister, had been a nickname she'd always associated with the cruelty that Grandma had shown her—when she was punished, when she was forced to run away. But the name had also defined her. It had made her who she was.

That day at her parents' grave, Mother looked at the crimson flowers staining her fingers, and then back at the sea of blossoms covering the mountainside. Suddenly, she understood, and the words flowed as freely as her tears.

"I've been such a foolish child! Ma must have forgiven me long ago. Otherwise, she wouldn't have planted all these rose balsam flowers to wish me well. Of course she loved me. Of course she was worried about me. She didn't even know if I was alive, but she was always thinking about me. She was my ma. What could change that?"

Grandma had never really hated my mother. She'd planted rose balsam and wished her daughter well day and night. The straw dam that had stood between mother and daughter for all those years was swept away. My mother's heart surrendered completely to Grandma. Filled with remorse, she couldn't stop crying. But it was no use. Grandma wasn't about to rise from the dead. The old saying was wrong: Fortune did not favor those with goodness in their heart—not in a country where lies had become second nature to everyone from the lowest peasant to the head of state.

A few years after Grandma's death, a great famine ravaged the whole of China, and even the blessed land of Sichuan was not spared. In Zhongxian County, people starved to death every day. First they slaughtered their livestock, then they ate insects. Some villages grew so desperate that people even resorted to eating their own shit or the bodies of the dead.

Those who had the strength departed for other regions to beg for food. But no matter where they went, they found no sustenance to fill their bloated stomachs. Those with money found no food to buy, and those without money were compelled to steal scraps to survive. Many people ate bark and tree roots that grew wild along the edges of the fields. Wild carrots and celery were the most palatable, but they looked and tasted almost identical to poisonous starwort and cowbane. Anyone who ate these had fifteen minutes to get treatment or face certain death.

Back then, several villages would share a single doctor, who would be hard-pressed to make it to a patient in an hour, let alone fifteen minutes. And even if a doctor did make it in time, he was unlikely to have the proper medicines. Once, a whole family of seven mistakenly ate starwort. They writhed on the ground, foaming at the mouth, their faces purple and hideously contorted with pain. The parents clasped their five children to them, and they died together in a heap.

After the wild vegetables were gone, the people began to eat the yellowish clay soil. One of my maternal aunts ate clay and, unable to defecate, she swelled up until the blockage finally killed her.

In the early days of the famine, the villagers would make crude plywood coffins for the dead, but once the numbers grew too great, they just wrapped the bodies in old bamboo mats or lengths of cloth and threw them into pits. Eventually, there were too many corpses to even wrap them up anymore.

But one night, patches of edible *Nostoc commune* grew around Grandma's grave. My mother said it was Grandma's way of saving the lives of Elder Uncle and Younger Uncle from beyond the grave.

When my mother heard about the Three Gorges Dam project, she was plagued by fears that it would someday flood Grandma's grave. Our relatives in the countryside wrote to say they'd have to move—the famous Stone Treasure Fortress near their town and an area stretching for miles around it would soon be under water. For a whole year, my mother tried to find out where they were moving. Then, one day, Mother said that Grandma had sent her a dream. She said that there were red water-level marks all around, and that Grandma was soaking wet and freezing cold. She insisted that she had to go to Zhongxian County to have the grave relocated before the water reached it.

Younger Uncle decided that he would accompany her, and then Elder Sister and Third Brother said they wanted to go too. However, they all wanted my mother to pay the travel expenses. Mother asked Second Sister if she had any ideas, and Second Sister suggested that I should pay. The discussion dragged on for years until the autumn of 2004, when it was finally decided that Younger Uncle, his wife, and my mother would all go together during the National Day holiday.

However, shortly before the trip, Mother suddenly fainted, wetting herself. They rushed her to the hospital, where they were told she was suffering from severe malnutrition. She asked Younger Uncle to go anyway, but he insisted on waiting for her to get better. The trip was put off again and again until a year before my mother's death, when the water level reached five hundred feet and submerged the whole village. Younger Uncle called everyone together for a meeting, and there it was decided that my mother must never know that the ancestral grave lay underwater.

Strangely enough, she never brought up the subject again. When the Spring Festival came around, she presented a red envelope containing a New Year gift of two hundred yuan to each person in the family, no matter how distantly related. Her generosity struck fear into the hearts of Third Brother and Second Sister. Perhaps Mother had intuited the truth through some sixth sense, or Grandma had told her in a dream.

Mother's concern for Grandma never waned. Her soul will wade into the vast waters of the Three Gorges reservoir to find Grandma, and I think Grandma will forgive her this time.

CHAPTER 3

I

I slept poorly all that night, turning things over and over in my mind. Voices of the mah-jongg players rose with each win or loss. There was always someone coming into the bedroom to look for something, the door banging loudly as they shambled in and out. Thinking about my mother closed up in that coffin downstairs made it all the more difficult to fall asleep.

Suddenly, there was a burst of firecrackers, signaling that more old friends had shown up. It took a while before the courtyard finally grew quieter.

I thought to myself, *I've got to get some more rest so I won't be a mess tomorrow.* But then I heard Elder Sister's voice.

"Relatives from Zhongxian County are here, and they brought peanuts. Come on! Get up and help shell peanuts. Mother sure got the best she could out of her death, timing it just right to make sure all her children were back to do their filial duty. They're all here, right down to the youngest grandchild. Is there anyone within a hundred miles of Chongqing as fortunate as her?"

Second Sister took offense at the words. "Listen to yourself! You're supposed to be the oldest among us, the wisest, but you're so tactless. Can't you ever keep your mouth shut?"

Affronted, Elder Sister stomped over, grabbed Second Sister by the arm, and pulled her out of bed. "Come on. Enough beauty sleep! Come help me shell peanuts."

The bed was much more spacious now, so I rolled over. Fourth Sister, emerging from Mother's bedroom, said unhappily, "Hey, Elder Sister, you woke me up."

"Guess you couldn't have been too sound asleep then, huh?" Elder Sister laughed.

Wind blew in through the gap at the top of the window. I got up and tiptoed over to close it, shutting the bedroom door on the way, muffling my sisters' voices as they headed down to the dining room.

This room, formerly my father's, still held his old rattan bed. He liked to sleep on the side facing the door. Whenever I passed him, I'd see my father with his eyes closed, pondering. On June 8, 1999, a week before his death, he unexpectedly released the pair of nightingales that he'd kept in a bamboo cage by the window. He had a mild cough, but refused to take any medication. Then, one night, he coughed a few times and closed his eyes. Mother, sensing something was wrong, went into Father's room and called to him, but got no answer. She walked over to him and, touching his hand, found it stiff. She clasped him to her and began to sob.

My mother held my father more tightly than she ever had when he was alive, and she wouldn't let him go even when my siblings arrived. She was shocked to realize how much she'd depended on him and was deeply haunted by her past disloyalty.

Long ago, during the famine, my father left to work far downriver, and my mother didn't hear a word from him for several years. A young man helped our family survive, and they fell in love. That was how she came to have me, her illegitimate child, the endless source of trouble. She was even dragged into court because of it. But she chose to stay with my father and her six children. I met my biological father when I turned eighteen, but shortly thereafter, he passed away. Many years later, I wrote my first memoir based on those events.

In the past, when I'd flown home from London, my mother would sometimes mention my biological father to me, so I knew that she missed him. However, after my stepfather, the man I called "Father," died, my mother spoke of him much more than she had of my biological father, often going back to the memories of their early days together.

When she was young, a mob boss in Chongqing saw Mother at a factory, married her, and fathered Elder Sister, but he was never good to my mother. And so, in the spring of 1947, Mother made her second great escape, this time with Elder Sister in her arms. She found a place to live by the side of the Jialing River, and began taking in laundry to wash, living a quiet life. One day when Father was steering his tugboat up the river, he saw a young woman carrying an infant, standing in the water near the bank washing clothes. He began to bring his clothes to her, even when they weren't dirty, just so he could be near her. He would cradle the little girl, sometimes whistling a song from his hometown to make her laugh.

Father always liked to dress neatly, but even when he got back too late to change out of his uniform, he would go straight to buy a basket of oranges and roasted chestnuts and take them to the river for Mother and her child. He wore his uniform well, with his strong, straight back and long legs. His angular boatman's cap made him look extremely handsome. His eyes were especially striking. Mother had to be careful not to be consumed by those eyes. She would drop her gaze demurely and continue with her washing. The water was receding, making the riverbank broader and revealing lush moss. The three of them looked at their reflection in the deep green waters, and they saw a family.

When my mother described those beautiful days, it was clear she'd loved Father as much as he did her. It must have torn her apart to fall in love with my biological father as well, especially since she only realized the depth of her love upon the death of each man, when it was already too late. I can only imagine how Mother must have hated herself.

Out in the dining room, Elder Sister was defending herself to Second Sister, and even through the closed door, I could perfectly imagine how she lifted her chin haughtily. "We're such filial sons and daughters, and grandchildren too. Before I even finished what I was trying to say, you go jumping to conclusions, ready to judge me." Her fiery temper hadn't cooled one bit over the decades. Mother used to call her "The Rod of Heaven" for her sharp tongue.

The voices of my three sisters suddenly fell silent, leaving only the sound of breaking peanut shells. After a moment, Fourth Sister began crying.

"Don't cry. That jerk humiliated you and got himself a new plaything. He doesn't deserve tears—we should throw him in the Yangtze to feed the fish."

It was Second Sister, speaking solemnly, ferociously. I couldn't help but sit up.

Fourth Sister cried even harder. Second Sister lowered her voice, and the three women seemed to be huddling together. After a few minutes, Fourth Sister sobbed, "All right, I won't cry."

"Just find a way to get him here," said Elder Sister. "People need to learn what happens when they go around harming others."

They lowered their voices again, and I only caught snatches: ". . . disgusting . . . Don't tell Little Six . . . We'll help."

In the bed, Third Sister-in-Law coughed, as if to tell me that she was asleep and not eavesdropping. The conversation outside turned toward the next day's arrangements. More guests were expected to arrive from out of town to bid Mother farewell. Twenty tables wouldn't be enough to seat them all, but more would mean an increase in Potbellied Cat's fee.

"If he charges more, don't worry about it. Anyway, Little Six is back. She's got more money than any of us, so she should pay."

"Oh, come on, Fourth Sister. Don't cry. Can't Little Six help you with him?"

"She doesn't care about what happens to me."

"Ugh! How can she be such a bitch?"

I couldn't sleep through slander like this. I got dressed and peered through the crack in the door.

Fourth Sister's eyes were red, her face streaked with tears. She didn't even bother to wipe them away as she spoke about her long affair with Tang, professor of Chinese Culture and Literature in London. He'd been drawn to Fourth Sister's distinguished bearing and her kind, patient disposition. But what he liked most of all was that she'd dote on him, care for him in his old age. The couple seemed perfectly matched. They'd happily give up eating or sleeping for sex or watching soccer. Other times, they'd sleep in all day just for the pure joy of it. Things were so good that she promised him she'd fly immediately back to Chongqing for a divorce. Her estranged husband, happy to obtain his freedom, hadn't contested the divorce, even giving Fourth Sister sole custody of their daughter, Tiantian.

Fourth Sister and Tang lived together for eight years—a common-law marriage under English law. But the previous May, he'd been invited to give a series of guest lectures at a university in South China. The receiving committee had arranged for a young doctoral candidate to accompany him on a scenic tour of the mountains, where they discussed ancient and modern philosophy. For years, this woman had been working on a dissertation about the American poet Sylvia Plath. She was frustrated with her thesis advisor. He wasn't half the scholar that Tang was, she said, and she needed guidance. Tang tried to help, telling her that her thesis had potential to be quite good, but that it needed some reframing. Beginning with Sylvia Plath's suicide following the breakdown of her marriage with Ted Hughes, he spoke of her inner world and her art. He continued, tracing a line through contemporary British and American poetry, moving from Plath's "bee" poems to feminist theory. He then connected Hughes's *Birthday Letters* to the anxieties of masculinity. From there, he moved on to Walter Benjamin, Max Horkheimer, and Theodor Adorno, expounding on them in a manner that was simultaneously profound and unassuming.

The woman had listened in a daze, nodding in agreement, bursting with admiration. She begged him to help her, and he said he'd be honored. His hand accidentally brushed hers. When he went to draw it back, she grabbed it tightly. Their flirtation had been like lightning bolts setting fire to the ground, and now oil had been poured on the flames.

A few days later, Tang announced he had to leave town to deliver a lecture. In truth, though, he went to rendezvous with the woman. In hopes of avoiding calls from the university and Fourth Sister, he turned off his cell phone and hid out in a cheap hotel with the woman until it was time to return to London. It wasn't Tang's first lie or his first affair, but this was the first time he'd been so out of control in his cheating. He didn't even understand himself, so how could others hope to understand him?

In July, he went back to China for a week on the pretense that he needed to sign a contract for a visiting-professor position at a Chinese university. Once again, though, he holed up in a hotel with the young woman—the contract was never signed. After he got back to London, they e-mailed and talked on the phone constantly.

One day, Fourth Sister came home sick from work. When she arrived, she heard Tang on the phone upstairs, talking in a strange voice. Out of curiosity, she picked up the phone in the living room, realized what was going on, and promptly fainted. When she awoke, she found the previous month's phone bill and scrutinized it. Most of the calls were to and from one number, and all of them occurred when she was out. She sat there for a long while, her mind a blank. Then she got up, slowly climbed the stairs, and confronted Tang.

He denied everything and even accused Fourth Sister of spying on him. She said she knew he'd been having an affair, that it must have been going on for months. When she showed him the phone bill, Tang exploded with a roar.

"Go and investigate then! Get to the bottom of it!" His face was distorted with anger. He was so furious that he did not speak to Fourth Sister for two days.

Listening to the sad story over peanut shells, Elder Sister cursed Tang, saying he was a wolf in human form. Second Sister didn't say anything, but her face was grim.

2

Not wanting to hear any more, I opened the door, and my surprised sisters fell silent. They quickly made space for me, and I sat down.

Second Sister, pulling part of a quilt over my legs, said, "It's strange. It's only October, but the nights are already so cold they cut right through you."

Sitting on the quilt was a sack full of both unopened peanuts and nuts already plucked from their shells. A ceramic bowl contained the discarded shells. My sisters grabbed handful after handful of peanuts, deftly removing the shells and throwing the nuts back into the sack in one practiced gesture.

As they did so, they chatted about the customs from Mother's hometown, where the tradition was to throw peanuts during the funeral to ensure a good afterlife, with the promise of plenty of food, clothing, and bright prospects for the future.

"Mother liked peanuts. Didn't she call one of her brothers' grand-kids 'Peanut'?" Elder Sister said to Second Sister, trying to make amends for their little fight earlier.

Second Sister and Elder Sister didn't think much of each other. Elder Sister was insecure, with a hot temper and a big mouth, whereas Second Sister hid everything inside and was always sure of herself. She'd always believed that Mother and Father favored Elder Sister over her. She didn't think it was fair, especially since she was the couple's first biological child together, but she never complained about it. If she mentioned it, that would be tantamount to admitting defeat to Elder Sister.

Second Sister had been a primary-school teacher until her retirement two years earlier. She was delighted that she no longer had to corral kids all day. Her marriage was stable. Her husband, handpicked by Mother, loved her very much, and their two sons were always well behaved. Her daughters-in-law were equally lovely. With no grandchildren yet, her days were peaceful and leisurely.

Elder Sister, on the other hand, had been married and divorced several times, giving birth to two sons and two daughters, who were now scattered all over the place. The year I turned eighteen, Elder Sister reunited with her first boyfriend, with whom she'd lost contact for more than ten years. Without hesitation, she left her job at the coal mine, divorced her husband, moved back to Chongqing, and married her first love, just as she'd always wanted. Elder Sister's second daughter Xiaomi came to Chongqing to live with them.

But Elder Sister and her new husband were not happy together, and they fought more and more. One day, in the heat of an especially bad argument, they began to divide up their things, progressing from the furniture to the bowls and chopsticks, then finally to the single bedsheet. They were each holding one end of the sheet, ready to tear it in half, when Elder Sister suffered a stroke, leaving her unable to move her legs or speak. Her husband was transformed. He spent every day at the hospital taking care of her and massaging her legs. So great was the apparent power of love that, after just three months, Elder Sister made a full recovery.

Sitting together over shelled peanuts, I reflected on the unbreakable blood ties that held the four of us sisters together. There we sat knee to knee in the middle of the night, with our similar large eyes and oval-shaped faces and broken hearts, shelling peanuts for Ma's funeral.

Had we ever felt so close before?

When I was small, the family gathered around the dinner table at Chinese New Year, but I'd always been relegated to a stool in the corner, told that little kids weren't allowed at the big table. When I was finally old enough to join everyone at the table, my older siblings had been sent down to the countryside for their Communist re-education and, every year, at least one of them couldn't make it home for the festivities. Later, when we'd all started our own families, if we came home for holidays or Mother's birthday, it would be a hodgepodge of relatives. I couldn't remember a time we sisters had sat together, just the four of us.

I could feel Mother still walking about the house. I could practically smell her. If only she'd been sitting there with us, but she was lying alone in the coffin downstairs.

I tried to imagine what life was like for Mother when I wasn't there.

She always wore comfortable, flat cloth shoes. Up at dawn each day, she would do her morning exercises on the balcony. Afterward, she would go to the bathroom and clean up, then pray to the Goddess of Mercy before eating the breakfast of noodles or rice Fifth Sister-in-Law had made her. She especially loved buns and soybean milk, which Fifth Sister-in-Law didn't know how to make, but she would sometimes buy it for her from the stall on Middle School Street. After breakfast, Mother would go out, sometimes strolling by the river, sometimes participating in activities organized for the elderly, such as tai chi. Later, she'd have a long lunch with her grandson, who was in secondary school. After the boy headed back to school, Mother would pass the time knitting, helping Fifth Sister-in-Law prepare dinner, or playing mah-jongg downstairs with the neighbors. Fifth Brother and the grandchildren would come home for dinner, and she'd chat with them about her day—whom she'd seen or what she'd done, bringing them up-to-date on all the local gossip. They would sit, three generations together, harmoniously sharing a meal. When they'd finished eating, Mother would take a walk, play with the neighbor's puppy or kitten, or maybe she'd call a relative. Then she'd watch TV, or occasionally go to the theater. At bedtime, she'd bathe, then remove her false teeth and clean them. On the weekend, all of her nearby children and grandchildren would come to see her, perhaps taking her to one of their homes for a few days. They would make plans to visit Youngest Uncle, or maybe her godson, Shouli.

When it was time for the Qingming, or Grave-Sweeping, Festival, they would all tend to Father's grave, and Mother would take everyone out for dinner. During the Dragon Boat Festival, she'd get up early and find five colors of string to tie about her wrists and ankles. She'd call each of her children and grandchildren, not wanting them to ever forget their ties to home. She'd direct Fifth Sister-in-Law to place herbs over the doorway, holding two handfuls while circling the room, all in hopes of keeping spirits away. She would meticulously tie strings around her family members' wrists, saying, "Long limbs, long life. Many colors to chase the ghosts away and to bring you good fortune and good health." Patiently, she explained to each of them that they must throw the colored ribbons into the river only when the first heavy rains of summer came. She would teach them to fold the soaked glutinous rice into meat dumplings, showing them how to pinch them just right so they looked good and held together when cooked. Teaching her family these customs always made her happy, and she'd end these festive days by sharing a cup of rice wine with my siblings and their spouses.

At the Mid-Autumn Festival, Mother would make tea with the best leaves and lay out a big spread. After setting out the bowls and chopsticks, she'd wait for the children to come and present her with mooncakes. Before dinner, they would offer a cup of wine to Father at the family altar. After the meal, they would let her grandson take a family photo.

Mother didn't care too much about the Double Nine Festival—it was the Spring Festival that was significant for her. She would begin preparations early: doing her spring cleaning, decorating the house, buying new clothes, preparing gifts. Every year, she would visit all her relatives, and extend invitations to each of them in return. Most importantly, she would go to visit the graves of my grandparents, my father, and all of our ancestors, burning incense for them, as she had not been able to do before. She would ask for protection and blessings for all of her children and grandchildren. Then, dressed in new clothes and seated at the head of the table, Mother would bask in the good fortune of being surrounded by many children and grandchildren. She was generous when handing out the red envelopes filled with money, the traditional New Year gift, and then everyone would watch the special holiday programs on TV, with Mother adding her own commentary here and there, making everyone laugh. They would massage her back and cut her an apple. Everyone and everything revolved around her. Surely even the matriarch in *The Dream of the Red Chamber*, with her view of the Grand Garden, could not have been more fortunate than my mother!

All of this was what my family told me about Mother's later years. They said her days were so full of joy that she was the envy of all the old ladies in the neighborhood.

If it was true, I had nothing to worry about. Whenever I called home, Mother always said, "Little Six, I am doing very well. Your sisters, brothers, and sisters-in-law are all very devoted. Don't you worry. You just take good care of yourself." She was always concerned I was spending too much on the long-distance calls. "*Ai-ya!* These phone calls are too expensive! Trust me. I am well. Good-bye, Little Six." And she would hang up.

And I'd taken her word for it. But now, having seen the state of her old body, I'd begun to wonder. Perhaps her later years hadn't really been like what I saw on my occasional visits home or heard in the reports from my family. I'd never before doubted that she was happy, secure, and worry-free.

For the first time, I questioned whether Mother truly spent her days relaxing with friends and family. Was there a side of things my family wasn't telling me? The thought was deeply unsettling. I remembered how she'd once lost two teeth and had to have some false ones made. Then next time I came to Chongqing and saw the pain the false teeth were causing her, I'd taken her to a renowned dentist and bought her some good dentures. What had happened to those? The dentures she had in her coffin were obviously made by a quack. Even though she must have been suffering terribly, she'd never breathed a word.

I was determined to find out the truth about what had been going on.

3

Just before sunrise, a man arrived. About fifty years old, he had a pleasant demeanor, wore a fedora and a three-piece suit, and looked worn from travel. He removed his hat and kowtowed three times to Mother's coffin, then he handed over a red envelope and, without another word, turned and walked away into the first glimmers of the dawn.

Third Brother was standing in the center of the room, describing the event like a storyteller. He cleared his throat dramatically. "I recognized him as Uncle Jian's son at first glance. He's the spitting image of his father. Mother was lucky to have him as one of her godsons. He's really got a way about him. And what a hefty red envelope—six figures!"

Third Brother picked up a pack of cigarettes and made his way back downstairs.

Fourth Sister said, "I remember Uncle Jian. Didn't he and Mother . . . ?"

Instinctively, she looked over at me and fell silent for reasons that I could not fathom.

"Hah!" Elder Sister gave a dry laugh. "I heard Jian's been dead for years. Who'd have thought his son would be so filial—that's very good of him." Elder Sister tried to throw peanut shells into a bowl but missed. She continued. "It's true, though, Uncle Jian and Mother were lovers. He was chief engineer on a cargo ship. There wasn't much firewood available back then, and he often brought some to Mother."

"When was that?" Fourth Sister asked, picking the shells up off the floor.

"'74 or '76. I walked in on them once when I was visiting," Elder Sister said.

Indeed, I had seen Uncle Jian with Mother even earlier than that. Mother had been suffering from anemia at the time. While working as a porter at White Sand Dune Shipyard, she got dizzy and fell off the gangplank more than once. One time, she appeared to be dead, her hands and feet stiff, her face ashen. Her heart had stopped beating. They performed CPR, and she slowly came around. The factory doctor said that Mother had a heart problem in addition to high blood pressure. Only then was she moved to a new post stoking the furnace. One time, when Elder Sister arrived in Chongqing unannounced, she gave me ten cents for the ferry and sent me to go and tell Mother. Down at White Sand Dune, I found Mother with a man in his forties. Mother told me to call him Uncle Jian.

I don't know why, but I refused.

Mother turned to the man and grumbled, "I don't know what's wrong with this one—she never listens to a word I say."

The three of us went to the canteen to get some food: cauliflower and pickled vegetables. It was the best cafeteria meal I'd ever had. The cauliflower, having been simmered in rice soup, smelled wonderful. We sat down to eat at the little table in Mother's boiler room. People kept coming in to fill their thermoses with hot water. Uncle Jian struck me as a proud and upright man, taller than average. He must have been six feet tall, but he limped a little on his left leg. He spoke in an accent similar to Father's, and must have come from downriver as well.

He smiled at me as he said, "Well, stubbornness in children shows character. What year are you in at primary school?"

I answered him, and then asked him if he knew my father. To my surprise, he nodded his head.

Uncle Jian was obviously good to Mother. He poured water for her as we ate, and refilled my bowl. His eyes twinkled when he looked at her. After dinner, Uncle Jian patted me on the head and left, just like that.

I expected Mother to warn me not to tell Father about Uncle Jian when I got home. But on the boat ride home, Mother was silent. She held my hand tightly, closed her eyes, and turned her exhausted face toward the river.

"Mother must've had . . . that sort of thing with the personnel man at the dockyard as well . . ." Second Sister paused, looking for the right words, but she couldn't find them, and just gave up. "I mean, something must have been going on, otherwise she'd never have gotten promoted from a temp position to full employee and been reassigned to such light work, boiling water."

I burst in. "Wasn't there a governmental policy mandating that all temp workers receive permanent employment? I remember Mother saying so."

Second Sister said, "Well, everyone at the factory says the same thing about Mother."

"That doesn't prove anything."

"Well, Sixth Sister, you're the writer. Maybe you should get on the case. Prove they were just slandering Mother," Second Sister said in a flat voice.

Elder Sister waved both hands in the air and shouted, "Stop it, both of you, and listen to me. Mother was in her forties by then, and she was still a ravishing beauty. In a gutter of a place like the dockyard, she was even more of a rarity. Lots of men had their way with her. My father—the mob boss—Father, Shouli's uncle before Father, and Sixth Sister's biological father, Sun or whatever his name was. Who else was there? Oh, right. Uncle Jian. Heaven knows how many affairs she had. Old as I am, I've never met a person with as many secrets as Mother!"

Fourth Sister said, "It's true—we'll never know just how many lovers Mother had in her lifetime. My ex-boyfriend wouldn't marry me because of Ma's bad reputation at the dockyard. His family was against it. Father must have been so ashamed! It's no wonder Spectacles Wang and Auntie Shi were hard on Ma. She really did bring it on herself. But she is my ma, what can I say?"

"How come Ma's friend Wang Guixiang hasn't come to pay her respects?" Second Sister asked.

"Did anyone let her know?" Elder Sister asked.

"Third Brother must have notified her. I think she no longer lives in Chongqing."

"Wang Guixiang and Mother were joined at the hip. They used to share a carrying pole at the dockyard. She'd definitely come if she knew. Mother would have wanted her here," Elder Sister said.

"We'll ask Third Brother in the morning if he contacted Auntie Wang or not. What about her godson Shouli and his family?"

"Shouli already came. He knelt down and kowtowed as soon as he set foot in the door. He said his mother is sick in the hospital, and they can't tell her about Ma for fear it'll make her worse."

"And what about Auntie Mo? Mother and Father were close with her before they passed away. Did we let her know?"

Elder Sister flew into a temper, "How should I know? Go ask Third Brother. He thinks he's head of the house now—Mr. Big Shot, looking down his nose at everyone."

"Elder Sister, we must work together peacefully during Mother's funeral."

Elder Sister looked at me and said, enunciating each word clearly, "Sixth Sister, you have no right to tell me what to do. I don't care how many other men Mother had in her time—your father ruined the happiness of this family!"

I was caught utterly off guard.

"It's true. This family hasn't had a single good day since Mother gave birth to you, Little Six," Second Sister said.

My sisters had no problem telling racy tales about Mother, but they'd never acknowledge the love between Mother and my biological father. Even though he'd been dead for twenty years, they were still holding a grudge. My eyes brimmed with tears of rage. I wanted to stand up and let it out, to give them a piece of my mind. But since we were in mourning for Mother, I restrained myself.

Just then, Third Sister-in-Law piped up from the bedroom, "You ladies have a lot of nerve, gossiping about Ma's shameful acts in earshot of the children, not even caring that Ma's bones are barely cold!"

Her voice was full of indignation. All of us in the living room shut right up and looked at each other. But Elder Sister shot back, saying, "This is a family matter, it doesn't concern you as a daughter-in-law."

"How could it not concern me? I've been ruined since marrying into this family, going around with a bad name these twenty-seven or -eight years!"

"How has it ruined you?"

"Your ma only cared for her daughters."

As Fourth Sister tried to calm everyone down, I decided I'd had enough and ducked outside. The folks keeping night watch downstairs were all wrapped in warm clothes, playing mah-jongg to stay awake. Mother was still lying in the iced coffin, surrounded on all sides by paper flowers and fresh ones. The image of her in a Taoist nun's black cap lingered in my mind. The trace of a smile escaped from her tight lips.

Was it us she was laughing at or herself?

The idea made me shudder. Did Mother really have so many lovers besides my biological father? A new link was added to the chain of suspicions that had already formed in my mind. Second Sister's words had hit home. I was a writer. If I wanted to prove that Mother had been slandered, I'd have to come up with the evidence. I'd make them see just what sort of person Mother really was.

There was more than one thing I needed to get to the bottom of.

4

Two oil lamps had been placed beside Mother's coffin, their light flickering in the chill wind. Beneath the whitening sky, the whole neighborhood around Alley Cat Stream looked exceptionally peaceful, shrouded in sleep. The nearby Chongqing Cigarette Plant emitted its terrifying rumblings, just as it always had. Apart from the rebuilt Compound No. 6, where each household had its own modern bathroom, there was still only one public outhouse in the whole area. It stood on the site of the old toilet, which had been demolished, although the only real difference between them was the new ceramic tile. There were the same three pits for women and six for men. Each morning, people would queue up to wait their turn, a routine that had not altered since the day of my birth forty-four years earlier.

Even now, the outhouse had no proper plumbing or sewer. Only a heavy rain could dissipate the foul smell. At the same time, though, heavy rain would make the septic tank behind the toilet overflow. The residents who lived closest were used to the rank smell, but they lived in fear of the foul water rising right up to their doors. They had to constantly beg local farmers to come and cart the manure away.

Near the outhouse were some low shacks built out of blackened tiles, rotting wood, broken bricks, and oily felt. In the distance was the shimmering river. Nine years earlier, Chongqing had been promoted to the level of special district directly controlled by the central government and things had begun to change. Chaotianmen Dock on the opposite shore was rebuilt to look like a giant, cement boat. And thanks to massive investment, the banks of the Yangtze were paved with tarmac, lined with marble, and landscaped with dozens of species of imported trees. Upscale restaurants and teahouses opened along South Bank Road, turning it into a major entertainment hub. The mountains rising above the marble streets, however, were just as underdeveloped, depressing, and stinky as ever, dotted with innumerable slums. The Chongqing Cigarette Plant continued to befoul the air and water, the chimney rumbling like some kind of beast. The local authorities went all out to make Chongqing look good, but behind the new facade, nothing had really changed.

The pollution was hurting my lungs, and I turned to go back inside. But I stopped at the doorway. Trying to settle all sorts of old scores at once, my sisters were still fighting like feral cats.

The scene was all too familiar. When I left at eighteen, I swore an oath never to return. I was young then, rebellion coursing through my veins. Only later did I realize that running away like that, without a thought for anyone else, had cut me to the core. A person severed from home is bound to lose her way. When I came back years later, it was out of affection for my parents. Then I left the country for a long time and, when I returned again, I found myself forever a visitor in my own home. Then my biological father had passed away, and so had the man I considered to be my father, and now, my mother. I no longer had any place I could call home.

The very roots of my life were dying, I suddenly realized, and I was filled with terror at the thought.

5

My first love died before it even began, just like the embryo in my womb. I fell in love with my history teacher, and he killed himself to avoid facing the consequences of our affair. The tiny life we'd made ended in the Qixinggang Women's Hospital. At the time, I'd had no other choice. I was eighteen then, the age of a newly opened blossom, the age of fearlessness.

The man who'd gotten me pregnant became just a shattered image, fading more with each day.

My Fourth Sister fared a bit better. When her first love tried to leave her, she drank pesticide. The suicide attempt failed to kill her, but it succeeded in winning him back. They married, but their happiness had lasted just two months and ten days when, one night, his stomach began to hurt. Fourth Sister was working overtime, so he went alone to the emergency ward of the No. 1 People's Hospital at South Bank. As soon as he walked through the door, the doctors whisked him into an operating room. As they were removing his appendix, they discovered he had colorectal cancer. Unable to decide on a course of action, they stitched him back up and consulted a specialist.

Back then, Fourth Sister was strikingly beautiful and adored by whoever laid eyes on her. All the doctors, nurses, and patients felt sorry for this gorgeous young bride and her sick husband.

At the time, I was away from home at a vocational school. Second Sister wrote to tell me that Mother had to help care for Fourth Sister's husband. She had to prepare a special diet for the hospitalized patient—on top of looking after the whole family. The work took its toll on her. She lost twenty-five pounds in a month. Fourth Sister spent every night at the hospital, sleeping on the floor or in a chair beside the bed where her husband lay, stuck full of tubes and pumped full of fluids. Knowing he was going to die, his temper grew worse. He deliberately spilled the chicken soup that Mother had made for him, dumping it all over the bed and floor. Fourth Sister said nothing, just set about cleaning it up. Mother walked the half-hour journey back home, heated some more soup, filled up the thermos, and carried it back.

Then the hospital began to limit the man's painkillers, leaving him in such pain that he cursed profusely, calling indignities down on the heads of eight generations of his ancestors. Fourth Sister went around begging for people to sell her any kind of painkillers they had, but sometimes she couldn't get ahold of any. When the addiction was upon him, her husband would grab Fourth Sister by the hair and smash her head against the wall, spewing disgraceful curses all the while.

After he'd tortured Fourth Sister for more than six months, the hospital proclaimed the man incurable and discharged him. He returned to his mother's home in White Sand Dune, where Fourth Sister stayed with him until the end. Finally, he closed his eyes in her arms with infinite regret. Their love, like glittering fireworks, came with a bang and departed swiftly, extinguished before it ever really began.

Before long, she had moved on to her second husband, a colleague. He was a simple and honest construction worker. His younger sister, who also worked with them, had set the two up after she and Fourth Sister became friends. His mother would make delicious food, and the sister would invite Fourth Sister over. They'd even take food to Fourth Sister at work. With this new family taking such pains to look after her, it wasn't long before Fourth Sister's resolve never to marry again crumbled. She got married and moved to her mother-in-law's small apartment in the city center.

One year later, she gave birth to her daughter, Tiantian.

A few years later, her husband became a contractor, overseeing construction projects far from home. Fourth Sister's dead husband appeared to her in a dream, urging her to visit her current husband at once. As soon as she woke up, she grabbed her bag and rushed to the train station. She spent nearly twenty-four hours on the train. When she arrived, dawn was just breaking, and she caught him in bed with a young woman who worked for him. He assured her it was nothing. He was merely satisfying his sexual needs with the girl, whom he promised to fire at the first opportunity. Fourth Sister went back to Chongqing, but when she called her husband, she found his manner cold. She asked him to come back to Chongqing for her birthday, and he promised that he would, so she waited, but in vain. That's when she decided to commit suicide. The first time, she took pills and was rushed to the hospital to have her stomach pumped. On another occasion, she slit her wrists. She bled so profusely even her slippers filled with blood. It was Tiantian who found her and called the ambulance, and after that, because of her intense worry, the poor girl could barely get through school. As soon as class ended, on winged feet, Tiantian flew over the hills, afraid that her mother would be dead before she got there.

That marriage finally ended when Fourth Sister followed Tiantian to London, where she met Tang.

Tang was like a father to Tiantian, helping her with her homework and even legally adopting her so that she could stay in the country. He taught the girl English, giving her a quarter for each new word she picked up. Fourth Sister was getting on in years, and struggled to learn a new language, so she threw herself into cooking. The English know nothing about fine knife work or the tricky business of mixing vegetables with meat, whereas the Chinese are masters of the culinary arts. Fourth Sister had always been clever. She memorized the names of dishes and types of alcohol, and she practiced making cakes and desserts in the middle of the night when everyone else had gone to bed. She got top grades in culinary school, and during an internship at one of the best restaurants in the area, her outstanding performance caught the boss's eye. He asked her to come and work there as soon as her classes ended.

Tang was separated from his wife, but he never mentioned divorce. Fourth Sister didn't mind, devoting herself wholeheartedly to him. For many years, their lives were peaceful and happy. Who could have known that cruel fate would lead Fourth Sister right back to where she'd started? Tang turned out to be just like her second husband, suddenly running off with another woman.

Fourth Sister had always confided in Second Sister and Elder Sister. Even the expense of long-distance calls couldn't deter her. She told them everything about Tang's betrayal. Elder Sister and Second Sister despised him. They told Fourth Sister to leave him. Fourth Sister wouldn't, so they helped her come up with ideas based on the four-step strategy traditionally used by Chinese women for winning back their husbands: first you cry, second you threaten suicide, third you hang yourself, and fourth you beg for forgiveness. But no matter how hard she tried, resorting to tearful pleading or outright threats, Tang wouldn't leave his new girlfriend.

"Is that Tang's heart made of plastic or something?" Fourth Sister always liked to say.

Elder Sister walked over to where I sat, interrupting my thoughts. She looked smug, as though she'd won an argument. Stretching, she seemed about to say something to me when her second daughter, Xiaomi, came up the stairs. She was thirty now, a lovely young woman, wearing jeans and a patterned shirt.

Elder Sister said, "Little girl, it's daybreak. What are you doing up at this hour? And dressed like that! Aren't you worried about catching a cold?"

Xiaomi ignored her and turned around.

Elder Sister shouted in anger, "Xiaomi!"

I walked over.

Xiaomi addressed me in a gentle voice, "My dear Sixth Auntie!"

6

Xiaomi invited me to her home in Shiqiao to rest, and I accepted gratefully. I had been trying to figure out where I could go—even if it was just a crummy hotel or a spa to get away from my bickering sisters and be alone for a while.

Downstairs, I saw Third Brother and Fifth Brother attending to the guests. Potbellied Cat came in, carrying a rack full of steamed pork buns and bread, followed by a cook with a big pot of congee.

"Breakfast has arrived!" he crowed, ignoring the sorrowful faces of everyone else in the room. He got out bowls and disposable chopsticks.

Fifth Brother invited me to sit with him and eat some steamed buns, but Xiaomi tugged at my sleeve. I looked at her, and then told Fifth Brother that I had to go out for a bit.

Once we were outside the compound, I asked Xiaomi, "What's wrong? Do you think Potbellied Cat's food isn't clean?"

"Well . . . no harm in being on the safe side. Let's go and get some spicy dandan noodles. You must miss them, not having been back to Chongqing in so long! Besides, I need to get away from that so-called mother of mine."

Elder Sister's daughter was clearly good at intuiting others' needs. She was pretty as a flower, but her face was marked with a fine scar, collateral damage from Elder Sister and her second husband's fighting. Although the man was a miner, he liked poetry and had an excellent reading voice, which brought him a lot of attention from the ladies at the coal mine. One day, Elder Sister confronted him about his cheating. He didn't reply, simply smoked one cigarette after another. Elder Sister knocked his cigarette to the floor, cursing him, saying she wanted to leave him. In a burst of anger, he picked up the kitchen knife and began to chase Elder Sister around. She ran in a big circle but eventually returned to the house and hurried to shut the door behind her.

Xiaomi had been trying to ignore the fight, but ultimately, the hearts of a mother and her daughter are bound together. The crazed man broke down the door, and as he lunged at Elder Sister with the knife, Xiaomi threw herself between them. The knife slashed Xiaomi's left cheek, sending blood gushing everywhere. Stunned, the man stood there like a statue.

Xiaomi was taken to the coal mine's first-aid center, where they stopped the bleeding, and then they made an hour's journey to the county hospital. But the scar stayed. Xiaomi, being a smart girl, knew how to cover it with makeup so that it was barely visible.

Elder Sister inquired at the police station, and was told that her now ex-husband had committed a criminal act. For injury with disfigurement and using a knife with the intent to seek revenge, he would get at least two years in prison. He offered Elder Sister a five-thousand-yuan bribe not to press charges, and Elder Sister, greedy as always, accepted.

To pay for her hotheaded son's mistake, the man's kindly mother dug out the life savings she kept squirreled away in a jar under her bed, the bills mildewed after so many years. But it wasn't enough. She borrowed money left and right, finally managing to scrape together the five thousand yuan. Then, after handing the money over to her son, the woman hanged herself.

The son blamed Elder Sister for his mother's death. He hated her for it and would often harass her on her way to work.

One day, Elder Sister had had enough. She went home and raged at Xiaomi about his abuse.

Xiaomi replied, "You got yourself into this. If he'd gone to prison for two years, he wouldn't be here to shout at you."

Elder Sister said, "I only wanted that money to pay for the operation on your face. You're too young to know anything."

"Do you really have the nerve to claim you spent all that money on me? You're the sort of person who would sell your soul to be rich."

"How dare you! I've worked day and night to raise you. What have I done to deserve such a disloyal daughter? What karma! What rotten luck!"

"Karma is right! You're a bad mother, and you always have been!"

Elder Sister had moved from the countryside near the Three Gorges back to our hometown in Zhongxian County, where she gave birth to Xiaomi. She brought the baby to Chongqing when she was eighteen months old, dumped her on our mother, and took off. A couple of years later, when I still was in primary school, little baby Xiaomi came down with a serious illness, and it seemed like we might lose her to diarrhea and dehydration. Father spent all day watching over his sick granddaughter, and as soon as Mother got off work, she spent hours searching for medicinal herbs to save the baby girl. Nothing worked until Mother combined dried chicken gizzards, beehives, and yams. Mother crushed all the ingredients together, mixed them with water, simmered them over a low heat for a long time, and then fed the mixture a spoonful at a time to Xiaomi until the illness loosened its grip. Then, Mother scrimped and saved to buy eggs for her emaciated granddaughter. Over time, Xiaomi's face regained its healthy, rosy color, and she began to laugh again. There's no fooling the body of a child, and no fooling her heart. After that, she would always be closer to our family than to her own mother.

"I didn't even want to see Ma here," Xiaomi told me as we walked away from Alley Cat Stream. "It's Grandma who raised me—who saved me—and I don't mind the whole world knowing."

"I understand, Xiaomi, but she's your ma. You can't act like that toward her."

"She's not my ma," Xiaomi stated emphatically.

Middle School Street was already bustling with commuters and shoulder-pole carriers. The cobblestone street looked clean and fresh after the overnight rain. The shops and houses on each side of the stone steps were the same as I remembered, the old teahouses already open for business. There were a few men with graying hair sitting inside, necks drawn into their collars, clutching cups of tea in their hands. They stared blankly at us as we passed.

The primary and secondary schools soon appeared before us. The exercise field looked the same as before, but the old temple had been knocked down to make way for several new buildings. Students streamed past us, shouldering their backpacks. The classrooms were quiet, but I saw some students already inside, holding books in their hands.

Reaching a smaller road, we hailed a motorized rickshaw and climbed in. The pitted and potholed street made the rickshaw toss about violently and spray dirty water high into the air. It took us ten minutes to reach a paved road.

Before long, we arrived at Shiqiao, where skyscrapers towered high and billboards shone. Most shops weren't open yet, but cars were everywhere. The rickshaw turned down a muddy alley, both sides lined with fruit and vegetable stalls.

Suddenly, there was a loud bang, and the rickshaw came to a halt.

"My tire!" the driver shouted, and jumped off to investigate.

Xiaomi handed him some money and said we'd walk the rest of the way.

7

Elder Sister and Xiaomi had lived in the Dafo neighborhood of Shiqiao for five or six years. Mother had often gone to visit them before she died. It has long been said in China that, when a person dies, her spirit will fix itself onto someone who looks like her, and it will collect her footprints from all the places she went. Walking down the street to Xiaomi's apartment, I searched the crowd of strange faces for someone dragging her feet like heavy objects, one shoulder higher than the other, frizzy hair, a serious expression, and a curved spine. But there was no Mother there, no one the least bit like her. Since Mother had visited so often, Xiaomi must know something about her later years. Now that I was alone with her, it was the perfect time to ask.

"How was life for Grandma when I wasn't here?"

It was as if Xiaomi hadn't heard the question. I repeated myself.

"Grandma was very happy. Don't you know that?" Xiaomi said as she pulled me into a busy noodle shop.

Xiaomi spoke to the man who was tossing noodles into the pot, asking him to add some extra greens to hers. I could tell she must be a regular. I said I'd have mine without chili peppers.

Some people got up, so we grabbed their seats.

Xiaomi said, "I didn't see too much of Grandma, really, but Ma said that, for a while, Grandma thought about moving into a nursing home."

"What? How come I never knew about that?"

"Well, they took Grandma to see the nursing home. An elderly neighbor on their street had been sent there by her children. The residents there got watery food, meat and eggs only once a week, and no milk. They were clearly suffering from malnutrition, their faces thin and sallow. They slept in shared bedrooms, with only one bathroom and toilet for thirty or more people. The caregivers were obviously cruel, and the entertainment was limited to one color television, which was only switched on to certain channels during set times. The neighbor took Grandma aside and told her, 'No matter what, don't come here. It's like being in prison. We're all just waiting for Yama to take us to the afterlife.' So Grandma went back home."

I couldn't think of anything to say. Before long, someone brought over our noodles. I had asked them not to put chilies in mine, but there they were anyway. I dropped my head and began eating. I was suddenly hit by the reality of Mother not being in the world any longer, and my tears fell splashing into my noodles. I used a tissue to wipe my eyes, but my appetite was gone.

Xiaomi insisted the meal was on her.

We left the noodle shop and walked another ten minutes, entering a compound of five or six apartment buildings squeezed tightly together around a scraggly garden. Several old ladies sat there, watching their grandchildren and soaking in the sun on stone benches.

"I'm afraid there's no elevator," Xiaomi said apologetically. "At least the building's not real tall."

We climbed the stairs to Xiaomi's fourth-floor apartment. It felt spacious, with an open living room, two bedrooms covered with Japanese-style tatami mats, an eat-in kitchen with a dining table, and a modern bathroom.

Xiaomi said, "It's just me and my son here now. Ma and her husband moved out."

Aha. They must have had a serious falling-out.

"They took most of the furniture with them when they left."

No wonder the apartment seemed spacious—it was empty.

"Then where does Elder Sister live?" I couldn't help asking.

"They live in Huangjueya now, in a slightly smaller place."

Xiaomi poured two cups of water and passed one to me. She sat down and said in a flat voice, "I bought that furniture with my hard-earned savings from when I worked down south. My ma had the apartment renovated before I bought the furniture. She's not like a real ma at all. Sixth Auntie, tell me, what kind of mother doesn't have feelings for her own daughter? What kind of a grandma doesn't have feelings for her own grandson?"

8

Elder Sister had been out of work ever since returning from the coal mine to Chongqing in search of her first love. After getting remarried, she lived with her third husband and aging father-in-law in a tiny studio apartment in the Dafo Textiles Factory dormitory near South Bank. They built a shed to use as a kitchen and dining room. Her husband's younger brother fought all the time with his wife, and after each fight he'd come stay with them for a few days. Elder Sister complained nonstop about the lack of space. Her husband told her to deal with it. Their fates were as bitter as the bitterest medicinal herb. She was born into the wrong family and married—yet again—to the wrong man. Both had a match-like temper, easily ignited. They quarreled often.

When I came home from England to visit my mother and we all sat down together to eat, Elder Sister started to complain before we could get through a single mouthful. She said she'd wanted to buy a skirt that cost thirty yuan, but she'd had no money and the clerk had ridiculed her.

In front of everyone, she began to sob, "Love isn't worth shit! We're so goddamn poor we can't afford cloth to cover our butts. We haven't got a clue about what happiness is. The other night I dreamt I was arrested for not being able to pay for some hot pot I ate."

Mother made her stop and said we'd talk about it after dinner.

That was 1992. I had only been in London a little over a year. I was in Chongqing for Mother's birthday. Father had gone blind and couldn't get around easily, so Mother didn't want to go out to a restaurant. She said for her birthday she'd be happy if everyone just got together for a meal. Mother sliced sausage and made seaweed and pork ribs soup, and Second Sister bought hot chili chicken and some other cold dishes. Younger Uncle and his entire family showed up, and we all squeezed in around the table, with the kids seated at a smaller table nearby. During the meal, Mother went to the kitchen and cooked dry-braised green beans. I went to help her.

Mother said, "Your Elder Sister wants some money. If you've got some, lend it to her."

I didn't reply.

Mother changed her tone and said, "Ma knows your money is earned one word at a time through your writing. It's not easy for you either. Never mind—don't pander to your Elder Sister. She's a useless creature anyway."

Third Brother came running in, warning me, "When it comes to financial struggles, we've all got problems. She's not starving. Don't go messing with the status quo. It'll only bring trouble."

I understood what he meant. If you give money to one person, everyone will want some.

"Anyway," he said, "it's Ma's birthday. What's Elder Sister crying for? She's so inconsiderate."

After dinner, Elder Sister took me out to the corridor alone. She leaned against the railing and looked into the distance. The river had grown wider with the rising spring temperatures. A motorboat came over from the Jialing River, speeding into the Yangtze, trailing a long white wave.

"I have a good friend at the Chaotianmen Shoe Wholesale Market. I'd like to open a shop there," Elder Sister said, pulling at my hand, her eyes full of hope.

I asked her how much she needed. She named a figure. I turned and went to Mother's bedroom, took my wallet out of my bag, and counted out a wad of US dollars. I walked back as if nothing had happened, through the living room to the corridor outside. I put the money in Elder Sister's hand, saying, "You can exchange that at the bank for over thirty thousand yuan."

"Call it a loan to your elder sister," she said, counting it carefully. The joy spreading over her face could not be concealed. "Little Sister, you're so good to me! I know I haven't always been a great success in the past, but things are different now—you'll see. I'll pay my little sister back as soon as I can. And I won't tell the family it was your money, to save them all bugging you for a handout."

I said, "All I want is for you to be good to the family, and to stay out of trouble."

She held up her hand, promising me.

Before long, the shoe shop had opened. Elder Sister went bright and early to the shoe factory to buy stock, opened the store on time, and poured her heart into her business. Whenever anyone from the family went to buy shoes, she refused to charge them, and friends only paid half price. Second Sister wrote me to say that Elder Sister had opened a shoe store, that she was working hard, and that her business seemed to be doing well.

Second Sister also said that whenever they asked Elder Sister, whose pockets had never jingled with excess coins, where she got the money to open a shoe store, she swore that it was a loan from an old friend who had hit it big in the city. My elder sisters and brothers made no comment. I don't know whether they really believed her or were just letting the lie stand.

I couldn't help but breathe a sigh of relief. I thought to myself, *At last, Elder Sister's done something right. She's turned over a new leaf. Thank goodness.*

Xiaomi couldn't find work in Chongqing, so she went with a good friend to Wenzhou to study hairdressing. Before long, she moved to Shenzhen. Elder Sister told everyone how capable her daughter was, that she'd found a Hong Kong businessman, and that after they were married, he was going to buy her a two-story villa.

About six months later, Second Sister wrote to say that Elder Sister had given up the shoe store and gone to Shenzhen to see Xiaomi. When Elder Sister returned to Chongqing, she not only brought back Xiaomi, but also her one-year-old grandson. When our brothers and sisters asked where the child had come from, Elder Sister's answers were full of holes and inconsistencies. Knowing that she was losing face, she fell out of contact with the family.

A year later, when I returned to Chongqing to see my parents, I asked about Elder Sister. The family went on and on about it.

"Xiaomi was that man's mistress! Hong Kong businessman nothing. He was just a Wenzhou businessman who traveled to Hong Kong sometimes. The child hadn't been born five minutes when he disappeared into thin air. Even a bird would have left a shadow. Oh, there was a villa, but it was his elder brother's, and he sent someone to kick her out."

The only real information about him that Xiaomi had was a phone number. She tried to call, but got no answer, so it was as good as having nothing at all.

Hearing that I'd come back, Elder Sister made a fuss about bringing her grandson over. She was just like before, her poverty the first thing on her lips. Xiaomi's son looked bright. He didn't cry or fuss. He ate grown-up food and was very obedient. It broke my heart to know that he had no father, so I gave him a red envelope.

Elder Sister didn't mention anything about returning the money I'd loaned her, nor did she mention the shoe store. Instead, she told me that Xiaomi had moved into her cramped little home and opened a small hair salon nearby. Elder Sister looked after her grandson and helped out at the salon.

Elder Sister's father-in-law's home was slated to be demolished. As compensation, he would get a state benefit home, its value calculated according to his years of employment. The problem was that he'd have to come up with tens of thousands of yuan to make up the difference between the value of the old place and the new one. Elder Sister's husband said they had no money, and he wanted Xiaomi to come up with the cash. The eighty-year-old father-in-law had one condition. "If Xiaomi comes up with the money for the new apartment," he insisted, "then she should be registered as the owner."

Elder Sister started working on her father-in-law that very day, arguing that she should be registered as the owner instead. She said that if Xiaomi got married and the man turned out to be a scumbag, he could steal the house and drive them all out. Her father-in-law insisted that whoever put up the money would be the owner. Elder Sister said that the house belonged to her and her husband as well, and she insisted that her father-in-law break his word to Xiaomi. For once, her husband was on her side. Her father-in-law flew into a fury saying, "What sort of way is this for parents to act?"

As a sort of revenge, they'd sent the old man to a nursing home, but they couldn't stop him from putting the apartment in Xiaomi's name.

I'd only had a vague idea about all this before hearing Xiaomi tell me the story now. I did not know what to say about Elder Sister's antics. It was fortunate that Xiaomi had been able to keep her name on the deed. A year after Elder Sister, her husband, Xiaomi, and her son moved into the new house, the father-in-law died in the nursing home, and my brothers went to pay their respects, giving Elder Sister the opportunity to reconnect with our family.

9

Our conversation was interrupted by shouts from outside. Xiaomi opened the door to yell at some neighbors noisily moving furniture.

"It's eight in the morning," she hollered. "Keep it down, will you!"

Coming back to sit with me at the small table, she sighed and continued to fill me in on everything that had happened.

"Ma used to come by when I was running the salon. She only cared about collecting the cash. She even made me pay her for the time she spent looking after my son. I worked so hard at the salon, but with all the money going to Ma, I had no choice but to shut it down. I was unemployed and couldn't find a job, so I applied for public assistance, but two hundred yuan a month doesn't go far. Luckily, I'd squirreled away a little money from the salon that Ma didn't know about. Raising a child is so expensive. I'm worried sick about it. I don't know how I've made it this far."

Xiaomi turned to me expectantly. "Sixth Auntie, can you think of some way to help me find my son's father? We're not legally married, but the boy is his. I've struggled so hard to do it all alone these past nine years. School fees go up every year. I've pleaded with lots of people to track that bastard down, but none of them could find him. Recently, I managed to get his elder brother's cell phone number, and I got through, but as soon as I gave my name, the jerk hung up on me."

Hearing now for the first time about everything that had happened, I really did want to help her. But Xiaomi knew nothing of the man's background: where he was from, what kind of business he did in Hong Kong, where he lived. Absolutely nothing. Even if I had superhuman abilities, I'd be hard-pressed to find that cold-hearted man. Who would have thought such a lovely girl could be so foolish? I sighed and sighed again. Her child was nine years old already. Doing the math in my head, I realized that, nine years earlier, Hong Kong was right in the middle of the Asian financial crisis. The man's company almost certainly had gone bankrupt.

Xiaomi sat rocking in the chair, saying to herself over and over, "What am I going to do?"

I tried to get her to think of any other details she could give me to help her search for the man. She couldn't sit still.

"There's no need to worry," I said.

I looked around the apartment. The dinner table and the chairs we sat on were solid wood. The floor was laminate, but not bad at all. Though not extravagant, the furnishings weren't exactly cheap either. When Elder Sister got the keys to the place, it had been unfurnished and in bad shape. Who'd paid to renovate and furnish it? Had the money for this come from Xiaomi's pocket too?

When I asked her about it, she hesitated.

"You've been hearing the rumors, haven't you?" she asked.

"Rumors?"

"Yes, the rumors. Grandma shouting out in her sleep, 'My eldest, how could you be so heartless? How could you do it? Stealing the money Ma worked hard her whole life to save? I just can't understand!'"

Xiaomi appeared to be waiting for my response. I was shocked, but I tried not to show it.

"There are plenty of people besides my ma that could have taken Grandma's money," she continued. "Look at how Third Uncle and his family live—one room and a lean-to for a kitchen. Thank heavens you've helped their daughter go study in England. Then there's Second Auntie. She, her husband, and their two sons all live in one room in a run-down old courtyard attached to the primary school, and they always have relatives staying with them. Second Auntie had to get two bunk beds, and they have to share a toilet with everyone else in the courtyard. Fourth Auntie used to live with her mother-in-law in that crowded little two-room house at a turn in the road. One summer, a drunk driver crashed right into their house and just barely missed them. You can't get a good night's sleep in a place like that. You have nightmares. And Younger Uncle hasn't got anywhere to live at all. His family, all three of them, are stuck at Grandma's. Everyone's desperate for something better."

She shook her head in despair. "They all say Mother took Grandma's ID card and savings book to the bank and withdrew one hundred thirty thousand yuan, using it to renovate this apartment."

"If your mother didn't take it, then who did?" I asked.

"Sixth Auntie, I really don't know."

"Xiaomi, I'm not accusing your Mother, but I need to know everything that happened."

Slowly, the story came out. My brothers and sisters had accused Elder Sister of stealing Ma's money. She'd denied it, but no one believed her. They could tell from the savings book that the money had been taken out, but not where it went. They dragged Ma to the bank to investigate, and made her wait in a long line. Then they wrote a statement on Ma's behalf, signed with her fingerprint, that gave Third Brother power to act as her representative. They wanted to see all the transactions for Ma and Elder Sister's accounts. The bank said that information was private unless Ma went to the police, but she refused. She didn't want to get anybody into trouble.

Throughout the whole ordeal, Xiaomi told me, my mother had been morose and silent. While Mother appeared confused about the details of the accounts it had been spread across, she remembered the total clearly: one hundred thirty thousand yuan.

According to Xiaomi, Third Brother and his wife did remember the details. In 1999, the year my father died, they were tidying up his things and discovered that Ma had stashed the bankbooks in his pillowcase. They took them straight to Ma. They said there'd been four accounts altogether: three fixed term and one instant access. She'd opened the accounts in the seventies with just five hundred yuan. Over time, Ma's savings increased, but there were also large withdrawals—mostly for her grandchildren's school expenses. None of Ma's grandchildren managed to get into a good secondary school based on their grades, no matter how hard they tried. So the family had to pull strings and buy their way into school, the amount of the bribe depending on just how bad the grades were.

Xiaomi said that everyone knew my mother had kept a close eye on the bankbooks, getting up in the night to change their hiding place, as if guarding against thieves.

"But everyone who lived with her was her own flesh and blood," Xiaomi told me. She considered the possibilities. Fifth Uncle would never do anything bad, but what about his wife? She might steal money to support her family in the countryside. Their teenage son was hooked on the Internet and online games, so he was also a suspect. Apparently, he was always going into Grandma's room, and afterward, her wallet would be ten, twenty, sometimes even one hundred yuan lighter. When she confronted her daughter-in-law, Fifth Auntie and her son denied everything and suggested that Grandma put a lock on her bedroom door if she didn't trust them. Of course, Grandma had refused, and so she continued to lose money. If Grandmother ever complained, Fifth Auntie would pout and give Fifth Uncle a hard time. Fifth Uncle would begin to recount his son's faults, saying that he didn't work hard at school, that he spent too much time playing games. His son would then throw a tantrum and fling his schoolbooks to the floor. Finally, poor Grandmother would wind up apologizing, saying that she was old and useless and had a poor memory.

My heart was pounding at each new revelation Xiaomi shared. How could this be? I knew I had to remain calm if I hoped to get to the bottom of it.

"So maybe Fifth Auntie and her son were pilfering from Ma's wallet. But that's not looting her savings account, is it?" I said.

Of course, Mother knew as well as I did that the person she had to guard against most carefully was her eldest daughter.

"Xiaomi, your mother must have talked to you about this? You must have had your own suspicions?"

Xiaomi remained silent, her eyes flicking from side to side.

"Where did she say she got the money for this furniture, Xiaomi?"

"She said Grandma gave money to her. It was a secret between them."

"Go on."

"My mother had gone to see Grandma for several days in a row, talking about how difficult life was for her, that she never had anywhere nice to live, that three generations had to squeeze into a tiny space. Finally, thanks to my good fortune, they had a little place. But with no money to furnish it, she said it was no better than living on the street. She begged Grandma to lend her two thousand yuan. She said that Grandma wiped the tears away from Mother's face with her handkerchief, saying to her tenderly, 'Eldest one, don't cry. Ma will give you the money.'

"Grandma and Mother went together to the bank and got the money out, then went back to Grandma's to have lunch and take a nap together. Two days later, Grandma discovered that there wasn't a cent left in her accounts. Anger made her blood pressure spike, and she collapsed. For two days, she refused to eat and wouldn't go to the hospital. She just clutched an old photo album containing pictures of her children.

"I heard that Fifth Auntie tried to force her up, saying she either had to eat something or go to the hospital. Grandma ignored her, murmuring to herself, 'My eldest girl—it's all my fault. How did I fail so horribly with your upbringing?'"

Xiaomi looked at me blankly. "That's how it started. The accusations. Fifth Auntie tried to coax Grandma to say more. Grandma just closed her eyes, her face went blue, and her hands wouldn't stop trembling. In the end, Fifth Auntie had to call the family together to discuss the matter."

"Including your mother?" I asked.

"No," she answered softly. "Mother did not attend. She was busy finding a redecorating team, buying paint, tiles, a toilet, lights, and appliances. She said she was so busy she wished she could grow an extra set of hands and feet. In two months or so, the work was complete. Without even waiting for the paint to dry, we bought furniture and electronics and moved into the new home. I paid for the furniture.

"Mother's brothers and sisters came looking for an explanation. Mother answered all their questions confidently. 'My daughters pulled together their savings to decorate the place for me,' she told them.

"'Elder Sister, give back the money you stole from our mother!' Second Auntie said, 'Do you have any idea how upset she is?'

"Mother just stared at her stubbornly.

"'You really don't have a heart in there after all, do you?' Third Uncle shouted. 'First you take Ma to the bank to show them that you're related. Don't deny it—I know that was your ulterior motive for wheedling the two thousand out of Ma. Making sure the bankers would recognize you. Ma didn't know what she was doing, but you did!'

"Then it was Fifth Auntie's turn," Xiaomi told me. "She said, 'Elder Sister, you stole Ma's ID and bankbook while she was asleep. You rushed to the bank and arranged the transfer. Then you hurried back home, lay down on the bed, and pretended to wake up with her as if nothing had happened.'

"Of course, all that made my mother really angry. 'How dare you go to the bank to check up on me?' she yelled.

"Mother threw the glass she was holding onto the floor, and looking deadly serious, she said, 'You all listen very carefully. First off, I'm not that sort of character, sneaking around like a rat. Ever since I was little, I've owned up to whatever I've done. Second, if you come after me, I'll cut myself off from you just like that, and I'll sue Little Six for emotional damages over that book she wrote!'"

My head was throbbing.

"Thank you for telling me all this," I murmured. "That must have been hard for you."

Xiaomi lit a cigarette with shaking fingers. "I didn't say she did it."

"Of course not," I said.

I waited in silence as Xiaomi continued smoking, gazing blankly out the window. Her shoulders shook a little. When her cigarette was finished, she stubbed it out on a plate.

"Do you want to hear the rest of *my* story?" she asked sadly.

"Very much," I said.

Through friends, she had been introduced to a boyfriend who was ten years her senior. Dressed in a business suit, he seemed an honest man right down to his toes. Although he didn't have a proper job, he was very caring toward Xiaomi. Once, when I was back in Chongqing, I saw him myself, carrying Xiaomi's bag for her. Seeing the weather change, he took off his own jacket and put it around her shoulders. Any woman in the world would be pleased with such a boyfriend, even if he had his faults. But Elder Sister and her husband were against him. They said he wanted to mooch off of Xiaomi. Xiaomi told them it was none of their business, and her relationship with her mother got so bad that Elder Sister told Xiaomi to take her son and get out. Xiaomi said that the apartment was in her name and told Elder Sister to move out herself. Elder Sister said that she knew this day would come sooner or later. She refused to move. This lasted for several long years, the whole family living in simmering anger. In the end, Xiaomi took out the last of her own money and bought a small house to move her mother into. Thankfully, the price of housing in Chongqing hadn't yet skyrocketed.

"I earned that money working in a hair salon in Wenzhou. I was on my feet from nine in the morning till eleven at night. My feet were always swollen. I was too busy to eat lunch. Every penny I earned was soaked with my sweat."

"Is your boyfriend good to you?"

Xiaomi suddenly started crying. She'd faced too much pressure from her parents, who were so nasty to her boyfriend that they almost came to blows. In the end, she'd had no choice but to break up with him. Now Elder Sister was always finding opportunities to berate her for being a single mother, all alone without a man. Xiaomi didn't know what she'd done to deserve such a selfish mother.

10

I went to the bathroom.

I stretched out my hand to wipe away the layer of dust on the mirror. The face that looked back at me was pallid with eyes bloodshot from lack of sleep.

Xiaomi's underwear was soaking in the washing machine. There were baby pandas on the wall tiles. I wondered whether they'd been paid for with the money Elder Sister stole from Mother. Presumably everything in the room—the washing machine, the toilet and sink, the patterned tiles, the dark-blue floor tiles, the big round mirror—had all been paid for with the money that Mother had struggled her whole life to save.

I went to the bedroom, pulled the curtains, and got into bed.

Xiaomi came in and knelt down beside me. "Sixth Auntie, you can see how pitiful I am. I've never asked you for a single thing in my life, but today let me beg one favor of you. Find me a partner abroad. It doesn't matter how old he is or what he does, if I can get away from Chongqing and my damn mother, I'll marry him with my eyes shut."

I tried to lift her to her feet, but she was determined not to get up until I'd promised. I could only say, "Okay, I'll try."

She stood up. "Sixth Auntie, thank you. You've always been better to me than my own mother."

"Xiaomi, life abroad isn't heaven."

"But abroad is abroad. It must be almost heaven. Otherwise, why do so many people want to go there? I've already started learning English." She pointed to her son's room. "I bought an English-Chinese Dictionary and language tapes. I'm serious about this."

"I can only try. Finding the right partner depends first on what sort of person you are looking for and what you yourself have to offer. And after that . . . it's luck."

She listened, her face taut with nerves. After a while she sighed, saying, "Sleep well, Sixth Auntie. May we both dream of better days to come."

CHAPTER 4

I

It felt surreal. On the morning of the second day of my trip home for my mother's funeral, I was lying on Xiaomi's bed. Light shone weakly through the curtains. I found myself staring at a poster of Princess Mononoke from the Japanese director Miyazaki's anime film. In her silver fur cloak, she was riding on the back of a white wolf, holding a spear and a slender wakizashi sword. Her short hair flew about her face, which burned with a fearsome intelligence. I thought it was beautiful.

The tiny bedroom suddenly seemed like mine alone, and I felt my whole body relax a little. My mother was born in the Year of the Pig, making her eighty-three when she died. I was forty-four, born in the Year of the Tiger. My mother had me when she was thirty-nine. In the film, I recalled, Princess Mononoke says she has nothing to her name, that the whole human race has abandoned her. I remember being profoundly shaken by her words. My earliest impressions of the world were much the same.

But the truth was that I'd had my mother, and while she may have been tough on me, only after half a lifetime did I realize that she'd never abandoned me for an instant.

I wrote the story of most of my mother's life in my memoir, *Daughter of the River*. I started writing it in London in 1996 and continued through the scorching summer in our Chongqing home on the south bank of the Yangtze. My mother would get up at the crack of dawn to make congee to which she would add mung beans, winter amaranth leaves, or preserved eggs and shredded pork. By noon, the congee had cooled down and was ready to eat. She'd also make a different cold dish every day—fried chili peppers with lettuce, a couple of tender slices of young ginger, or blanched water spinach with chili paste and garlic salt. There were also spare ribs with sweet-and-sour eggplant, simple yet perfectly delicious.

Mother must have been seventy-three that summer. My father's death in 1999 changed her life forever. Without him around, it was hard for me to get reliable reports about how she was doing. I would have to do my homework carefully to find out how things had really been for her in her last years.

The 1996 visit, when I went with my husband back to Chongqing to visit for almost two months, was the longest I'd ever spent. One day, I was violently nauseated, and thought I might be pregnant.

My husband's response was, "Well, if you really are pregnant, we shouldn't go through with it. Children are a lot of hassle. You wouldn't be able to cope with being a mother, and we don't have the time, never mind the ability, to take responsibility for a child. I already have a daughter anyway, and it was hard enough bringing her up. Think about it. She's not even around to take care of us. She has her own job. She's married. She only calls every six months, if that, and then only to ask for money. There's no benefit to having children at all."

The test was positive, of course. Without my husband's support, I had no choice but to have an abortion, and, like a repeat of the one sixteen years ago, I went to Qixinggang Women's Hospital. The only difference was that this time there was anesthetic.

On the same day, my husband flew to Shanghai to see his ex-wife. They were both Shanghainese, and she had come back from Canada to visit her family. My mother came back from the market early that morning with an old hen, which she had planned to cook to help me get my strength back. But she couldn't bring herself to kill it because she had always been scared by the sight of blood. She led Father, who by then was blind, into the hallway and put the knife in his hands. She was so scared of blood that she was still shaking when he handed her the carcass. We were the same that day—both terrified of taking a life. If my father hadn't killed the poor old chicken, my mother would have simply stared at it helplessly, and I would have gone hungry.

My mother was annoyed that my husband had taken off, but only mentioned it once. I was having trouble writing, sitting there staring at Southern Mountain in the distance, when I heard her sigh and remark to Father that they might not be perfect together, but at least she could rely on him for the rest of her life.

Without waiting for Father to respond, she muttered, "A family is only a family when you have children. Without children, you're no more than a couple of shadows drifting where the wind takes you. Well, Little Six has always been miserable. It's best not to say any more about it."

I sat there dumbstruck. There were so many things I wanted to say to my mother. I felt as if she had never given her blessing to my marriage. When I brought my wedding photos home to Chongqing, she had barely looked at them before going back to her TV program.

2

My husband was my ex-boyfriend's colleague. The two of them had gotten to know each other at the office and eventually became like brothers. In 1989, my ex-boyfriend made it his first order of business to escape from China, and ended up leaving me to go study in the United States.

Once, I saw a letter from his colleague, my future husband. He had beautiful handwriting, the delicate characters written in the style of the ancient calligrapher Zhao Mengfu. The tone of his writing was modest, intellectual without being pretentious. The two friends had been working on translating an avant-garde poetry collection, but couldn't find a publisher.

At the time, I was in Beijing to participate in a writers' workshop at a famous university. A friend heard that the colleague had gotten divorced and come back from London to Beijing in order to meet a Chinese woman to marry. I was recommended.

And so it happened that, one summer day, I knocked on the door to his room. He opened it and looked at me in a way that was at once warm and oddly familiar. That steady gaze sealed my fate. He shook my hand and motioned for me to sit on the sofa, while he sat at the foot of the bed. He looked younger than I'd imagined—nineteen years older than me, but seeming more like ten. Solidly built, he appeared taller than he actually was, and with a pair of fancy-looking glasses perched on his nose, he was every inch the wise Confucian intellectual. His eyes were laser-focused on me the whole time. I was overcome with such nervous excitement that I fidgeted and shuffled my feet, unsure how to respond.

He told me he'd been worried I wouldn't actually come to meet him on such a scorching-hot day, and that the way some women played with men's feelings was terrible. But I was different, he said. He asked me if I was a virgin. I told him I wasn't, and maybe I never had been. He told me I was the one he'd been looking for.

I was amazed at his bluntness. He began to tell me about his adventures at college in San Francisco, about how he'd caught the tail end of the sexual revolution of the 1960s. He talked about his many girlfriends, mentioning slyly that he'd even taken one of them to a sex club. He asked me if I'd be shy about going to places like that.

Why would I be? Sexual liberation had come to China in the 1980s. I told him that when I was growing up, nobody dared speak of love, not even to say "I love you" to their own parents. Love was a sin, and sex was a disgrace. A lifetime of political pressure and sanctimonious moralizing had left my generation physically and emotionally repressed, spiritually empty, and desperate for emancipation, for rebellion against convention and tradition. We would organize "lights-off dances," where, intoxicated with alcohol and cigarettes, we would recite foreign poetry and discuss the philosophy of Nietzsche and Sartre. The women all worshiped the feminist theories of Simone de Beauvoir. We experimented with all kinds of art forms, danced naked, and picked any guy we felt like to be our partners, and the next day we might throw ourselves into someone else's arms. Once when I was drunk, I read a poem about a child in danger. The notes of fear and fearlessness in the poem made me feel as though it was written just for me, and it gave me comfort for years thereafter.

He grinned in delight, and I suddenly realized that this man was the author of the poem. I had always wanted to meet him, to be close to someone like him.

He said we must have been destined to meet. I was embarrassed.

Not five minutes had passed before he asked if I would marry him.

I didn't say yes, or even that I would think about it. I just grinned with sheer happiness.

That afternoon, he asked to see my body. I said it was only fair if I could see his too, so we both undressed, and he embraced me from behind. I led him over to the mirror and turned halfway to look at his body. He wanted to make love, but I said I wasn't ready for that. He nodded his head in understanding.

We went out and walked for ages in search of a restaurant with air conditioning. Eventually our patience was rewarded, and we found a clean, quiet little place. The friendly waiter brought us ice water and recommended the sautéed river snails with ginger, which he said had been brought in fresh that morning. We also ordered mushu pork and a tofu dish. Our food arrived swiftly, and the river snails really were particularly good. We drank a toast, albeit with water, to meeting at last. He asked me to tell him about myself, and he listened attentively to everything I said. Once we had finished eating, he called a taxi to take us to Beijing University so we could visit a well-known professor there who was a good friend of his. The professor was very kind. She peeled a pear for me to eat and even said that I reminded her of herself when she was young. It was obvious that he'd brought me there to get her approval.

Early the next evening, the doorman called to say that someone was asking for me. I ran outside, and there he was. I walked with him along Jingshun Road, the route to the airport. The street was lined with trees and flowers. He asked me if I would have dinner with him and, although I had already eaten, I readily agreed. He told me that the professor had given me a nearly perfect score and suggested he choose me. After introducing me, he'd also brought a very pretty artist to see her, but his friend hadn't rated her highly at all. I told him I was leaving for Guangzhou the following day to visit a friend for a while.

While I was in Guangzhou, I watched the florist across from my hotel every day. Many types of flowers came and went. The jasmine blossoms disappeared; chrysanthemums took their place. I thought of him, but found I couldn't remember what he looked like. One day, I answered the phone and was surprised to find him on the other end of the line. The first words out of his mouth were to say that he was headed back to London. The next were to ask me to marry him.

I told him I needed time to think it through.

I went back home, where he sent me letter after long letter urging me to come to England. So, the following spring, I boarded a plane to London. Although his two-bedroom apartment had its own garden, the kitchen and bathroom were so small that there was barely any space once he got the dishwasher in. Nevertheless, it was a cozy kind of small—just right for two people. There was a park nearby with a stream so clear you could see right to the bottom, as well as the studio of the famous nineteenth-century socialist and artist William Morris. On Sundays, by the ancient water mill on the stream, there was a market selling handicrafts and Mediterranean and East Asian foods. The biggest supermarket in England was also close at hand, although the nearest Tube station was a good twenty minutes' walk. For someone who had never really had a home, it was simply heaven.

The wardrobe contained a couple of coats and some skirts and underwear that he'd bought for me at a secondhand shop, all of which fit quite well. That first evening, he cooked chicken thighs with potatoes and steamed rice. Then, that night, we made love. It wasn't as good as I had expected, perhaps because we didn't yet know each other well enough. I hoped it would get better with time.

Spring nights in London were cold, so we made good use of the fireplace. He took a lot of naked photos of me bathed in the flames' warm glow, most of them underexposed and artistically blurry. The only nonblurry one showed me holding a red apple while posed on the bed with my eyebrows raised, perhaps because the apple was a symbol of the sins that God couldn't forgive.

He told me he'd met a dozen or so women in Beijing, some of them part of the literary crowd, people whose names were familiar to me, and none of them compared to me. He had cast a wide net in the hope of finding someone who could be a good wife to him. Some of these women he had met before he met me, others after. He had taken the pretty artist out to talk about marriage and gotten intimate with her right there in the park.

I wasn't terribly upset. Although he had already proposed, we weren't married yet. Even if we had been, he had the right to change his mind, or to be with other women. It's not like you wouldn't let someone try on a few outfits before picking the one that made them feel most comfortable.

Over the course of our first few nights together, I told him about my life, about my childhood, about leaving home at eighteen, and finally about what happened in the summer of 1989 due to the Tiananmen incident. His eyes damp, he said, "Poor thing, having to pick up the pieces again and again. You can trust me. I'll be good to you. I'll always love you."

He took great interest in the stories and poems I wrote, giving me excellent advice, and even editing them for me. I discovered I couldn't stop talking about 1989, about the student uprising, about everything that had happened to me. He said, "Why don't you write it all down?"

As I began my first novel, that infamous square, which had retreated into distant memory, seemed to draw close again. Every single person there had hoped their destiny was about to change, that the country we loved would change. I'd yearned for the same, but never truly believed that change was possible. Now, all I wanted was to be with him, and for him to keep me far away from Beijing, far away from China. I was utterly disillusioned with my country.

He said he couldn't afford to support me, so I should find a job, on top of school and my writing. My English wasn't very good, so I was worried about finding anything decent. He told me I had a lovely figure and suggested I try modeling for photographers.

Sometimes he would come with me, and other times I would go on my own. One fashion magazine with particularly exacting standards told me I was too chubby around the hips and needed to diet. For a week, I ate only fruit, drank only water, and did sit-ups religiously.

Before long, I was able to start earning some money. He got more and more into the idea and hunted through the yellow pages for companies I could work for. One day he told me that doing private films would be even more lucrative, and he'd found a company that paid by the hour. The very first customer, a middle-aged British man with curly hair and a handheld video camera, wanted to film me doing nude sex scenes. I was so angry I shoved the door open and walked out.

When I got home, he made his disappointment plain. He made me watch video after video of sex scenes until my dreams were filled with all shapes and sizes of penises and vaginas, endless naked bodies piled on top of one another in orgies. I didn't find it sexy at all. On the contrary, the actors seemed to me more like machines than like people. It had been three months now, and I had to decide whether I should get a residence permit by marrying him, since he had British citizenship, or try to extend my student visa. In spite of all his initial confidence, now he was hesitant about the issue.

Should we get married or not? He lay sprawled on the carpet, agonizing like a tormented Hamlet until a British friend of his finally asked him what in the world he was afraid of. It wasn't such a big deal, she said, and so he took me to look at wedding rings.

We went to see the vicar at the local church. According to church rules, we had to attend the church for two weeks. The vicar could then announce that these two people wished to be joined in marriage and ask whether anyone objected. If nobody objected at the end of the two weeks, we could get married. Leaving the church after our second visit, we decided to go for a walk in a nearby park. It started raining, so we ducked underneath an old oak tree. The vicar walked by carrying an umbrella and smiled at us. Then a rainbow appeared in the sky.

My soon-to-be husband gazed at the rainbow for a long while and then pronounced, "This is a good sign!" and pulled me close.

On the morning of our wedding day, we went to a favorite haunt of artists and the black community, an area where there was a market virtually every day. I picked out a pale-pink dress inlaid with silver flecks. It looked like a Chinese cheongsam without the lace-up neck, but it fit me perfectly and the vendor only wanted five pounds for it. I found a white hat at another stall, which was less of a bargain at three pounds. Once I tied a purple ribbon around the hat, the outfit seemed to take on a soul of its own.

The vicar had assumed this was just another case of a Chinatown business-owner bringing a girl over from China for a fake marriage. When he confessed this to us, we merely exchanged glances and smiled at him.

All the female wedding guests told me how beautiful my outfit was and asked me where I had bought it and how much it cost.

What was I supposed to say? What would they think if I told them I had gone through this, the most important ceremony of my life, in an outfit bought at a secondhand stall for eight pounds, or just over a hundred yuan? Even if they didn't turn up their noses, they were bound to think that I was beyond redemption—how could I let the most significant day of a woman's life go by like this? Even if she didn't make the man pay a fortune for a fancy wedding, or get a diamond ring out of him, a woman should at least get a new dress.

All I could do was smile demurely and say nothing.

It was true that I was filled with dreams of elaborate white dresses. But dreams are dreams. Not wearing a white dress felt like leaving a space in which to think and reflect quietly on myself. That summer, I wanted nothing more than to marry that man. On our wedding night, he spoke at great length about how much he loved me, about how our marriage would be different from other marriages. We would be absolutely free. We were not slaves to one another, and we would keep our finances separate. We wouldn't let marriage be the death of love. Marrying him would be the beginning of happiness.

So this marriage would not be like those of our neighbors when I was a child, who simply got married to have children and share the burden of life's hardships. My life with him would be an adventure, an art, a primal place where our imaginations could run free. It would be like *Gravity's Rainbow*, a dazzling display of fireworks shooting out toward a higher plane of existence.

The following day, we went to Brighton for our honeymoon, and he took me to the nude beach. He was happy, intoxicated by the envious stares of all the other men. Dark thunderheads descended, so we hurriedly put our clothes back on and made a break for the safety of a friend's house. The black clouds gave chase, flashes of lightning and peals of thunder striking all around, so loudly it seemed as if a vast and unstoppable army was closing in, ready to swallow us up. I wasn't scared. Love had struck me faster and harder than the thunder and lightning. I loved this man. What reason could there possibly be not to love someone you had sworn before God to entrust your happiness to for the rest of your life? I was willing to stay with him in this foreign land, for better or for worse, until death do us part.

3

I shut myself up indoors and wrote for three straight months until I finished my first novel. It was almost like a diary, documenting the experiences of a handful of young people in Beijing in 1989. After a series of betrayals, the female protagonist is taken away when the police track her to a going-away party for friends moving abroad.

My husband wanted to celebrate, so we went to Paris. We met up with two friends who appear in the novel, as well as a writer who would later win the Nobel Prize for literature. Much to my surprise, the writer liked my novel and wrote a long foreword for me. The Taiwanese publisher asked me to rush my revisions so he could get the book out as soon as possible, and he also arranged for a Scandinavian critic to write the preface. Both the publisher and the critic were friends of my husband.

A British-run Chinese-language newspaper published extracts from the novel. The editor hired an English-language translator, but the work never seemed to get off the ground. My husband said we shouldn't wait any longer and translated it himself. We sent the draft to a number of British publishers and agents, but only a few replied, and even then only to say they weren't interested, so I gave up on the idea altogether.

To someone like my husband, who came of age during the celibate Cultural Revolution, promiscuity was always a rebellious act. He once said to me, "You can sleep with anyone you want, men or women, but you have to tell me about it, and you have to use a condom. If you do that, I'll treat you even better. And if you don't fall in love with anyone else, I'll always love you."

Every night after he fell asleep, I did the dishes and cleaned our apartment. In those days, his friends would often come to stay with us, and sometimes he would ask me to have sex with them. Afterward, one of his friends told me right to my face that he didn't even like me. After the guests had left, I'd have to change the duvet cover and pillowcases. We didn't have a washing machine, so I would hand wash everything in the bathtub and drag it out to the clothesline in the garden.

One winter we went to New York. When we walked by a swanky club, he said that his fantasy was for the woman he loved to do a strip-tease dance for him in a place like that. He asked me if I would make his dream come true. I was more than a little reluctant, but nodded my agreement when I saw how disappointed he looked. After a few minutes of negotiation, the club owner finally agreed. I'd only seen this kind of dancing in films, and I'd certainly never danced like that in public. So, that afternoon, with only two or three customers there besides him, I threw on a red wig and walked out on the stage. Because I was dancing out of love, I felt passion and embarrassment in equal measure. In the end, I stopped short of stripping completely.

I ran back to the dressing room and put on my clothes.

When I came back out, he pulled a sour face and said, "Too bad you didn't go all the way."

Another time, we went back to Chongqing for him to meet my parents. Compound No. 6 was still standing back then, but the second floor was uninhabitable, and my parents both lived downstairs. They insisted that we take the bed. When I got up, I realized that my mother had already gone out to get baskets of fresh fish, meat, and vegetables from Stone Bridge Market. By eight o'clock, all my brothers and sisters had arrived to meet my husband. We stayed at the house for two days before moving to a nice hotel in the city center.

My husband said, "You've come home a success, and you've done your duty as a daughter. Now it's time to show them you made a good decision in marrying me. Showing them we can afford a fancy hotel will go a long way toward preventing your family from saying you married a useless old codger."

Fourth Sister brought her daughter, Tiantian, to our hotel room to try the fancy shower. My husband took lots of photographs of them and kept saying how beautiful my sister was, how it was a waste for her to be stuck in Chongqing.

After we'd been in London for a few days, he told me he'd gotten in touch with that pretty artist from a few years back, and that she'd come to meet him at the house when I wasn't there. She still wore a velvet qipao, he said, but this time, the dress was dark blue and she had her hair up in a bun, which highlighted her slender neck. She'd said she wasn't very interested in sex, but she really liked being naked. When she undressed, he saw that her breasts sagged and she wasn't as slim as she had been a few years ago.

Why did he invite her over when I wasn't there? And why did he only tell me about it after the fact? Extremely annoyed, he snapped that I shouldn't be so jealous. I complained that he hadn't kept his word.

4

Over the next five years, I made a few friends of my own in London. One of them, Ni, had been in London for nearly a decade and lived in a rambling house in Hampstead. He'd dined in the fanciest restaurants in town, yet he once told me that nothing they made was as good as my twice-cooked rib and radish soup. I mentioned my novel to him, and he said he knew a pretty good literary agent. He offered to take the manuscript and see what he could do.

It didn't take long to get a response. The agent read the draft and called to arrange a meeting.

That day, Ni, my husband, and I arrived at the agent's Victorian house together as arranged. As we climbed the stairs, Ni explained that this agent had originally made her name as a publisher, but she now ran a literary agency with her partner, an industry veteran who had published a certain book about three generations of Chinese women that had gone on to become a global bestseller.

We arrived at the fourth floor and were met by the agent, Ms. F, who was a strikingly beautiful woman no more than forty. She said she really liked the novel and that her business partner also wanted to meet us.

It wasn't long before Mr. Y arrived. He was a tall man of around fifty. Upon hearing that I didn't yet have an agent, he said he wanted to represent me.

At this, Ms. F's expression changed, but she didn't say a word.

The meeting lasted about half an hour. When we came out, my two companions were even more excited than I was. I was bewildered by the way they looked at me—it was as if I were already a bestselling author.

The agents took my husband's preliminary English translation to the Frankfurt Book Fair and managed to make deals for rights in a dozen or so countries. They took me out to dinner to celebrate, and Mr. Y offered to drive me home.

The next day, my husband opened a letter from Mr. Y, which was of course addressed to me. The letter was very short, but it was friendly almost to the point of tenderness. My husband flew into a rage. He insisted that something must have happened between me and Mr. Y. I told him that was absurd, that Mr. Y was a professional. He was a shrewd businessman, and he'd already been able to get me a publishing deal and an advance on my yet-to-be-written memoir.

After our fight, my husband went to Australia to see his daughter and ex-wife. I realized that I was pregnant again and had another abortion, alone. That night, a terrible storm rolled in, and I curled up in the dark, miserable, listening to the noise of the old oak tree lashing against the window.

Over the next few years, I was frequently invited to various European countries to promote my latest book. My husband stayed behind, handling all my correspondence, my checks, bank accounts, and credit cards.

Once, while he was out of town for a conference, he phoned me one afternoon to complain that the friend's play I'd recommended he read was a waste of his time. Not only did he have to spend time on me, but on my friends too. He said that all he did at the university was teach basic facts about China to a bunch of Westerners, and he wanted to move back to China. I refused.

"You keep saying you'd rather die than put up with me. If that's what you want, then go right ahead!" he said.

I said I would, but he said I was full of shit.

After hanging up, I swallowed half a bottle of his sleeping pills and changed into a knee-length, white cotton outfit. I combed my hair and lay down on the bed, silently thanking my husband for giving me permission to end things. Life was too hard. Nobody loved me, and I was not capable of loving anyone.

The playwright friend in Paris called at that exact moment. I got off the phone quickly, but he knew something was wrong, and he called back. When I didn't answer, he tried in vain to reach my husband, and then called everyone he knew in London. His friends called their friends until they found the people nearest to me. They broke the door down as the ambulance arrived outside.

The sleeping pills had started to take effect, and they had to carry me to the ambulance. As if in a dream, I heard someone say, "Her husband's here," and I forced myself to open my eyes. He stood there on the curb in the twilight, his heavy black satchel slung over his shoulder. He gazed in my direction with a mixture of innocence and helplessness. He looked so alone, so sad, that all I wanted to do was cry my heart out. I have no idea what happened next.

When I awoke the next day, he was sitting at my bedside. He told me the doctors had pumped my stomach, and I would be fine. He wanted to take me home so that I could rest properly. He seemed to have aged ten years overnight, making me feel terribly guilty. I told him I was sorry.

He heard me and seemed to be about to say something, but then stopped himself.

The hospital would only release me on the condition that I had twice-weekly meetings with a psychiatrist. The gray-haired man asked me a lot of questions about my life, my childhood. He was the kind of person who insisted on getting to the bottom of things. He was curious about the Chinese Cultural Revolution, the Great Famine, and Tiananmen Square, as well as Chinese emigration, modernization, and economic development. Our therapy sessions turned into lectures on modern Chinese history.

While I was in London tutoring my therapist, my youngest sister had left her job to live with her husband while he was overseeing construction sites away from Chongqing. However, before long she caught him with the worker he'd promised to fire. She dragged her husband onto a bus back to Chongqing, where they were robbed at knifepoint. The robbers were about to kill her husband for refusing to hand over his wallet, but my sister threw herself between them, and in the scuffle, her right hand was nearly severed. Surgeons were able to save it, but it ached and was of little use. At first, her husband was moved enough by her heroism to break things off with his mistress, but it didn't last. Fourth Sister resolved to follow him whenever he went out of town, even though it meant hanging around building sites every day with nothing to do. When I got a letter from Second Sister telling me all about this, I invited Fourth Sister to come to London the following summer to have her hand treated. I hoped a change of scenery would do her good and that seeing her would do me good. I missed my family fiercely.

The summer came, and my sister got a visa to visit London. My husband took the two of us to the seaside at Brighton. As we approached the nude beach, I couldn't help but recall being the young woman posing naked by the sea, her husband frantically adjusting the camera as he took shot after shot. The girl that I was then was afraid of the water but still went in. She started to laugh, and he nearly stumbled. She stopped laughing and yelled, "Be careful!" It seemed to have happened in another lifetime.

As we pulled into the parking lot, I suddenly burst into tears and couldn't get out of the car. Without a word, my husband slammed the door and strode resolutely toward the sand, refusing to look back. My sister followed. The seagulls squawked madly above the car as I watched the two silhouettes recede, gradually becoming one with the sea.

Six years ago, he and I had come to this beach on our honeymoon. We had run hand in hand to take refuge as thunder crashed and dark clouds rolled in all around us. But now that the wind was still and the sea was calm, he was nowhere to be seen. I knew then that I had lost him, and that he had lost me.

5

Since leaving home at eighteen, I'd told my mother as little as possible about my life, hiding behind truisms and formality. It wasn't that I was afraid she wouldn't understand, just that I couldn't bear to make her worry.

But being my mother, she thought nothing could get past her. After all, I was her own flesh and blood. At the same time, her love for me had always been repressed and misdirected, tempered by the shameful circumstances of my parentage and the treatment she'd received for daring to raise me. For my part, I never tried to close the distance between us when I had the chance.

Still nestled in Xiaomi's bed as all these memories washed over me, I thought back to the hellishly hot summer of 1996 when I'd traveled back from London to Chongqing to spend two months with my parents, the longest I ever lived with them as an adult. I was rushing to put the finishing touches on the first draft of my memoir, *Daughter of the River*.

That summer, Chongqing's factories were in the middle of a crisis and couldn't afford to pay their workers. A magazine that was publishing a new novella of mine wired the royalties to a post office in the city. Since I was still recovering from the abortion, my mother insisted on going for me. First thing the next morning, she put on her straw hat and headed out for the hour-long trek. As the impossibly hot day dragged on, I flitted between the balcony and the front passageway, looking for any sign of my mother on Middle School Street. My father paced back and forth in his room. She was seventy-three already, and we both feared heat stroke.

By the time my mother returned, the sun had already sunk deep into river. I told her my father and I had been worried sick, and brought her a cup of herbal tea.

As I took the money from my mother, I noticed that she seemed annoyed. I went to my bedroom, took some money from my purse, and bundled it together to give to her.

My mother tried to refuse, but I insisted. She said it was too much and that she wouldn't accept it for herself, but that she'd save it for me.

When she finished drinking her tea, she finally explained what had happened.

"After I left the post office, I took the ferry across the river to Chaotianmen. A big group of retired folk staged a sit-in in solidarity with the factory workers."

I instinctively glanced out the window at the river stretching into the distance. Chaotianmen was still visible, and I pictured the old men and old women demonstrating all day under the harsh sun.

In Chaotianmen, she'd run into Wang Guixiang, the lady she'd shared a carrying pole with during her days at the shipyard. Wang Guixiang was a few years younger than my mother. Her father had been a clerk in a police station before the Liberation, when the Communist Party came to power, so he was a prime target for the political purges that followed. He was convicted as a member of the bureaucratic classes and sentenced to three years in prison. Later, exiled to a remote village and ordered to serve as a primary-school teacher, he was overcome by depression and illness and soon passed away.

Wang Guixiang's husband had been a technician. During the 1950s campaign to "Speak freely and air one's views fully," he'd authored a poster detailing twenty of the party's wrongdoings. He was thrown in jail and given twenty years at the Sunjia Garden No. 2 Provincial Prison near Stone Bridge. The prison factory made parts for electric fans, so he continued working as a technician while he was inside. There, he'd been complicit in another prisoner's escape—an unpardonable offense—and been executed by firing squad. My mother told me she'd had to stop poor Wang Guixiang from killing herself on a number of occasions back then. The two of them became close friends.

"Didn't anyone get heat stroke?" I asked my mother.

"They did, but luckily, the protest wasn't far from the hospital. Your Auntie Wang and I were so hot there was smoke coming off the tops of our heads. That foreman is a nasty piece of work. He hasn't paid anyone's salary in months. We've gone over there several times to demand some answers. We went all that way just for those ungrateful idiots to scold us like they were teaching their grandchildren a lesson. They talked to us like we were three-year-olds, saying we're a bunch of useless old fogeys hanging on past our time, and that we're just making a nuisance of ourselves because we have nothing better to do!"

My mother said she'd only come back because she didn't want us to worry.

"Auntie Wang's still sitting there. These big bosses are really evil!" She sighed indignantly.

I was ashamed at how petty I'd been. My mother had given me the royalty money the moment she walked through the door, but I had the nerve to think that she was annoyed because I had accepted it. She went into the kitchen to make dinner, and I tried to help her, but she told me to go back to my writing.

My mother wasn't a strong reader, so she never knew too much about my work. She had a red notebook that my biological father had given her, and she used it to keep track of monthly expenses, which of her grandchildren had been ill and seen a doctor, and the formulas for various herbal remedies. Her cursive handwriting was very difficult to read, but with some effort, I could make out most of it. After she died, the notebook was nowhere to be found.

That summer, as I sat writing in my mother's bedroom on the south bank of the river, an overwhelming sadness would often pull me up short. My mother always did her best not to disturb me. If she wanted to bring me tea or get something from the room, she would peek around the door frame and only come in if I wasn't writing anything at that moment.

The memoir about my childhood took me a year in total. It was first published in Taiwan, where it was named book of the year. My mother never read it. Neither did my father. That book, *Daughter of the River*, was finally published in China in 2000. The book spoke to ordinary people, its popularity exceeding my wildest dreams. In Sichuan in particular, that magical land where the book was set, news of it spread by word of mouth and newspapers rushed to print excerpts. When I was signing copies at bookshops in Chongqing and Chengdu, there were readers who gave me gold necklaces and chanted, "Long live Hong Ying!" The line outside the Xinhua Bookstore at Jiefangbei was so long it held up traffic, and the police had to come to restore order. Jealous local authors went to the authorities to demand that I be prohibited from coming back. Readers, on the other hand, came to the Jin Jiang Hotel where I was staying and secretly paid my bill, while others sent fruit baskets to my room and offered to personally drive me back to Chongqing.

My eldest sister was the first member of my family to go and buy a copy. She took it to show our mother, reading certain passages out loud. My mother's eyes reddened as she listened, her handkerchief clutched tightly in her hands, but she never said a word to me about it.

Third Aunt and Second Sister howled, "Readers in foreign countries are one thing, but now all of China is reading Sixth Sister's book! Our dirty laundry is being aired all over the TV and newspapers. How dare she shame us this way!"

The family felt, of course, that I shouldn't have written about us, saying that it was bad for me and for them. Elder Sister told them I was a writer, and anyway, it was presented as fiction.

"Why did you defend me?" I asked her.

"I was worried you might ask me to pay back the money I borrowed for the shoe store," she replied.

My eldest sister was at her most loveable when she was candid.

On more than one occasion, I thought about reading the book to my mother, but I never did. Every time I was about to suggest it, someone always arrived to interrupt us. When Father passed away, I took a copy of the book to his grave as an offering.

Finding out I was "illegitimate" was like a huge earthquake, an eight on the Richter scale—the very earth was pulled out from under me. And, from that traumatic moment on, I understood why my siblings had been so mean to me, why Mother had been so hard on me, that things would have been so much easier for my family if I'd just never been born. Father could have quietly suffocated me, or been like those people who hate their adopted children so much that they beat them to death. But he didn't.

Throughout my childhood, I had a recurring dream. In it, my father was hiding under my bed, brandishing a kitchen knife. One night, I woke up screaming, thinking, *My father doesn't want me!* I was afraid of him, but at the same time, I wanted desperately to be close to him. I couldn't say a word, but woke everyone with my terrible sobs.

My father spoke quietly from one of the other beds. "Let's all get some sleep. The sun'll be up soon."

From then on, each time I had the dream, I explained to myself that he was hiding under the bed with that knife to protect me, in the hope that it would turn out to be true.

For his part, my father never so much as raised his voice to me. Once, Third Brother and I ran home from the river soaking wet, only to find Father at the entrance to the courtyard, anxiously calling our names. I stopped dead in my tracks, but Third Brother pushed me in front of Father, who slapped me across the face. It really hurt, but I covered my face with my hands without making a sound. Father may have thought I was Third Brother—his eyesight never was good. But I've always hoped he knew, because then it meant we were actually close enough for him to be willing to hit me.

I consider myself a person without a father, and yet, Father was more important than Mother in how he shaped my life. That ill-fated relationship with my history teacher was a textbook example: I was searching for a father figure. I wanted someone to love me, no matter how implausible it was, no matter how dangerous. Even if the price was my life, even if I had to sacrifice the whole of my existence, I just wanted a father. Every relationship I've ever had with a man, including my marriage, has been part of this search for a father. My distorted psyche meant that I was destined to fail, destined never to find happiness, destined to have my heart broken.

That I should be so twisted up about all this is evidence of my innately flawed nature, especially since my father accepted me as his daughter. All those days and nights when my father had gazed at me with mournful eyes, he hadn't been ruing my existence—he'd actually been worried about me. To his dying day, he cherished and cared for me, this child born of the love between his wife and another man. If only I'd been able to truly feel his affection.

CHAPTER 5

I

My mother never called me because she never knew my number or where I was. She had dreams about me, though, envisioning me marching as fast as I could down a rough path, my whole body drenched in sweat while I struggled under the weight of a backpack. "My sixth little girl is one of those people who's always on the road," she would say when people asked after me.

For many years, I would call my mother every time I arrived in a new place to tell her I was safe and ask how she was, but toward the end of her life, I called less and less. Fourth Sister kept me up-to-date on her health and welfare.

About two months before my mother's death, I was sitting in front of a laptop in a small Italian hotel. Outside the window, emerald-green mountains stretched into the distance. The hotel was situated deep in the vast mountain range of central Italy, surrounded by centuries-old pine forests. The buildings were even older than the trees, dense layers of ivy and vines winding their way across the stonework. There were hot springs less than an hour away, and it was a short drive to the coast.

The beautiful hotel was a treasured secret of the chicest Italians. The chef there had formerly been in charge of the kitchen at Harry's Bar, the famous (not to mention extremely pricey) Venetian bar where Hemingway himself had watered his fertile imagination night after night while writing *Across the River and into the Trees*. He drank himself into such a stupor there that it was the worst novel he ever wrote.

I had been working on a novel off and on for a good six months. Set in old Shanghai, it told the story of a young boy, a young girl, and a magician. Only here, deep in the mountains of Italy, was I finally able to relax.

From July to August, in observance of a local holiday, a stage was erected in the town square at the foot of the mountain to host various performances. Amid the lively atmosphere this created, I checked my e-mail on the hotel computer. One day, wading through endless and mostly useless messages, I found a note from my second sister's son:

> *Ma asked me to let you all know that Grandma is bedridden and has barely eaten anything for weeks. Ma says it's because she's worrying herself sick about Fourth and Sixth Aunties. Not a day goes by without Grandma talking about how much she misses them.*

I took the antiquated elevator back to my room and called my mother. It was one in the morning in Italy, early morning in China. My fifth sister-in-law, who was caring for my mother, answered. She told me Mother had been in the hospital for a while. She'd just come back home and still wasn't eating. I asked her to put my mother on.

Mother asked me where I was, saying how much she missed me and how much she wanted me to visit.

I told her I was in the mountains in Italy and it would be September before I could finish the novel and go back to China.

"Little Six, I'll wait for you," she said.

Those words made me very uneasy.

The next time we spoke, she said, "I've been eating, I swear. Come back soon, Little Six. I have things I need to say to you. Phone calls are expensive, and your old ma knows things are hard when you're far away from home. Make sure you look after yourself." With that, she hung up.

My eyes were filled with tears.

2

Ten days after that second phone call, I caught a flight to Beijing and rushed straight to Chongqing.

The neighbors watched me climb the stairs, gossiping in hushed tones. I pushed open the door and ran to my mother's bedroom. Her eyes were sunken, her face withered and misshapen. She sat up in bed and gazed at me with a dazed expression. Tears began to roll down my face at the sight, so I quickly turned away. When I looked back, I managed to force a smile.

She exclaimed, "My sixth daughter is back!" before lying down again.

The center of the bed had caved in so much that it squashed her into a little ball. The mother who had managed to support this big family on nothing but her own strength was gone. Her hair stuck to her pallid face as she lay incapacitated on the bed. She could no longer eat or dress herself, let alone cook or do laundry.

The bed was littered with piles of clothes and linens. Beside the bed, a chair sagged under a similar mound. Only Fifth Sister-in-Law, my mother, and I were there for dinner that evening.

Fifth Sister-in-Law brought my mother's dinner to her bedside and fed her one mouthful at a time.

"Your ma's appetite is better than usual," she said.

The desk by the bed was the one I'd bought when I came home in 1996 to write my earlier book about the family. Next to it sat a dust-covered picture frame, still in its cardboard packaging. An equally dusty photo of my father, roughly twenty inches across, hung on the other wall.

Third Brother and Third Sister-in-Law had had the photo enlarged when my father passed away in the summer of 1999. He was around eighty, with a wispy beard and mustache, wrinkles clearly visible at the corners of his eyes and on his neck. It was the face of a good man who had been through more than his share of life's ups and downs. I remembered my father's eyes being brighter than in the photo, shining with the wisdom, kindness, and tolerance with which he always conducted himself.

Dark came early that day. In the glare of the lamplight, the first thing I did was to put away the extra quilts and blankets. Next, I carried a bucket of water into the room and wiped the dusty surfaces down with a damp cloth. I was going to take the cardboard off of the picture frame, but my mother was leaning against it as she gazed out the window, and I didn't want to disturb her.

Fifth Sister-in-Law obviously hadn't cleaned the place in ages. I took down the curtains and threw them in the washing machine. The potted rose balsam plant and jasmine bush on the balcony were parched and yellowing. Part of the awning above them had rotted away and moss was growing beneath the damaged section. Bamboo mats were piled up in one corner with a few plastic sheets, all of it coated in a thick layer of gray dust. Three old-fashioned trunks sat against the wall, covered with a grimy red cloth. When I was a child, those trunks had seemed inviolable, sacred. Every time my mother took something out, she would immediately lock them again. Once, my eldest sister, finding the house empty, took the opportunity to pry open the lock and carry off a basket full of things. My mother scolded her, saying that unless she learned respect, she'd never grow into a responsible adult.

The desk was also unbelievably grubby. The drawers were filled to the brim with bottles, jars, sticky rice sweets, and piles of old newspapers. A quick inspection showed that all of them dated from 1996—they were the newspapers I had read when I was living at home. My mother had kept everything from that summer—the pencils, ballpoint pens, scraps of paper, buttons, needles, thread, paper clips, squeezed-out tubes of toothpaste, ends of soap, toothbrushes, erasers, correction fluid. I wrapped the heap of garbage up in a cloth.

"Don't throw that away, Little Six," my mother called out.

I looked at her for a long moment and then returned the items to the drawer.

"You can use them when you come back to do more writing," she said.

"Do you really think I'd be able to write anything in this mess?" I retorted irritably.

My mother seemed about to say something, but stopped herself.

"Why don't you tell them to clean up a bit for you, Ma? Couldn't you at least say something?" Now I was angry.

My mother just looked at me without replying.

Fifth Sister-in-Law walked in and said, "I'll clean up, Sixth Sister."

I told her there was no need; I was almost finished anyway. I asked, "Are there any clean sheets? Let's change the bed for Ma."

Fifth Sister-in-Law brought clean sheets and a duvet cover. I put my arms around my mother and lifted her up. She was startlingly light, no more than ninety pounds. There was a dark stain on the sheets where she had been sleeping, which stank horribly when I moved closer to it. I looked my mother over carefully and realized that her pants were stained with shit, and her fingernails were a greenish-black color.

Fifth Sister-in-Law changed the sheets, duvet cover, and pillows, and I removed my mother's dirty clothes before laying her back on the bed. I got a fresh bucket of hot water and scrubbed her clean, washing her hands with soap, and changing her into clean pajamas. I got angrier and angrier as I went. Why didn't my mother stand up for herself? What had Fifth Sister-in-Law been doing all this time? She'd been a shop assistant for a while, but she had quit to become a full-time housewife. After the old compound had been demolished, she and my brother moved into the new condo I'd bought. I sent two thousand five hundred yuan a month to cover living costs for my parents and their caregivers, as well as any medical costs while my mother was ill. First, it was Third Brother and Third Sister-in-Law taking care of my parents, then my eldest sister's daughter Xiaomi, and finally Fifth Brother and Fifth Sister-in-Law. In the end, Fifth Brother was considerate enough to tell me that I didn't need to give them so much, since our mother's pension covered most of their expenses, and if they were short, they could ask Second Sister, who handled Mother's money.

My mother had always been a stickler for cleanliness. Knowing she would come back from the shipyard on the weekends, Fourth Sister and I would do a major cleaning job every Friday, dusting the bedside tables and saving the water we'd used for laundry to wash the tables and chairs. If my mother had been able to live in this filth without complaining, she must really be getting old.

My mother seemed surprised when I told her I was going back to Second Sister's house that evening. She propped herself halfway up in bed and looked at me quizzically, as if asking why I didn't sleep there with her.

So why didn't I? Was it simply that I couldn't stand to sleep in a bed that smelled of my mother's piss and shit? I told her my luggage was at Second Sister's place and that I needed to use the Internet there. I promised I'd be back first thing in the morning, and she seemed satisfied.

The next day, Eldest Sister, Second Sister, Third Brother, and the grandchildren all came over. My mother was overjoyed and ate much more than usual. Later, as we sat around on the edge of her bed, she told us that sometimes she was constipated for days on end. She would work herself into a panic until she finally had to use her hands to dig the waste out. Eldest Sister said she would go and buy some kind of herbal laxative, but the distance from the bedroom to the toilet was too far for Mother to manage. We sent Third Brother to buy a comfortable bedpan and a rocking chair, and we made plans to clear off the balcony so that our mother could sit outside and get some fresh air.

I had recently put twenty thousand yuan into her account. "These new purchases can come out of the money in that account," Second Sister said.

"Leave that money alone," I replied. "It's bound to come in handy someday."

I took five hundred yuan out of my purse and gave it to my mother. She put the money in her pocket, saying that she would give it to Third Brother to pay for the rocking chair.

Later on, while we were eating, she wet herself. When we changed her pants, Third Brother caught sight of the money and asked, "Do you want us to use this money to buy you a rocking chair?"

She nodded, and Third Brother took the money.

After a few days, I went back to Beijing and buried myself in work on another novel. When my birthday came later that September, I thought of calling my mother, but forgot. When I finally did call, she told me not to worry, as she was eating and sleeping better now. I had nearly wrapped up the novel about old Shanghai and was negotiating a contract for its publication. Second Sister later told me that Mother had been looking for the five hundred yuan I gave her, terrified she'd lost it. She sat only once in the rocking chair that Third Brother had bought. She did appreciate the bedpan, at least.

3

After having slept for less than an hour at Xiaomi's place, I woke and lay on the bed, gazing once again at the Princess Mononoke poster. Thinking back on it, I realized that the still-wrapped frame I'd seen the previous month in my mother's room must have been used for the portrait at her funeral. If I had been paying a little more attention, I might have realized that my mother was getting ready to die, and I wouldn't have been in such a rush to leave. And if I'd stayed in Chongqing a little longer, maybe my mother wouldn't even have died. *The Wolf God had the company of his spirit daughter, Princess Mononoke,* I thought, *just like my mother had her children.* But since none of us ever really stayed by her side, it was as good as having no one. She had raised us—a pack of heartless, ungrateful wolves—for nothing.

I walked out of the bedroom to find two bowls of egg and tomato soup on the table. Xiaomi had changed into a black floral tank top but still wore her jeans. She smiled at me apologetically, explaining that the soup was left over from the day before, and she hoped I didn't mind.

"Of course not. Time to get back to your grandmother's place," I said.

Just as we finished the soup, my phone rang. I was surprised to see that it was Tang—Fourth Sister must have called him. He told me he was flying in from Nandu that day, as he was the only one who could pick up the keys to my mother's new condos.

The six-story building my mother lived in, the one built on the foundations of the old Compound No. 6, was slated to be demolished to make way for an even newer high-rise. So last year, I'd bought a pair of two-bedroom condos on South Bank Road. They would be ready to move into by autumn. One was meant for my mother, the other for Fifth Brother, who would take care of Mother.

Since I didn't have Chinese citizenship anymore, Tang had agreed to let me buy the condos in his name. Right after the sale went through, though, my mother passed away. Now, if Tang didn't come, we wouldn't be able to take possession of the properties.

At first, I worried that Tang was calling to say he couldn't make it, but my fears were unfounded. Not only was he coming to help with the condos, but he wanted to pay his respects to my mother. I was moved—maybe he wasn't such a bad guy after all? Even the deepest enmities and the bitterest feuds should be forgotten at a time like this. In the *Godfather* movies, vendettas are always put on hold until after a funeral. During celebrations, baptisms, and other happy occasions, the characters do what they have to do. But never at funerals. The deceased command the ultimate respect.

I turned around to find Xiaomi eavesdropping on my phone call with Tang.

"Sorry, but I can't help wondering: Why is he calling you instead of Fourth Auntie?"

It was a good question, but I couldn't explain everything to her. Some things were better kept secret. I said I didn't know.

Then Xiaomi told me the story of how Fourth Sister had come back from London a month earlier not because of our mother's illness, but to find Tang.

Tang had taken early retirement from the university in England and returned to China to teach at Nandu University. Fourth Sister wanted to go with him, but he told her he would go ahead of her, and she could follow once everything was settled. After hearing nothing for a month, she e-mailed him, but got no reply. She called, but no one answered. Fourth Sister feared that what Tang had said in London was just a way to extricate himself from their relationship. Sick of being made a fool of by this man, she decided to go to Nandu herself and find out what was going on.

When Fourth Sister arrived in Nandu, to her amazement, Tang pretended not to know her. He refused to let her through the door and threw her luggage into the street. It was inconceivable to her because, before his departure from England, the two of them had shared the same bed and made love. Tiantian had wanted to go with her mother to the airport to see him off, but Tang had insisted that Fourth Sister take him to the airport alone. Before he went through security, he'd embraced her tightly, as if unable to bear the thought of being apart.

When she arrived in Nandu, though, she found his characteristic courteousness had turned to cruelty. At first, she was stunned by his refusal to acknowledge her, but when she came to her senses, she confronted him. It was quite a scene: he ran across the campus, trying to flee away from her, with Fourth Sister giving chase like her life depended on it.

Tang was sixty, much older than she was, and his body quickly began to give out, but he sprinted onward with no regard for the consequences. Fourth Sister was so heartbroken she stopped chasing him. When she got back to his house, a gust of wind slammed the door in her face. She had no key, so all she could do was wait outside. Soon it became clear: however long she waited, he wouldn't be back. She called his cell phone, but it was turned off. She tested the apartment's flimsy door, and she found the old lock too warped to hold. Inside was a one-bedroom, 1950s-style apartment with a living room, tiny kitchen, and squat toilet.

It was really miserly of the lousy university to treat a famous scholar like that. Fourth Sister gave a snort of contempt and felt indignant on Tang's behalf. She carried her suitcase in and sat down on a stool, unsure what to do next. Abandoning his job in England for such an awful place could only mean that Tang had another woman. The woman that had phoned him flashed into Fourth Sister's mind. She must have put him up to all of this. How had she been so blind? The disgusting pair had been planning this all along, lying to her. Tang had made himself a stranger to her, severing all ties to show devotion to his young lover. Fourth Sister began to cry, lamenting her own stupidity, bemoaning her loneliness and the cruelty of men. If he'd wanted so badly to break up with her, there was no need for him to move to another country, let alone run across campus like a madman. Was he really that scared of her? She beat her hands on the table until the skin was bloody and broken, but she didn't feel any pain.

A little clock on the wall ticked on and on. After half an hour or so, she had cried herself out. Only then did she notice the broken skin on her palms and bandage her hands with a handkerchief. Just as she stood up to pour herself a glass of water, there was a heavy knock at the door. She went to open it.

Outside were two policemen. They told her they had received a call about a home invasion. They grilled Fourth Sister about who she was and threatened to take her to the station.

Fourth Sister informed them she was the tenant's wife of ten years. Taken aback, the policemen looked at each another, not knowing how to proceed. At that moment, Tang strode in. He told the police that he had no wife and didn't know this woman. Fourth Sister was furious. She cursed him for his ingratitude, and then proceeded tearfully to recount the whole sorry tale. The police listened, unable to make heads or tails of her diatribe. Finally, they asked for ID.

Seeing the pair's British papers, the two policemen exchanged another look, then, saying that they weren't interested in British people's domestic squabbles, turned on their heels, and left. Fourth Sister went to the bathroom to wipe her eyes, and when she came out, found that Tang had disappeared again. It was late, so she figured he must have run off to hide in some cheap hotel. Fourth Sister went out to search for him for a while, but in the end had to go back to his house. She had no friends in Nandu. All she could do was call Chongqing and pour her heart out to her sister.

Tang didn't show his face the next day either, so Fourth Sister went to look for him in the building where his classes were held. Not finding him there, she returned to the house just as he was sneaking in to retrieve his laptop. She demanded that he tell her what was going on.

He insisted they go to the university's Foreign Affairs Office. There, Fourth Sister exposed Tang's dual citizenship, which was not allowed in China, as well as the details of their common-law marriage. Tang must have wished that the ground would open up and swallow him. The

Foreign Affairs Office said Tang had to choose between Chinese and British citizenship or go to jail for breaking the law. Tang said he was so sorry everyone had been put to so much trouble on account of his private business, and he offered to treat them all to lunch at a nearby restaurant. After Tang had ordered the meal, he pretended to go to the bathroom and ran off again, leaving Fourth Sister to foot the bill.

Filled with contempt for Tang, Xiaomi concluded, "If there's a next life, I want to come back as a man. I'd show all these scumbags how a real man behaves."

Tang hadn't mentioned Fourth Sister's trip to Nandu on the phone, and I hoped his willingness to come to Chongqing showed that it wouldn't be a disaster for him and Fourth Sister to be in the same place.

"Should we go now, Sixth Auntie?" Xiaomi asked.

I put my shoes on, picked up my backpack, and nodded.

4

Since no bicycle rickshaws came by, Xiaomi took me on a shortcut through the nearby streets.

The Water Café, a little restaurant in the middle of Stone Bridge where I'd bought steamed pork buns for my eighteenth birthday, had been demolished. The photography studio, department store, stadium, and Xinhua Bookstore—all the old familiar haunts—were gone. Not a trace remained of the world I remembered. Billboards hung from the tall buildings on either side of the road. Pop songs played in every store, and sale signs were plastered in every window.

I caught my reflection in the shop windows. The shoulder-length black hair, the short black coat, and the flower-embroidered hem of my red skirt seemed at odds with the sad face that wore them. Twenty years seemed to have slipped by in an instant. A steady stream of people passed by. Then suddenly, there he was, his nose long and straight, his eyes gazing fixedly at me. He smiled as if he were a little surprised to have finally found me. I felt myself transformed back into a pigtailed young girl in a black skirt and white blouse.

It was very hot that long-ago summer day. Sweat beaded on my forehead as I let myself be swept off my feet. The crimson sunset clouds illuminated us. There were a dozen or so people in the square practicing Western ballroom dancing. He stopped and watched for a while, before stretching out his hand. "Come, dance with me. There's nothing to be afraid of."

In a surge of confidence, I began to move my feet in time to the rhythm. "One, two, three. One, two, three. Raise your head. Chest out." He looked at me and smiled. For that shy girl dancing with the first man in her life, everyone else vanished. The music suddenly changed. The waltzing couples abruptly began to fling their arms and legs wildly, in a collective revolutionary dance. He disappeared.

He had been my history teacher. His brother had died in the factional fighting on the Yangtze, and the blame fell on his shoulders. On top of it, he himself had been active in the Red Guard and, in the post-Mao backlash, was deemed one of the three types of "undesirables": rebels, factionalists, and killers who had joined in armed warfare during the Cultural Revolution. Rather than carry the burden of his past, he chose to end his life. He also did not want to face the consequences of our affair.

I'd spent years trying my best not to think about him, about where he was buried, about anyone who had known him. His family probably hadn't even kept his ashes.

I believe that death is final, like blowing out a candle. On the other hand, I don't deny that the restless souls of the dead sometimes send us messages after they have passed on. Standing there with Xiaomi, I was sure I'd seen his reflection in the window, that I'd been with him once again for a few fleeting moments. But we'd never really danced like that, in public. Maybe his soul had been wandering nearby when it ran into mine and, seeing my despair, did what I had secretly wanted him to do all those years ago.

Shouldn't a girl at least be allowed the fantasy of dancing with the man she loves?

I realized then that I had loved him. Over time, I had come to understand that a man's love has the power both to sap the will and to warm a damaged heart, even if he is already a ghost.

And what about my husband?

I am good at looking into the distance, but bad at seeing what's close at hand. The closer I get to the present moment, the blinder I become. It's like peeling an onion. The more layers I remove, the more the tears come. It was easy for me to go over everything that happened before 1997. What happened after that year, though, I didn't want to remember.

From childhood, I'd always harbored depths of unhappiness in my heart, and I grew up to be a bitter person, always angry with the world. I felt justified in my intolerance of others' faults. I was so obsessed with cleanliness and purity that it infected my heart. I had an extreme need for beauty and perfection, so much so that I didn't care if I humiliated my husband in public. For example, if he wasn't telling the whole truth, I would point it out immediately, leaving him no room to maneuver. He liked me to dress in sexy clothing, and he liked to take sexy photos of me. But I wanted to dress according to my own personality, rather than to please him. Once, I bought a sturdy, nice-looking suitcase. He thought it was too expensive, and tried to make me return it, but I wouldn't. When he then went through quite a few cheap suitcases while mine held up beautifully, I mocked him mercilessly. He said I was self-righteous and intolerant, that I could never let anything go. Looking back, I feel I was a complete failure as a woman. I can only imagine how dissatisfied he was with me.

During a fight once, I locked myself in the bathroom and said I'd only open the door if he'd give me a written guarantee that he would treat me well. The stalemate ended with him kicking the door down. I cried, but he didn't even deal with me. He simply grabbed his bottle of sleeping pills and went to bed. I heard the sound of snoring coming from the bedroom and felt a chill in my heart. So this was marriage—watching someone who loved you turn into a complete stranger. I stood in front of the mirror and looked at myself. I had never felt as panicked or pathetic as I did at that moment.

After that, I didn't want to argue with him anymore. I simply threw the door open and went out to wander the streets aimlessly. He never came looking for me. I walked until the middle of the night with no place to go. I didn't even have my keys, so all I could do was yell to him from the doorstep to let me in. He was quite annoyed to be woken up.

Upon hearing all of this, the British therapist I was seeing said something that shook me to the core.

"You poor child, you have to get out of that house. Maybe then you can find yourself again."

I did as he suggested and took a vacation so I could relax. Prior to that, I had only traveled for book tours, which were always packed with interviews and readings from morning till night. For my getaway, I took the Eurostar from London to Paris, where I spent some time with an old friend. Then I took a train to Munich to see another old friend. We sat at the edge of a calm lake and drank ice-cold beer as we watched the wild ducks spread their wings and skim over the water. Where was my husband at that moment?

I arrived back in London just in time for the publication of the English version of *Daughter of the River*. The *Sunday Times* had previously serialized an excerpt. My British publisher had also done a good deal of publicity for the book, which had made its way onto quite a few bestseller lists. At that time, the sales figures even surpassed *Harry Potter*, though this was before that series had truly taken the world by storm.

Then, in May, I received an invitation to the Sydney Writers' Festival, which happened to coincide with the publication of my memoir in Australia. I flew from London to Sydney, with a stopover in Bangkok. The trip took nearly twenty-four hours. I expected someone from the writers' festival to meet me at the airport, but no one showed up. My luggage lying at my feet, I noticed a man who looked as weary as I was tying his shoes. They looked ordinary at first glance, but a closer inspection revealed them to be unusually elegant.

A tall, well-built man in his early forties, he had short hair and wore black jeans and a meticulously tailored suit jacket with no tie. Hoisting my luggage onto his cart, he introduced himself as P, a famous historian and a professor at a British university.

I told him a little about myself, and he marveled at the coincidence that we were on the same plane and going to the same event.

By now it was dark out, and we were surrounded by other passengers. Having resigned ourselves to the fact that nobody was coming to pick us up, we went outside to hail a taxi. It was just a short ride to the designated hotel. The lobby was brilliantly lit and filled with huge vases of fresh flowers. Someone showed us to our respective rooms. I could see the ocean from mine, and the publisher had even sent a lovely bouquet of flowers. A welcome card with a schedule lay on the table.

In the morning, I came down to the lobby and ran into P again. The writers' festival had arranged a shuttle for us to spend some time at the writers' camp. Our group was about twenty authors from all over the world. I sat in the front row next to the window. P asked if he could sit next to me. I nodded.

He called me by my name. I joked that I wasn't her; I was her little sister. He laughed, revealing perfectly white teeth. His smile was enchanting, sensitive, and very kind. When he wasn't laughing, though, his face seemed melancholy, as if he were always pondering something—just like me. I was stunned to find my English unusually fluent. Words I didn't normally use came to me effortlessly. We talked until we reached the writers' camp, which was in a beautiful spot. I and another author, a woman from India, would be staying in two chalets connected by a corridor. Our bags were waiting at the door.

At that moment, an old friend from China arrived. She was teaching Chinese literature at an Australian university and had driven over to see me. I took her to a place where we could drink and talk. P joined us and, throughout the day and evening, he didn't leave my side, not even when we moved to another place for dinner. The other writers all returned to their rooms, but the three of us sat up late into the night drinking and talking, P telling joke after joke. The wind whispered through the trees on the mountains as we walked back along the path, which was lit by sparkling little lamps. We reached a fork and said good night under the moon. He took a few steps toward his room, but then rushed back and embraced me tightly. We looked at one another, and then he turned and walked away. My friend said he was in love with me.

I shook my head. Love had been absent from my life for so many years that I scarcely believed in it anymore.

I could make out the faint sound of the Indian woman next door chanting scriptures. That night my friend filled me in on the recent bad luck she'd had at her university, as well as the trouble that had resulted from her translation of a poet's biography.

She had to get back early the next morning, and after she left the Indian writer and I took a walk. There were kangaroos everywhere, big and small. They were really sweet, and not the least bit shy. I didn't see P at breakfast. Word was he'd accidentally eaten some garlic the day before and had an allergic reaction.

It was afternoon before we saw each other again—the shuttle returned to take everyone back down the mountain to the hotel in Sydney. We stopped at a vineyard for a tasting, and everybody bought a few bottles of wine.

When we got to the hotel, the head of my British publishing house came to see me. She told me she was from New Zealand, so visiting Sydney was almost like going home. She asked me if I knew anybody else there. I told her I had met P, and she smiled as soon as she heard his name. It was obvious they knew each other well.

That evening there was a cocktail party that doubled as the opening ceremony of the festival, and everyone was expected to attend. I wore a knee-length skirt with matching high heels and put my hair up. I met a lot of reporters, writers, publishers, bookshop owners, and literary agents, and all of them wanted to toast my book. I had already drunk close to half a bottle at the wine tasting that afternoon, and I was beginning to realize just how much alcohol was in my system when I caught sight of P. He was dressed in a suit so smart it made him look like a new man. He gazed at me warmly. Beaming, I asked if he would like to have dinner with me.

He said he would be honored.

That evening, P was very attentive. The editor took us out to dinner at the Authors' Club, where P showed himself to be a perfect gentleman, taking excellent care of me. The dinner went quite late, and it was close to midnight by the time we returned to the hotel. As we passed the hotel bar, P asked if I would join him for a nightcap. I looked into his earnest face for a moment, then shook my head and said we should have breakfast together the next morning instead.

Why didn't I say yes? I regretted it immediately. I couldn't sleep for hours, and when I did finally drift off, he filled my dreams. We were in Chongqing looking for a restaurant. Every place we looked at wasn't good enough for him. I was starving, but he still refused.

I woke and sat up, shaking my head uncomprehendingly. I went to the breakfast room, and sure enough, he was there. He handed me a glass of iced tomato juice, and I told him about my dream. He laughed. A publisher walked over, saying she'd just seen the newspaper, and she congratulated him on the high academic honor that the British establishment had conferred on him. She asked him jokingly why he was sitting with me, commenting that the two of us looked like we were close. He said it was because I was a genius.

I congratulated him too. He looked overjoyed. That day was a turning point in his life.

I had two talks to give that day, as well as several interviews. His schedule was even busier than mine, but we agreed to meet in the evening.

The day flew by, and it was half past ten by the time I returned to the hotel. I took a shower and changed into an all-white outfit. The phone rang, but there was nobody there when I answered. I decided to go downstairs to send a fax. On my way back up, the elevator stopped at his floor, and I ducked out on impulse. As I stood in the hall wondering what to do next, he came out of the other elevator holding a fax. When he saw me, his eyes lit up. We moved toward each other and fell into an embrace.

We were fish, and we needed water, he said. And I would come to realize that he was the water, the very reason for my existence. That incredible night marked our first of many together. Later, he told me that he'd had everything in his life but me, that he'd always been waiting for me. It was love at first sight, a love that made us young again. Every blink of our eyes, every word we spoke, every move we made, and every inch of our bodies revealed our joy.

The next day, we were booked all day again. I stole away from my commitments to hear his poetry recital, after which there was just enough time for him to catch my talk. We were forced to spend the afternoon apart. When we stole a brief moment to talk at the conference center, he told me he couldn't wait to see me that night. It was the last night of the festival, the last of our magical time together. I got back to the hotel very late and then had to get up before dawn the next morning. He helped me get dressed. I was leaving for Melbourne, and then on to a few other cities to promote my book, while he had to catch a flight back to London.

In each new city, I would clutch the essay collection he'd given me, feeling happy as I read every word. For the first time in a while, I found myself able to sleep without pills. I missed him—really missed him. I was dying to finish the trip and get back to London to see him.

When I got home, I found a letter waiting for me. In it, he said that it felt like the end of the world when I left. He described his feelings on reading my memoir, saying that it was on par with the works of Dickens and Tolstoy and so on. And he told me he couldn't wait to see me again.

My husband had opened the letter before I returned, and he had an odd expression on his face when he saw me. After some time, he said he wanted to meet P. I told him I would see if it was convenient.

We went to P's house the day after I heard that my father had passed away. P had invited several of his close friends. It was also the first time I meet P's wife, A. She was a painter and a trustee of one of London's top galleries. She was also a strong personality and, to me, rather forbidding. I wondered if he needed a mother figure in his life. A was just such a woman.

As I watched P playing Ping-Pong with my husband in the garden, I reflected that my husband wouldn't want to give me up, and that P might not want to leave his wife either. Should we be lovers? It didn't seem like a good idea, but I wasn't sure how else I could be with him.

My family said that the weather was so hot they'd have to cremate my father immediately, and I couldn't get a flight to China in time for the funeral. My husband told me that there were different ways to attend a funeral, that it was enough that I had expressed my feelings. I wrote a long piece about going to the funeral, in which I also talked about P, who thought I had gone back to China. I needed time to get some perspective on our relationship.

My husband and I decided to buy a new house. I found one on Hazel Road with three bedrooms and two living rooms, gardens in front and back, and a kitchen complete with dishwasher, washing machine, and dryer. The garden was huge, with nearly a thousand square feet of lawn in addition to a big greenhouse. There were two apple trees, lavender bushes and hydrangeas, three tall pine trees, and lots of rosebushes.

The aging wooden shed looked like a true antique. The house was only a few minutes' walk from the Tube, and there were plenty of shops nearby, as well as a sizable library.

We rushed to buy it, using the advance from my novel. I wanted to redo the floors and paint the walls, but my husband insisted on moving in as soon as the papers were signed. By the time we'd arranged the furniture and cleaned up the garden, we were exhausted. The two of us had always had different ideas about houses, but this time he supported my choice completely. Maybe he really did love it as much as I did. Or maybe it was because of P.

One day soon after, I stepped off the escalator from the Tube station, and P was there waiting for me. I felt like I was being lifted up from hell. He pulled me close and embraced me. We went to eat in Chinatown. He kept saying he wanted to run away with me, that nothing mattered as long as we were together. He was unhappy to hear about the new house.

Once, we went together to a lecture he was giving that his old school had arranged for him, followed by dinner at his teacher's house. It was late by the time we got back to London. On the train, he told me I was just like his first wife, and that his colleagues and his teacher all thought so too. He said life was too short, that he wanted to start over immediately. He had resolved to leave A, and to tell his children about us. He said meeting me in Australia was like winning the lottery. He couldn't wait any longer to move in together.

Then, A called and told me a number of alarming stories about P. I was unmoved—P had already told me everything. He was overjoyed that I hadn't been scared off by A and that he'd found someone who could stand up to her.

Not long after that, I went to a conference in Canada, and by the time I got back to London, everything had changed. While I was away, my husband's lover had come from China and was staying in our new house. At the same time, P had rented a hip loft in an old factory on the canal called the Eagle's Nest. Without even waiting for my return, P moved in. He sold the enormous, antique desk his grandfather had left him and used the money for new furniture, including a metal-framed glass desk, a beautiful rug, an antique-style coffee table, and a stylish screen.

He wanted me to move in with him right away and even reserved a moving van, but I felt too guilty. My husband was going through a difficult time, and I didn't want to make things harder on A, who, on top of the breakup, had just lost her father. So I lived in both houses, spending some nights with P, and some on a little sofa bed in my study on the top floor of the house my husband and I had bought.

P was upset. He kept pressuring me to move out and divorce my husband. For his part, my husband was very supportive. He impressed upon Fourth Sister what a big deal it would be for me to marry P, as if P were an English prince. Fourth Sister was naturally excited by this surprise development. My husband took the matter very seriously. After some discussion, we filed for a divorce on the grounds that I had committed adultery. We awaited the court's consent.

As this was the first Christmas since P had told his kids he was starting a new family, we agreed that he would spend Christmas with them. He planned to make it up to me with a trip to Spain to celebrate the New Year. But P missed me, and he only lasted until lunchtime on the twenty-sixth before rushing over to my place. When A found out, they had a huge fight, during which she threw a glass at him. She called me and yelled for an hour without taking a breath. Each time I hung up, she called back, over and over again. It was like she'd lost her mind.

For New Year's we went to Madrid. We rented a car and meandered from the north to the south. He called A to check in, and I called a girlfriend, but P accused me of lying and calling my husband. I had to put him on the phone to prove to him it really was a woman. Later, my husband did call, asking P to polish up his translation of my novel. Although P agreed, he was furious, railing against my husband for deliberately sabotaging our trip. I said maybe P just didn't want to do the work. That night we had our first real fight, and I stormed out of the hotel room.

The whole trip was plagued by interference from A and my husband, and the two of us never managed to fully get out from under the weight of London. I told P I'd be happy just to be his lover, that I didn't want him to leave his children. Of his four children, his eldest was only fifteen and the youngest was ten. I didn't want him to go through with the divorce. P said it meant I didn't really love him.

When we got back from Spain, he seemed very unhappy. He went to see his children, and I went back to my own home, even though my husband's new partner was there. We saw each other again a little while later at my husband's university. P had heard that I was going there to see a friend who was returning from America and wanted to make sure I wasn't cheating on him. Upon seeing that the friend was a woman, even he admitted he was being ridiculous. His jealousy was getting worse.

The lease on the loft was nearly up, and P was resolved not to move back in with A and the children, so we saw several places together in the space of a single weekend. We eventually settled on an apartment in Highgate, and this time, despite my trepidation, I agreed to move in with him. He was very pleased and suggested we celebrate with a movie. We decided to ride on the open-top deck of the bus so that we could take in the London sights. We arrived at Charing Cross to find the theater was showing *The End of the Affair*, adapted from Graham Greene's novel. When it was over, neither of us could say a word. The tragedy of the film enshrouded us.

That Sunday, he went to see his children.

Maybe it was fear for my future, maybe it was pressure from my husband, or maybe I really wasn't ready for such a huge life change, but that Sunday I felt restless. I got an "I love you" fax from P, saying that A had a new lover who had given her a huge ring. I felt deeply sad. I sent a fax to my husband to say that I was in the new apartment on my own and P had gone home. My husband wanted me to come home right away. My fourth sister had come to visit, and they were both concerned about P's increasingly possessive behavior. They said I should leave P. They wanted to drive over and pick me up.

Everything that happened next felt like a dream. Late that night, I took a long walk along the canal, returning covered in dew. In the morning, I called P, and he said he was coming over immediately. Without waiting for him, I wrote a long letter telling him to go back to his children. I put the letter on his desk and left without looking back.

Why did we break up? To this day, I still haven't figured it out. Nothing big happened. I just knew that his wife and four children and my husband would always come between us. We couldn't harden our hearts to them. We wanted to leap over the abyss and into a new life together, but we didn't make it across.

I had plenty of opportunities to spend some time with him again, but I never did. I could at least have gone by the apartment—I knew he was there—but I didn't. He left me messages, but I never called back. My departure was total, but it was never really directed at him. In truth, I was leaving everything: P, my husband, London, England. After nine years, I was sick of my life there, and I wanted to bring it all to an end.

And so it happened that, just as my memoir was being published in China, I found myself moving back to Beijing. On my way to the Chinese embassy to get a visa, I called P to tell him I was leaving the country. He begged me to meet him in the doorway of a church next to the BBC building. I saw him there, looking frantically for me. I came around behind him, and he swept me into his arms. He took me to the pub next door.

He ordered us two gin and tonics and sat down facing me. He said he had moved back in with his wife and children. He brought me the many presents he had given me that I'd left behind, in particular the hand-woven Eastern-style silk nightdress he'd hunted for at Christmas. He started to cry, and then I started crying too. He pulled out a handkerchief and gave it to me to dry my eyes. He said we should only publish what we had written for each other after we were dead, including the collection of my poetry that we'd translated together. Otherwise, he said, we would bring unnecessary trouble on ourselves. He was often the subject of unpleasant articles in the tabloids.

We took a taxi to Paddington station and went into a pub for another drink. He looked a little happier. He kept kissing and hugging me, reminding me to write to him from China. We walked to the train together, knowing that it was time to go our separate ways. He started to cry again, but this time I managed to control myself. Later, though, as my eyes followed his train out of the station, the tears fell like rain. That night, I wandered through London like a ghost. Finally, late that night, I returned to the house that had never really been my home.

Before my departure for China, I went to a literary festival held in Marguerite Duras's former home in the south of France. The hotel was situated at the top of a small hill, and you could see for miles. I unpacked my camera and took some pictures from the window, then lay down to stare at the thick, heavy blinds. It was only then that the weight of everything I'd lost truly hit me. I slept for eight hours, nearly missing my evening talk. There were quite a few Chinese authors present, and they'd also invited other well-known Chinese expatriates, such as Wei Jingsheng.

Next, I went to the International Women's Festival in Sweden. P had originally wanted to go with me to meet the poet Tomas Tranströmer, but of course, that was no longer possible. While I was at the conference, Tranströmer sent me an invitation to dinner. Everyone was amazed, as he'd been famously reclusive since becoming wheelchair bound and losing his speech. I went to his home, the Blue House, for dinner. On the train there, the friend I'd invited to accompany me commented that the Tranströmers probably expected me to bring my boyfriend. Maybe they wanted to find out who he was. In reply, I only said that life was unpredictable.

And so, after nine long years as an expat in London, I flew to Beijing and began renting a friend's house in the Xibahe area.

My husband came to visit during his summer break. He told me the court had granted our divorce petition, but that the divorce would not go into effect if either party objected. He proposed that we stop the proceedings and remain husband and wife. He offered to leave his lover and move back to China, and he proposed that I buy her a house in recompense. She refused. In those days, he was very unhappy. He'd had no luck finding teaching positions in China, as various people jealous of his achievements always did their utmost to stand in his way. He brought up the whole business with P again, making everything out to be my fault. He said he hadn't wanted to be with his lover, but I had forced him into it. There was nothing he could do.

We had a huge argument. I reminded him that seeing other people had been his idea, so how could he blame me now? Moreover, he'd been the one who first broke our agreement not to fall in love with anyone else.

We made a new agreement, an attempt to start over, but within a couple days, he was already calling his lover again. I told him it just proved that he'd never been sincere in his commitment to me, that I'd never truly believed him in the first place. He said he'd taken a sleeping pill and needed to go to sleep. I said we had to talk everything through, but he refused. He said P was selfish. I retorted that P had said he was always trying to control me, to brainwash me. In response, my husband said something so offensive that I went berserk. I took a notepad from the bedside table and hurled it at him. He tried to dodge, but its wooden binding struck him squarely in the eye. He yelped with pain and fell down on the bed.

As he lay motionless, I phoned his lover and told her, "I killed him."

Just as sobs exploded from the other end of the line, he suddenly sat up. He picked up a mirror to look at his eye, and I shot across the room to examine the damage. He had a black eye, the skin around it beginning to swell up. He looked at me with hatred, grabbed the phone, and called his sister. I told him it would be better not to get other people involved, that I would take him to the hospital, but he wouldn't speak to me. I was very upset. I apologized profusely, but he continued to ignore me.

His sister and her husband arrived first thing the next morning. They gave me a harsh dressing down before taking him away. They arranged for him to stay at their daughter's house in a distant suburb of Beijing, but they wouldn't give me the address or phone number. After making a string of calls, by the afternoon I'd managed to find out where he was. I took a forty-minute taxi ride to get there.

He refused even to let me in, so I knelt at the door, pleading for forgiveness.

Still he ignored me. I was walking away, tired, hungry, and angry, when I suddenly fainted. The guards and passersby crowded around pointing and debating about what had happened. Catching sight of the commotion from his window, my husband came out and helped me into the house.

He gave me a glass of water, and I begged him again to forgive me. For a long time, he didn't say anything. Eventually, he agreed to come see me in a couple of days to work things out.

He also asked me to go with him to see his lover. While I was there, they went into the other room to have sex. In this way, I came to tacitly accept their relationship.

I helped the lover to sort out all the immigration paperwork for her move to the UK with my husband. After I saw her off at the airport, I decided to walk rather than take the bus home.

I walked along Jingshun Road for almost three hours, exhausting myself, and reflecting on the summer of 1989, when I had hidden nearby. Maybe that was why I always wanted to stay here when I came back to Beijing. Jingshun Road was lined with huge trees, and cars, bicycles, and horse-drawn carts passed by from time to time. I didn't shed a tear the whole way home. When I arrived, I collapsed on the bed and went straight to sleep.

As soon as I woke up the next morning, I went house hunting. One of the few remaining buildings in Wangjing community just off Jingshun Road had condos for sale, and I found one that was exactly what I needed: airy, open and spacious, with two bedrooms, two living rooms, and two bathrooms, all of which faced the garden. I bought it on the spot. It was September 21, 2000, my thirty-eighth birthday, so I chose a floor and unit number that matched the date: 921. It was the first time I'd ever had a place of my own, a refuge from the storm.

I decided to live in Beijing and visit my husband in London from time to time, sleeping once again in the study of the sweet garden house I had bought with my royalties.

"You never were an ordinary woman," my husband said. "You're determined, intelligent, and tough. You don't care about conventions like marriage. This arrangement gives you total freedom and plenty of time to focus on writing. At home, she will be my wife, but you and I will still be husband and wife in the eyes of the rest of the world. And if we don't go ahead with the court proceedings, we can stay legally married."

"You're my family," I told him. "Even though I have family in Chongqing, I'll never be able to communicate with them the way I do with you. As pathetic as it sounds, you're the only real family I have."

"You'll always be family to me too," he replied.

I was moved by what he said, even though I knew no man would ever love me the way P had, and I would never love anyone like I had loved P. Plus, there was another, more selfish reason for me to tolerate this arrangement with my husband. A "husband" served as protection from the unwanted attentions of other men, and I just wanted to live quietly by myself.

I never imagined that once I started living in Beijing, six years would go by in the blink of an eye.

5

My mother never asked why I moved back to Beijing. I redid one living room of my new condo as an enormous study with a long row of bookcases, and installed a bathtub and a huge vanity mirror in one bathroom and a steam sauna in the other. In 2001, I invited my second sister, her husband, and my mother to visit me. My mother had plenty of time to ask me questions then, so why didn't she? Once, she came in to use the bathroom attached to my bedroom. A little irritated, I asked why she didn't just use the one by her own room. She said the toilet was lower, then turned around and walked out, never coming into my room again.

Maybe she'd just wanted to talk. I was always holed up, writing in the bedroom, so using my bathroom was a good excuse to catch me alone. But I'd brushed her off, missed the chance to open my heart. How I wish I'd talked to her, revealed the pain I was in. The grand, two-bedroom, two–living room house had no furniture besides a potted bamboo plant, a small sofa, and one chair. There was one plate, one bowl, one teacup, one bedside table, and one lamp—one of everything that should have come in pairs. Once my family had arrived, I hurried to add a sofa bed, three chairs, and extra dishes.

My mother could always see through the happy face I put on, and she surely knew how sad and lonely I was. I told myself I shouldn't burden her with the details of my sorrows, but now I realize that not knowing just made her worry more.

P e-mailed intermittently to tell me how he was doing. He'd taken a trip to Japan, he said, and seen a lot of Asian women, but none of them were me. He missed me. I told him that my mother had come to visit me in Beijing, and how I'd bought an extra air conditioner and a nice sofa bed to make sure she was comfortable. He said he was sorry he hadn't been able to be there to help out, but he was glad that I'd been able to spend some time with my mother. He wanted to meet the translator who was going to work on my novel so that he could show her particular issues to watch out for. Each time I wrote a new book, he would write to congratulate me. He remembered my birthday, even sending a card with a photo taken while a sculptor was making a bust of him. He also sent audio recordings of his novels so that I could listen to his voice.

At one point, he was attacked by the media. He got involved with a female student in his creative writing class, and she took the affair to the school and the newspapers, making things extremely difficult for him. I wrote him a letter to ask about it, and he told me not to believe her story. He said he was writing a book about his youth, in particular, the period from his mother's hospitalization following a horse-riding accident until her death. It had been his first training in life and in writing.

After that, he wrote to say he'd found a new girlfriend, a novelist. Sitting at my computer, I was as heartbroken as I had been when we first parted ways. I took a deep breath to stop the tears from coming. The more time passed, the further from him I felt.

6

Just before I'd left the compound with Xiaomi, Third Brother had turned to me and, in a hushed voice, said that since the weather was so hot, and now that all the children were here, we should proceed with mother's funeral procession and cremation.

Was I ready to say good-bye to my mother? Could I make a clean break with the past?

I thought back to a night in London. I was walking into the Dorchester Hotel to attend a party for Hogarth Press's anniversary. I recalled sitting down for dinner with the most celebrated British cultural icons, publishers, TV stars, and politicians. It was around the time when the *Times* had devoted several full pages to my novel, and the *Daily Telegraph* and several other British broadsheets had run full-page articles on the book. Virtually all the tabloids and magazines had jumped on the bandwagon. Life-size photographs of me and the book were all over bookshops and airports. I spent whole days and weeks doing promotional events. Everywhere I went, I was showered with flowers and applause. I had the gall to send my translator, in my place, to a dinner with famous editors. I had the nerve to ignore a powerful magazine's request to take revealing photographs of me. I declined interviews, didn't publicize the book according to the media's schedules, and insisted on being flown first-class by any organization that invited me. I was truly audacious. It was the peak of my life, and I was convinced of my superiority, swollen with arrogance. I felt as if the whole world belonged to me.

The canal by the Eagle's Nest apartment was always murky, disturbed only by gentle ripples when the wind blew. P and I liked to stand by the water to look for fish, but never spotted even one. Nearby, a few boats sat abandoned. I ran into him one day on that little, flower-scented path. I had been sitting on a bench when he suddenly caught sight of me. He crouched down and told me I looked like a refugee. I was a refugee, his love lifting me from the depths of misery to fly into the heavens.

I was so childish back then, so foolish, and so unaware of the complexity of the world. I never thought that one day the heavens would conspire to take all of this away from me, letting me fall back into the depths. Being raised up so high meant that when I fell, I fell into an even more pitiful state than I'd been in before, doing even more stupid things and getting further and further from myself. My education about life's cruelty had begun the moment I was born, and yet I was blind. Only when I was lying at the bottom of the abyss, when I realized that life was infinite darkness and pain, did I see it clearly.

I was so useless and so lonely. I didn't even have a cat or a dog for company, let alone a person! I thought about the man I loved on the other side of the world and what he would say: "People can only save themselves."

I had to save myself. The first thing I had to do was climb out of the hole I was in. I needed to sit up, learn to walk again, and make my way out of the hole, step by painful step. Unlike P, I had never been in love with anyone else. My husband had always been a stranger, and I'd always known that we'd part ways sooner or later. I looked at our relationship through the lens of time, trying to clarify my impression of him. In the years I had lived in Beijing after leaving London, I'd never really missed him. In staying married, I had been deceiving myself as much as anyone else. My friends' evaluations of him were always negative: "He's so old . . . his ideas are unbearably stuffy . . . he's arrogant, narrow-minded, stubborn, pedantic, and lacking in creativity . . . he has no joie de vivre . . . he drinks instant coffee . . . he never gives gifts or celebrates the New Year or birthdays . . . he's always so self-absorbed when he talks to people . . . he's never going to send you roses or chocolates . . . he walks like an old man . . . he smells like an old man . . . he has age spots on his hands . . . he never does housework . . . he snores . . . he doesn't like exercise . . . he doesn't like plays, movies, or restaurants . . . and he doesn't pay attention to how he dresses."

But no matter how I tried to get away from him, and despite what the people around me thought, in the end, this man was like a father to me. You can't choose your father, nor argue with his habits, his appearance, his likes or dislikes. Even if he's a murderer, as long as he doesn't abandon you, he's still your father.

When I first realized that my husband had a new lover, that he had been lying to me and treating me like a stranger, I'd wanted to shout at him, release all my long pent-up anger in a great roar. I wanted to tell him that he'd lost his dignity as a father figure. I wanted to tell him how cruel and callous he was, how I'd thought he was a great tree I could always lean on, and now I'd fallen to the ground. I wanted to tell him how much I hated him, and that I would never forgive him as long as I lived.

But I never did roar. Instead, in a voice as delicate as a thread of silk, every word perfectly clear, I told him: "I know what you've done, but I don't know what to do."

I am a heartless person, because he took my heart and broke it.

If only I had run to my mother in Chongqing right when it happened, thrown myself into her arms and let her soothe the hurt in my heart. But I didn't. If only I had called her and told her, maybe everything would have been all right. Maybe a few words of motherly wisdom or affection would have held the pieces of my broken heart together like some magical ointment. Maybe I would have been miraculously healed, or a new heart would have been born inside of me. But I didn't, because people without hearts are afraid—so afraid that their souls no longer seem to inhabit their bodies, and they become like the walking dead.

Oh Mother, what should I do?

Only now, when she couldn't answer, did I finally ask her. I hated myself for it.

Now, with the funeral procession nearly upon me, I decided to ask Third Brother and the others if there were any of our mother's friends from the old days who hadn't yet been informed.

My phone vibrated. It was a text message from Fourth Sister asking where I was and telling me to hurry back. I knew something must be wrong.

CHAPTER 6

I

The line of wreaths covering the courtyard of the old house at No. 6 extended out past the main door. When they saw Xiaomi and me enter, several people came over to greet us. Their faces looked familiar, but I struggled to recall their names. There were even more people than the night before, and endless neighbors, friends, and family members continued to arrive in a steady stream.

I walked up to my mother's coffin, knelt down, and lit some incense. All the people were looking at me, their faces wearing an expression that made me instinctively afraid. It was just like a scene from a short story I had written, which was based on an actual memory.

When I was little, my mother had taken me to get vaccinations at the hospital, but everyone in the neighborhood was convinced we'd gone to see my biological father. Even my father thought so.

When we got back, they turned the courtyard into a tribunal. In fact, the young policeman responsible for our neighborhood was there. They demanded that my mother account for our whereabouts every moment of the day, but she just stood there without making a sound. The mob turned on me, sure that a child would be easier to break. Scared out of my wits, I began to cry. Seeing my fear, my mother suddenly began to howl like a wounded animal.

I cried even harder.

That evening, my father sat scowling. He ate just two mouthfuls of rice before putting his bowl down with a demonstrative sigh. When she saw that, my mother smashed the bowl. My father cleaned up the broken fragments and threw them outside, where a small crowd had assembled to enjoy the show. They huddled around my father protectively. Was his wife always such a bad-tempered witch, they asked?

Uncle Shi yelled, "Throw the shameless old cow out! You indulge her too much."

My father didn't say a word.

My mother picked me up and walked out the door. She didn't start to cry until we reached the ferry dock. She said to herself, "I've always managed to keep myself under control. Why couldn't I this time? And your father didn't kick us out, so why am I running off like this?" Nevertheless, she still got on the ferry.

On the other side of the river, we changed buses several times and then walked for a long time. By the time we arrived at Uncle Liguang's house, the sky was pitch-black.

It was typical steelworks employee housing. Row after row of bungalows packed together, causing frequent power cuts. The people worked hard all day and went to bed very early. It was so quiet at night that you could hear the roars and growls of the lions and tigers in the zoo beyond the compound walls. I held tight to my mother's hand.

"The tigers won't eat you. Don't be scared," she assured me. Seeing the terror on my face, she said, "Don't worry. You're my good little girl. As long as I'm around, you will be too!"

The truth she couldn't have guessed was that I wanted to be eaten by the tigers. If I got eaten, then nobody could hate me anymore, and my mother and I wouldn't be stuck here, unable to go back home. Still, her words had their desired effect. There was a firmness to her tone that I didn't understand, but her protectiveness made me feel safe, and I began to calm down.

Uncle Liguang was the younger brother of my mother's first husband, who had been the head of the infamous Chongqing mob. Unable to stand her husband's womanizing and constant beatings, my mother had taken Elder Sister and run. She'd hidden out, supporting herself by working as a water carrier and clothes washer for the sailors by the riverside. As soon as Liberation came, her husband was arrested and eventually died in prison.

My mother hadn't had too much contact with Uncle Liguang, but Elder Sister identified strongly with this family connection, and so she'd sometimes snuck off to see him over the years.

Uncle Liguang let us in and lit a paraffin lamp. He had very dark skin and was scarcely taller than Auntie. He worked as a furnace attendant, the most exhausting and difficult job in the steelworks. The furnace was hard on the eyes, so he had to squint to see people. Forgoing pleasantries, he took a bottle of wujiapi herbal liquor out of the cupboard and asked Auntie to fry us a couple of eggs. My mother, suddenly seeming happier than normal, began to drink. They talked familiar names and places. He pounded the table merrily and clinked his glass together with Mother's, almost breaking it.

They didn't mention Father once, let alone me.

That night, I shared the single bed with Uncle Liguang's daughter, who was about my age. We slept with our heads at opposite ends. At one point, Uncle Liguang walked over and bent down close to me. I was so tense I didn't dare breathe. He stroked my face, bringing his body very near. He smelled of alcohol. His eyes were red and moist, and he was wearing a strange smile. Terrified, I clasped the duvet tightly, but suddenly, he stopped, turned away, and walked out of the room. I was covered in cold sweat. I wasn't sure what he was going to do to me, but I was instinctively afraid of men, something that never changed, even after I grew up.

As soon as I heard Uncle Liguang leave for work, I began to cry for all I was worth. My mother walked over and tried to calm me down.

Sobbing, I told her, "Ma, I want to go home!"

We went back to South Bank the next morning. There weren't many people on the ferry that day. I saw the shirtless boat trackers towing the boats from the sandbanks, humming as they worked. The sun shone brilliantly on the water. Throughout the trip, my mother sat, silent and sad, as if she had the weight of the world upon her shoulders. My father met us halfway up the hill. He told Mother he knew we'd come right back.

My mother ignored him. He extended a hand in my direction. Although he was just Father to me and not like other men, my mother shot me a look, so I withdrew my hand and followed along behind her.

2

Fourth Sister had texted me to hurry back, but she wasn't in the courtyard or in her room upstairs. From the balcony, I could see Third Brother and Fifth Brother busily greeting the guests below, so I went back down to help. A middle-aged woman waved to me: Uncle Liguang's daughter. She had been very good-looking when she was young, her eyes filled with a lively intelligence. Not a trace of her former bearing was now to be found on her densely freckled face.

Her tone was insincere, smarmy. "Wow, the great author returns! It's such a pity you weren't in the country when my dad died, but I lit some incense for him on your behalf. I requested a couple of songs for my dad from you too. You know, he used to be very fond of you. He used to talk about how you loved to read and always compared me to you. But I guess I just wasn't famous-writer material."

I nodded and thanked her.

She said it had taken her and her mother quite a few bus transfers to get to the South Bank. The rest of the family was busy, but they'd come that evening.

I asked if she still worked at the steelworks.

She told me the steelworks had cut back on staff, and all the female employees had been forced into early retirement at forty. She couldn't find another job, so she was making a living playing mah-jongg now.

"How much can you earn in a day?" I asked.

She said she could win fifty yuan if her luck was good, which meant a monthly income of thirteen hundred yuan or so. As long as she didn't eat delicacies, wear fancy clothes, travel, go to the movies, have children, or support her mother financially, it was enough.

Someone tapped me hard on the shoulder, so I spun around.

It was Elder Sister. She whispered into my ear, "I didn't tell anyone that you and Xiaomi had gone out. I know how to keep a secret. I have become more cautious about how others might look at us."

She beckoned enigmatically for me to walk with her, wanting to take a look at the old grain storehouse.

The old storehouse was covered in weeds, the building dilapidated and rotten. Rats darted in and out between the broken tiles, crumbling bricks, and torn hemp sacks. We could clearly hear the ditch water flowing toward the river.

Elder Sister said she'd called all of Ma's relatives and old friends.

"Ma was close to everyone, helping them out whenever she could and graciously accepting their favors in return. We should let them come and say their farewells to her. She always liked crowds. Unfortunately, we couldn't reach Wang Guixiang, Ma's best friend. And I wasn't able to get hold of Auntie Mo's family either. Third Brother is organizing everything and collecting the red envelopes. I hope he does a good job keeping track of things."

My mother had often talked about how she wanted everything to be like my father's funeral: hiring a band, gathering all her friends and relatives, and everyone sharing a meal before sending her off. Then she could die happy. Remembering this, I asked Elder Sister if there would be a band.

She replied, "Potbellied Cat provides full funeral services, which of course include a band."

Hearing his name, Potbellied Cat walked over, holding an ink bottle and writing brush. He said the band would arrive that evening. I relaxed a little.

"Great! They better be good, though," Elder Sister told him in a very severe tone.

"Don't worry, Elder Sister. I hired the best goddamned band in Chongqing," Potbellied Cat replied.

An oil-drum stove had been set up in the courtyard. The chef had lit the fire and was already making lunch for all the guests.

Elder Sister glanced around furtively and then switched to the topic she'd probably been working up to all along. "Little Six, listen to me. Whatever Xiaomi says, don't you believe a word of it."

"You're her ma. Why don't you take the high road and give in a little? You two need to work out your differences," I urged.

"You don't have a clue what's been going on, Little Six. That silly girl is so pigheaded." Elder Sister began to cry noisily. "Want to know why I was against Xiaomi getting together with that boyfriend of hers? Never mind that he didn't have a job—he smoked heroin! He played mah-jongg all day, scraping together just enough money to get high. When he realized Xiaomi had gone down south to Shenzhen, he thought she must be rich and he could just live off her. And you know how it is—you are the company you keep. Under his bad influence, she became lazy and greedy too. She even gave up her hair salon! Little Six, you're my sister. I don't have to hide anything from you. Think about the mess Xiaomi is in. She's raising an illegitimate child. It's not like she needs to support a drug addict too! When we were living together, they'd come home at three or four in the morning and do what men and women do. They made so much noise you would've thought there was an earthquake. They'd sleep all day like pigs and then go eat hot pot. They didn't care about the child's education, and they were always cursing in front of him—they thought it was trendy. I tried to talk to her, but she just argued with me. Your brother-in-law got so angry that he refused to let that disgusting freeloader drop by in the middle of the night. And then the junkie had the nerve to say that only Xiaomi had the right to tell him whether or not he could be in the house. Little Six, I don't think we'll ever get along."

I handed Elder Sister a tissue. She blew her nose and wiped away her tears. "Bad people get what's coming to them, at least. That bat-shit junkie started selling heroin! He was such an idiot that he got caught right away, though, and they gave him five to seven years. Lucky for him he wasn't involved in gang dealing or production, otherwise he would have been looking at fifteen years, or even the firing squad. I don't know what's gotten into Xiaomi: she's determined to wait for him to get out. Little Six, I believe in God now, and I do good things most of the time, but Xiaomi doesn't believe in anything. She only believes in that horrible, freeloading man. You have to persuade her not to wait for him. If she can find a good man and live a decent life—that will relieve some of my misery."

Seeing as Xiaomi had just asked me to find someone overseas to marry her, I was pretty sure she wasn't waiting like an imbecile for that boyfriend of hers. I told Elder Sister, and her face flushed with happiness.

"Did she really ask you that? You've got to help her, Little Six. If you help her, you'll be helping me, your Elder Sister. Marrying a foreigner would be great. Maybe she'll even take me on a trip abroad to enjoy the good fortune of having a foreign son-in-law. Hah! Your elder sister never dreamed she'd be able to go abroad, not even in the next life. Thank God! This must be a reward for believing in God!" She closed her eyes, crossed herself, and began to pray.

"Elder Sister," I asked, "does Xiaomi use heroin too?"

Elder Sister was taken aback for a moment, but then quickly answered, "Her? How could she? That's impossible."

I said, "Elder Sister, this is Ma's funeral. We shouldn't let anything inappropriate happen."

3

All the mourners went on about how lucky Ma was to have lived a long life and died in her own home. And I was sure my elder brothers and sisters held the same view. But when I pictured her lying in that coffin, pitifully frail and thin as a rake, I could no longer see it that way.

Had her final years ever been idyllic as my siblings had reported, or was it all solitude and stained sheets, even before the very end? The question was still haunting me.

Elder Sister was a terrible gossip, and she loved to go on and on about how badly Fifth Sister-in-Law and Second Sister had treated Mother, and how much Mother had wanted to live with her instead. Even though I knew better than to be misled by her one-sided version of events, I always listened carefully, trying to glean accurate information about my family. Once when I was back in Chongqing, she pulled me aside, and after glancing around surreptitiously, told me in hushed tones, "Little Six, did you know that Ma has kept in touch with your biological father all these years?"

"He's dead. What are you talking about?"

"I mean his family, not the dead guy."

Seeing that she had my attention, Elder Sister described how, once, some relatives of my biological father had come to see my mother, bringing fruit as a gift. Third Brother happened to drop in to see Mother and told them to get out. Mother was very hurt. She said to him, "Son, you need to think before you open your mouth and hurt people's feelings. If your dad were here, he wouldn't let you behave like this. You shouldn't treat people like that, especially when they've been kind enough to come and visit me."

"You might think they're here to see you, but that's not true. They're just trying to get close to Little Six now that she's a celebrity," Third Brother retorted.

Elder Sister said Third Brother had been right. Ma was too naive to see how quickly society was changing, how calculating people could be. She'd even brewed up the best Yunnan tuo green tea for them. Elder Sister told me she couldn't stomach the sight of that family. If Third Brother hadn't thrown them out, she would have done it herself.

Once, my brothers and sisters heard a rumor that I'd brought a big color TV back from England for my biological father's two sons—who were in fact my little brothers—and even given them some British pounds. The family was up in arms for some time, with my poor mother caught in the middle.

Of course, Elder Sister had started the rumor herself. She felt threatened because my mother had told her that I'd gone to see my biological father's mother.

That summer, my mother had given me my grandmother's address in Seven Star Hill. The streets there were bathed in dim yellow lamplight, and despite it being the city center, the area was as dirty and humid as the South Bank. It was a hot evening and the teahouses were overflowing. I found the stone steps and descended, then turned down a narrow passageway that led to the building and climbed a dark staircase. There was something malevolent and ghostly about the people seated around the mah-jongg tables.

I fumbled my way to the top floor and found an old woman staring blankly, small eyes peering out over a sharp chin in the feeble light of a fifteen-watt bulb. I asked her name, but she didn't acknowledge me. There was a litter of white newborn kittens in the room, and several cats sprawled vertically on the wooden staircase. Afraid of stepping on them, I panicked and ran outside. I staggered from one end of the alley to the other, certain that couldn't have been my grandmother but unsure where to find her.

The next day, my mother took me there. It turned out Grandma lived next door to the lady with the cats, and with her heavy eyebrows and big eyes, she couldn't have looked more unlike her. As soon as she saw us from a distance, she hurried outside. She stretched her arms out and took me by the hands.

I took Ma, Grandma, my aunt, and my aunt's daughter to a restaurant near their house. I told Grandma I had taken neither my adopted nor my biological father's name. I had made up my own.

Grandma expressed her approval over and over again. "That's wonderful, taking your own surname."

That day, Grandma cried. She said that she missed my biological father terribly and how happy he would have been to see us having lunch together. My aunt worked as a road sweeper in the neighborhood. She had a dark tan and spoke very little. Her daughter was in middle school, and was evidently quite disdainful about her mother's job.

When I went back to Chongqing the following year, my mother said sadly, "Little Six, your grandmother's gone."

Grandma had gotten sick no more than six months after our lunch together. She had been taken to the hospital, but didn't have money for surgery. As with my biological father, it seemed that we were destined to meet just once in my lifetime.

My mother looked at me as I cried, and I suddenly knew she wasn't finished. Sure enough, one day after Grandma had died, my aunt collapsed. It was late-stage cancer, and there had been nothing they could do.

I went white and rushed to ask, "What about her daughter?"

My mother sighed before replying. "Her parents were divorced, and her ma was taking care of her. Her dad's taken her in now, but there's a stepmother. I hope she isn't having too hard a time of it."

Shortly after I saw Grandma, I went to my biological father's village and had a tomb built for him. When my mother found out, she gazed out the window and squeezed my hand tightly. "It's raining. Rain is good, good for moving a grave," she said.

I left before dawn, feeling like I was betraying Father. I didn't even dare to look in his direction.

Passing the morning market, I bought a whole basket of calla lilies. Then I waited in Stone Bridge Square for a friend's car, which, like the flowers, was also white.

My biological father's old grave was in a wasteland halfway up a mountain. I use the word "grave," but it was nothing more than a ragged pile of stones heaped on top of his ashes.

Once the Taoist priest had finished performing the funeral rites, work on the new grave began. I laid the calla lilies in front of the gravestone I'd had carved. I was worried about offending his other wife and two sons, so I only included a single character from my name: Hong.

Nearby was a small village of maybe ten households. There was a pond and a bamboo grove. Crimson roses bloomed on the mountainside. The villagers came out to watch the ritual, three of them venturing over in the rain to chat with the friend who had driven me there.

"Is that his daughter?"

"She's really grown!"

"That woman sure got the short end of the stick. Her dad was desperately poor and in debt all over the place, not to mention having to send money for her on the quiet."

I caught sight of my biological father's wife, a very proper village manager with a sturdy build who smiled as she spoke. She had no objections to me rebuilding the grave, even admitting she'd felt guilty for never having the money to do it herself. She showed me a photo album full of pictures of her two sons. They looked a lot like our father, but not much like me. One of them wore glasses and the other was very thin. Of these two half brothers, one was in Shenzhen while the other worked in downtown Chongqing. Neither happened to be home that day. She offered to cook for me and my friend, but I politely declined and left as soon as I had given her all my contact information in Beijing and London.

Two years later, I was doing a book signing in a Chongqing bookshop when I spotted a familiar face. Some of the readers were lining up, while others were standing off to the side. I recognized one of my half brothers from the photographs, a woman holding a child at his side. I only caught a glimpse of them, and then they were gone. Elder Sister, who came to see me at the signing, told me later that she'd heard them say something to the children about going and asking Auntie for money. Fearing that they would make a scene, she had persuaded them to leave.

If they'd been talking, Elder Sister might have found out about me rebuilding my biological father's grave. And if Elder Sister knew, then the whole family knew.

What they didn't know was that one of the brothers had faxed me more than a few times to ask for money, saying that their father had paid child support until I was eighteen, which had made life harder for them. His family wanted to build a new house and his younger brother needed to have his eyes checked, but didn't have the money.

My husband wrote back to them, making it clear that their father's child support payments had been his responsibility as a father, not to mention they were paid under court order. He added that I had no obligation to support my siblings, let alone half brothers through an illegitimate family connection who hadn't been in touch for decades.

My half brother lashed out, saying I'd humiliated them in my memoir, and I owed them the money. My husband wrote back, warning him not to burn any bridges. They were better off having this family connection than not having it, as nobody knew when they might really need someone's help.

Once, over dinner, my husband told me the story of Marx's illegitimate son. Engels had placed the child in the care of a family in the East End of London, where the boy grew up speaking broad cockney. Before he died, Engels told Marx's daughters about their little brother, upon hearing which they went to see him. They found they had no common language and no feelings for one another. They were strangers. What does blood really mean? Without a shared upbringing, without shared suffering, without a true sense of kinship, it means nothing at all.

I wondered if it would be the same if I met my half brothers. We had all grown up with hardship, and we did speak the same language. Once we'd gotten the pleasantries out of the way, both my mother and their mother would be taboo topics. Instead, we'd talk about the father we shared, whose love they'd known. I remembered one of the photos I had seen, in which the boys lay on a bed, folding sweets wrappers with their father. His eyes were filled with a love and concern that I had never known. The brothers might also ask about my life in Britain. And how would I answer them? What could I say? One poorly chosen word might be enough to hurt their pride. In the end, the conversation would always return to our father, but they would never understand just how painful the topic was for me.

Elder Sister passed on the message that they wanted to meet me, although she was firmly opposed to the idea. She said she'd had dealings with them, and they were miserly village people who thought of nothing but money. There had never been any love lost between us, and yet here they were, pouncing on me for some cash. It could hardly lead to us developing any emotional ties as a family.

If Elder Sister was so disgusted by them, why would she have gotten to know them at all? The answer was simple: Elder Sister was a spy. I knew that if I gave them anything, she'd appear with her hand out. If I didn't give her what she wanted, she would stir up trouble in the family and take it out on my mother.

In order to avoid the whole mess, I never did meet my half brothers.

4

Elder Sister suddenly spotted Fourth Sister staring at us from across the courtyard. Elder Sister's right leg had always been a little stiff, but she positively flew over. She briefly discussed something with Fourth Sister, and the two of them shot me a glance. Then they began to argue. Elder Sister raised her voice, saying, "Do what I told you."

Fourth Sister gave me a sour look and walked away.

Normally, no one was the least bit scared of Elder Sister, but when she was in the right and decided to flex her muscle within the family, there was a certain crude ferocity about her that we'd all learned to be wary of. I didn't know what was going on, but clearly, it had to do with me.

The crack of fireworks echoed through the yard, and the air filled with the suffocating smell of gunpowder. I covered my mouth and nose with my hand and walked up the stone stairs to find out which friends or relations had arrived from afar.

It turned out to be the second son of my eldest uncle on our mother's side, who had rushed over from Wanxian County with his wife. They were exchanging greetings with Elder Sister. He was tall, slim, and appeared no more than fifty, though his hair was already gray. His elder brother had been Elder Sister's first husband. This younger cousin had done his military service in Chongqing, and our mother used to invite him over whenever she was making something nice for dinner. He didn't leave the military until he made battalion level. We were told that he had become the public administrator for a small county in the Three Gorges area. He walked over and shook my hand warmly.

"Little Six, you look just like when you were small. I've read quite a few of your books, and I often read about you in the papers too. It's wonderful! You've really made us proud!"

He was the very first relative at the funeral to admit he'd read my books, and I didn't know how to respond. It was also the first time I'd ever seen his wife. She introduced herself enthusiastically and apologized for the late arrival. A landslide on the road outside Changshou had held up their bus and made the three-hour trip take all day. Elder Sister offered them a seat at one of the tables, and gave them tea, peanuts, and sweets.

"Oh dear," I heard Potbellied Cat exclaim. "There's something really strange happening!"

The funeral director looked pale and shaky as he spoke to Third Brother.

"What's going on?" Third Brother's wife asked from behind Third Brother.

"The chef lit the fire to cook the rice, but even though the fire was roaring and the water was bubbling away, the rice stayed hard. It just wouldn't cook. It's really bizarre!"

I followed them outside the courtyard to the oil-drum stove. Simple wooden tables had been set up for cooking. Potbellied Cat nodded toward the chef, who stuck a calloused hand right into the boiling pot. He scooped up a handful of hard rice to show us, then wiped his hands on his apron, unsure how to proceed.

"Somebody must be playing a trick on us," concluded my third sister-in-law.

"Maybe someone should go buy some premade box lunches for this meal?" Potbellied Cat asked Third Brother.

"All right, but we can't have premade food for dinner," Third Brother replied.

"Don't worry," Potbellied Cat told him. "I'll go right now and get the yin-yang master to remove the curse. He knows all about magic."

In my grief the previous night, I had worried that someone would come to hurt my mother even more. Today it seemed that my fears had not been unfounded.

Who would do something like this during my mother's period of mourning? Besides Spectacles Wang, how many people could harbor such hatred? My mother was the kind of person who would feel terrible if she so much as stepped on an ant. How could anyone feel any enmity toward her?

5

No more than half an hour after Potbellied Cat had rushed off, he returned with two big stacks of boxed lunches. He and Third Brother dispensed the food and chopsticks. Taking the box he handed to me, I asked if he'd managed to get ahold of the yin-yang master.

"Little Six, your ma was born under a lucky star."

"You haven't answered my question."

"If he's coming, he'll be here in half an hour. If he's not coming . . ."

"Then he's not coming."

"Don't worry, we'll find some way to deal with it. At most, we just need to replace the stove."

"What if that doesn't fix it?"

"Things have a way of sorting themselves out. Anyway, your ma always had good luck. The immortals will keep her safe and sound," he said nonchalantly.

How could he be so sure? I opened the box. Perched on top of the rice was dried tofu and fried celery with shredded pork, along with some pickles. I tried a mouthful—it wasn't bad. Fifth Brother brought the teapot around, pouring tea for the guests. My mother's portrait gazed at me as I ate. She seemed peaceful and calm.

It wasn't always that way. Scenes of the courtyard before this white six-story building even existed flashed before my eyes. My mother returning home for the weekend when I was preparing for my university entrance exams—it must have been shortly before she retired.

She got home exhausted and angry, and she took it out on me. She said that girls shouldn't spend all day dragging books around. What was the point of reading? Did I really think I could make a living as a writer? That would take a miracle, and we had no chance of one of those since we hadn't picked good sites for our ancestors' graves.

"Little Six, I'm sorry, but you were been born into the wrong family! We're poor! We should be content if we have enough to eat!" she said. "What you need to be focused on is marrying a nice man. People from a family like ours shouldn't even dream of being famous. None of your siblings could get into college, so what makes you think you're so special? A grown-up daughter should help her ma with the housework instead of making her worry all day. Just stop being so ambitious and naive, get a job, marry someone decent, and get through life without too many ups and downs, and maybe you'll stop making your ma lose sleep!"

Later I came to wonder if she was putting on a show for my brothers and sisters, or if she'd just suppressed her resentment for so long that it had finally poured out all at once.

At the time, though, I simply didn't understand. That day, I hated her and wished that she weren't my mother.

6

I don't think I ever carried anything heavy for my mother. Many weekends, she would come home carrying the bundle of firewood given out to shipyard employees, struggling to catch her breath as she clambered up the steep slope from the riverside. And I never once helped her. She'd stride through the main gate of the courtyard at No. 6 and into the central room, where she'd drop the firewood and stand with her carrying pole grasped in one hand. With her back to the light, she looked like a stranger, her legs strangely thickened, her shoulders broader, her back beginning to hunch. Her sweat-matted hair covered half her face. She'd pretend she didn't see me.

Whenever I went back to Chongqing, my mother would sleep in the same bed as me. She would put out the lamp and chat with me before nodding off, her gentle, unceasing words like a light spring rain. I remember the time she told me about my father seeing his brother for the first time in almost half a century.

My father had been forced into the Nationalist army in 1939. After marching through eleven provinces, he had deserted his unit and become a sailor with the Chongqing Shipping Company. He must have sailed up and down the Yangtze hundreds of times, but he never did get back home.

My father was eighty-one years old the year of the reunion, his brother seventy-six. They spent two weeks together in the white house by the river on Chongqing's south bank. When it came time to part, they wailed as they clasped each other around the neck. My mother stood to one side, also crying. She said it was as if tears took the place of words for my father and uncle. They cried all the water in the Yangtze.

I like people who can cry, but I didn't like seeing my father cry. When my father cried, it was as if his heart was burdened with dark secrets and grievances he couldn't share—even with my mother.

Before illness forced him to retire from the river, my father had piloted the biggest passenger ferry between Chongqing and Shanghai. He could have gotten back to his old home in Zhejiang, but the boat wasn't allowed any farther downstream than the Three Gorges Dam.

Everyone working on the boat was checked and "rectified." They demanded that my father explain his role in running munitions for the Nationalist army during the Communist Party's liberation of

Chongqing in 1949. He explained that he had been forced to do it at gunpoint.

"You didn't have to do it. You could have made a glorious sacrifice instead," the person in charge of Rectification told him.

So my father was punished, transferred to cargo vessels traveling the upper reaches of the Yangtze, far from his wife and children. However, this by no means excused him from Ideological Remolding. The people carrying out Rectification demanded to know who else had transported munitions for the Nationalists.

When my father insisted he couldn't remember, the Rectification group declared that, since he was covering for other people, his crimes were twice as serious.

My father was so angry he stopped eating. He'd been malnourished to begin with, and his vision soon became blurry. He worked day and night until he started to see stars. He fell overboard and cracked his head open, but he was rescued and then taken to a county hospital in Yibin.

During his time at the hospital, my father became friends with a young nurse whose husband had died of starvation after being sent down to the countryside.

Meanwhile, my mother told me, she was working in the mountains with my biological father, who was not yet her lover. They had just finished for the day and were covered in sweat. She mopped her face with a towel. Just as my mother was saying that she needed to request time off to go and see her husband, she received a telegram about his injury.

My mother hurried to Yibin. The moment she set eyes on the nurse, she understood.

"She's more than just your nurse," she said.

My father didn't reply.

My mother found the nurse's home. When the nurse opened the door, she looked shocked to find my mother standing there. My mother saw my father's shoes under the bed and his clothing on a line out back. She had made those shoes herself, stitch by stitch, thread by thread.

My mother went home.

Once my father had recovered from his injury, the doctors determined that his eyesight wasn't good enough to work on the boats, so he returned to their home in Chongqing. He never went back to Yibin again.

More than thirty years later, my mother laid in bed with me, recounting every detail of these events. I asked what she thought Father had been thinking. She said she didn't know, but he'd sent money to the nurse and her daughter from time to time, and she'd always felt sorry for them.

7

I left home when I was eighteen, after discovering that I was an illegitimate child. Later, I entered a creative writing program in Beijing, which was disbanded in the summer of 1989. I fled from place to place around the city for three months before transferring to a university in Shanghai in October, where I would study in the Chinese department. I had no suitcase, so a friend gave me a big cloth bag. I cut the bag in half and stitched it into two, which were easier to carry. In these bags, I packed my books, manuscripts, and my few scraps of clothing. A whole bunch of friends saw me off at the train station.

When I arrived in Shanghai, however, there was nobody to meet me. I had to make two trips just to get the heavy bags off the train and then from the station onto the bus, after which I was soaked with sweat. Oh, Shanghai, Shanghai! My relationship with that city began in exhaustion and confusion, and that is how it was fated to continue. Almost all I read in those days were historical books on the gangsters and whores of the Shanghai foreign concessions.

Later, when I lived in London and would travel back to Chongqing, I never took much luggage. Other than a change of clothes, the only thing I carried was cash. I brought whatever I earned from writing, minus my own living expenses, to give to my mother and my sisters and brothers. My nieces and nephews were never smart enough to get into good schools on their own, and so they had to pay extra. Mother would put up the money, and then I'd pay her back when I visited. That way, she could give it to them herself and they would hopefully treat her a little better. Putting my siblings' offspring through school became my duty and my responsibility. As the years went by, not one of this next generation of children got anywhere in school, and neither did they ever say a word of thanks to me. Of course, people are forgetful. It's enough if they don't bear grudges.

When they did see me, the kids never said much. I suppose they were nervous. Their aunt was a writer, and they were worried about being laughed at if they spoke poorly—plus they didn't know how to sit still. They must have been influenced by their parents' view of me. This auntie of theirs had a bad reputation. She had brought shame on the family. Her lifestyle, words, and actions were unworthy of respect.

Virtually all of these children were here at the funeral, and at least they politely acknowledged me as "Auntie." My two elder brothers helped Potbellied Cat clear up the chopsticks and cartons from the boxed lunches, put them into a big garbage bag, and wipe down the tables.

"Little Six, be sure to tell me if there's anything you're not happy with." Potbellied Cat forced a smile in my direction.

"She's not in charge," Third Brother interrupted.

Potbellied Cat nodded and bowed toward Third Brother, but nonetheless turned around to reassure me that the yin-yang master would soon be here and dinner would be served successfully.

"Did you know that a woman from the back streets by Marble Rock died of a sudden illness? Bright-red blood oozed out from her coffin, so the yin-yang master wouldn't let them bury her," he said, mysteriously. "He poured amber powder into her mouth and burned safflower smoke in her nostrils, and just like that, he brought her back to life. That's how he got his reputation."

The strange funeral director never ceased to surprise me with his glibness. He raised his head and looked in the direction of the main entrance, before patting his chest in satisfaction. "Ah! Speak of the devil."

8

The yin-yang master was a little old man of around seventy. His face was completely expressionless, and he wore a long Chinese gown with black cloth shoes. On his head was a circular cloth hat. He attached a number of gaudy pieces of paper to each side of the oil-drum stove and laid a cushion on the ground, upon which he proceeded to sit cross-legged. He placed a copper basin directly in front of him, before producing, as if by magic, a shiny gold pot. He closed his eyes and drew an arc around his body. Then he stood up, brandishing a feather in the direction of the stove, all the while muttering incantations. He went on this way for ten minutes, before opening his eyes and murmuring something to Potbellied Cat.

Potbellied Cat waved over Third Brother, who was in the thick of the crowd of onlookers, and the two of them began whispering to one another. Third Brother called over Second Sister, Fourth Sister, and Fifth Brother, as well as some of the other relatives, including our maternal uncle. Eventually, the yin-yang master had Third Brother write a date of birth and an eight-character horoscope on a sheet of ritual paper.

The yin-yang master cupped the paper in his hands, exposing it to the heavens—first one side and then the other. A tongue of flame shot up abruptly from his palm and the paper began to burn.

"The great exorcism spell that turns heaven and earth!" His white head rocked back and forth so fast it looked like a rolling ball. The ball eventually slowed, and the shape of his head appeared normal again. He called toward the heavens, "Come, wind!"

A great gust of wind arose, sweeping the sheet of ritual paper into the oil-drum stove, where it vanished without a trace. The yin-yang master walked over to the stove and pressed his palms together in front of him, his eyes closed as he chanted an incantation. He nodded to Potbellied Cat.

"Everything is in order now. Let's get the water boiling and make some tea," Potbellied Cat called to the chef.

Potbellied Cat turned back to Third Brother and whispered something in his ear.

"That much?" Third Brother exclaimed.

"That's what it costs to call the yin-yang master."

Third Brother reluctantly took out a wad of hundred-yuan notes from his pocket, from which he carefully counted out twenty and handed them over. Potbellied Cat escorted the yin-yang master back out toward Middle School Street. As they walked, I noticed that a long wisp of gray hair had fallen out from beneath his hat. So the yin-yang master was actually a woman!

I asked Potbellied Cat about it when he returned.

He replied that it was difficult to say whether the master was a man or a woman, or most probably a hermaphrodite, and that the title "yin-yang master" was an obvious reference to being in contact with both the realms of the yin and the yang. The master, who used to be a witch, had inner eyes that could see the unseen and an understanding of the language of the dead as well as the magic arts. It would be more accurate to say Taoist priest, but everyone in the profession used the term yin-yang master out of respect.

Third Brother sat at the table in the center of the courtyard updating the accounts in a small notebook. Elder Sister started down the stairs, her face red and looking flustered. Before she even reached Third Brother, she began to yell, "What on earth is going on, Third Brother?"

Third Brother pretended not to hear.

"You're going to tell me exactly what happened," she shouted again.

"Can't you see I'm busy?" Third Brother snapped, burying his head in his ledger book.

She had always been a little afraid of him, so she stormed back upstairs. I followed her up to our mother's room.

"He burned my horoscope when I wasn't even there. It was your job to stop him, Second Sister. You all should at least have discussed it with me first."

"It was everyone's decision, Elder Sister. You're the eldest child, you should behave like it," Second Sister said.

Elder Sister spun around, saw me, and said, "Why didn't you burn Little Six's horoscope?"

"Hers wouldn't have been appropriate."

"Not appropriate? It's like you're her lapdog. You chatter behind her back, but really you're scared of her."

"The priest wouldn't take the horoscope of anyone who is menstruating or pregnant, or who is widowed," Second Sister quietly replied.

Elder Sister looked at me suspiciously, and I looked at them both in surprise. How could Second Sister's eyes be so sharp? If I had met those conditions, my horoscope would definitely have been the first choice.

Elder Sister still wouldn't shut up. She went on about how whoever had her horoscope burned for her mother would join that mother earlier than the other children. The curse on the stove had been dispelled at the cost of years cut off from her life.

"That's enough," Second Sister said. "All of us are trying to express devotion to our parents. Only an idiot would believe these crazy theories of yours."

"Enough my foot!" Elder Sister's rage grew with every word. "If you wanted to burn something, why didn't you burn yourself?"

"Are you cursing me?"

"That's exactly what I'm doing! You've always thought you were the head of this family, and I've kept quiet about it for decades, but Ma's not here anymore. I'm telling you, Second Sister, from this day on, you're dead to me. What are you going to do about it?"

"Stop it!" I yelled, cutting Elder Sister off. "Look what you're doing to her!"

Second Sister was panting frantically, supporting herself against a table, her face ashen. I called her husband up to the room, and he said Second Sister needed to be given oxygen at a hospital.

He carried her out the door on his back. Elder Sister started to follow, but I put my arm out to stop her. I told her it was better if I went.

CHAPTER 7

I

The South Bank District No. 1 People's Hospital was jam-packed. Numbers flashed up above every window, and the din made the intercom impossible to understand. Still, you could always pay a little extra to get into a specialist ward. Second Sister didn't want me to spend too much, but I insisted.

Second Sister's husband watched as his wife was given oxygen. He said he needed to pop out to get a few things and motioned for me to sit in the chair by the bed.

Just a few minutes later, Second Sister looked much better. She removed the oxygen mask from her nose and told me that this condition had actually become more serious since she stopped teaching and retired. If the air was bad, a little stress could be enough to land her in the hospital.

"You can't let Elder Sister upset you like that," I said.

"She makes me crazy," Second Sister replied. "How could our own sister be such a heartless ingrate? If you want the truth, it was Elder Sister who drove Ma to her grave."

I was shocked by her blunt accusation. Before I could ask what my mother's last few years had really been like, Second Sister began to tell me herself.

"Ma actually forgave Elder Sister for stealing all her savings. Then, well, as you know, Younger Uncle and Ma got along well—he was Ma's only living brother. His wife got breast cancer, but she was fine after the surgery. Younger Uncle was so happy that he invited all of us over for dinner."

Second Sister took a knitting needle and a ball of wool out of the handbag her husband had brought for her. Teasing out the end of the yarn and hooking it on to the needle, she looked at me for a long moment before continuing.

"While they were at Younger Uncle's house, Elder Sister started an argument with Fifth Sister-in-Law over something trivial. Our host, Auntie, politely tried to break up the fight, but Elder Sister just started in on her as well. Then Ma tried, so Elder Sister swore at Ma. Fifth Sister-in-Law said to her, 'If you'll even swear at your own mother, you'll get your retribution in time.' Then Elder Sister picked up a big earthenware bowl and tried to smash it on Fifth Sister-in-Law and Auntie. Auntie fainted from the shock. Younger Uncle was furious. Auntie's illness returned after that, and she died just three months later.

"Younger Uncle blamed Ma for letting Elder Sister get away with traumatizing his wife so grievously that it led to her death. Ma, fuming, tried to chastise Elder Sister, but she wouldn't have it. Elder Sister said that Auntie had never treated any of us children well, that she had always played favorites, and that she deserved to die. Ma was so angry she tried to throw Elder Sister out of the house, but Elder Sister said, 'You don't need to throw me out. I've got legs, I can leave by myself, and I won't be back. From now on, I won't have such a shameful excuse for a ma.' Then she stormed out. Ma was so upset that she got very ill."

"When did this happen?" I asked.

"Around December last year."

"And Ma never got better after that?"

"She was in terrible shape. She couldn't eat, couldn't keep anything down. She even went to the hospital for a blood transfusion at one point."

Second Sister told me Mother had been in the hospital for a month before getting a little better and going home to recuperate. When her younger brother called, all she did was apologize. She called Elder Sister to beg her to apologize to Younger Uncle, but Elder Sister refused. Ma said she had no conscience, and they had a shouting match over the phone.

"From that point on, Ma never really recovered."

"Second Sister, I've been dying to ask: Fifth Brother must have treated Ma well in her last years, but what about his wife?"

"Fifth Sister-in-Law? She's a villager who married into a city family. It was a giant step up for her, even if Fifth Brother has a cleft lip. We've always been good to her. What reason would she have not to be good to Ma? Anyway, I know she's hardworking, and she gets things done, not like Third Brother and Third Sister-in-Law. When they looked after her, they were always stingy with Ma's food so they could keep more of the money for themselves. Not Fifth Sister-in-Law. Whenever I went to see Ma, she always had chicken soup or rib broth stewing in the pot. Plus, she was very conscientious about keeping Ma's clothes clean. She always used the washing machine and never tried to skimp on the electricity bill. Fifth Brother would go fishing on the weekends, so Ma always had fish to eat. They even got Ma her own color TV, so they'd never have to argue over what to watch! Ma was very pleased with the way they treated her. When Elder Sister upset Ma and she got so sick, Fifth Sister-in-Law carried Ma to the hospital on her back. She always took good care of her. When Elder Sister heard Ma was ill, she rushed home and started moaning about everyone behind their back. Not that she did anything to help. All she did was create more work for Fifth Sister-in-Law, who had to cook for her. Elder Sister even complained that the food wasn't good enough, and said that eating slop like that must have made Ma ill from malnutrition."

I was relieved. Fifth Sister-in-Law had always seemed every inch the devoted daughter-in-law, but the filth in my mother's room on my last visit had frightened me. Maybe her life with Fifth Brother and Fifth Sister-in-Law really had been happy, and her depression had been the result of her conflict with Elder Sister and the eccentricity of old age. She had become garrulous, talking endlessly about every little thing, while her habits and temper had become increasingly strange. For example, she adored lima beans cooked with mixed flavors, and she always wanted to share them with her grandsons, but refused to give any to their mothers, her daughters-in-law. If you tried to talk to her about it, she would shut herself up in her bedroom to sulk, refusing to eat anything or speak to anyone.

Second Sister suddenly changed the subject. "Tang is one of those people who's all talk and no action. He doesn't seem like much of an 'intellectual' to me. I can't stand people like that. Fourth Sister should never have gotten involved with him."

Startled by her sudden declaration, I checked the time and realized that Tang must have just about arrived in Chongqing to help with the condo.

I wondered if my sisters had some kind of revenge planned, but shook my head at the thought. They were mostly decent people who lived simple lives. Still, Second Sister spoke as if she intended to teach him a lesson, or at the very least give him a tongue-lashing. She put down her knitting and clipped the oxygen mask back over her nose.

Outside the window, I could see two newly built hospital buildings. But the outpatient ward where we sat was still in the old building—a dilapidated bunker filled with worn-out spittoons and garbage cans. The stiflingly powerful smell of alcohol that hung in the air was enough to darken anyone's mood.

Taking the mask off again, Second Sister said, "This hospital reminds me of someone, and it's no exaggeration to say he got what he deserved. He never could manage to commit to Fourth Sister. He even wanted to break up with her just before the wedding!"

Second Sister was referring to Fourth Sister's first husband, who had been admitted here for bowel cancer years earlier, but she was also implying something about people in general.

"The wicked things people do cannot escape the gods' notice."

"But Fourth Sister loves Tang," I said.

"Well," Second Sister huffed, "she never could see clearly when it came to men." With that, she replaced the oxygen mask.

"It's all my fault," I said. "I should never have brought her to London in the first place. If she hadn't been in England, she would never have gotten together with Tang."

Second Sister looked at me with an odd expression. "Little Six, you have to talk to her! She needs to get over this relationship and move on somehow—like you did."

I didn't say a word. Second Sister talked about the years before I was born, about how Fourth Sister had never had it easy. She'd always suffered from one illness or another, and her chronic asthma meant that she always had to watch from the sidelines while other children played. Eventually, after a multitude of traditional remedies, she finally got better.

"Ma was running around with some guy named Sun at the time," she said.

I felt a chill run down my spine. Sun was my biological father—she just said it that way to remind me how much she hated him.

"You can imagine, Little Six, life at home was far from peaceful. Elder Sister started mouthing off, pushing us out of the room and slamming the door shut when she wanted to talk to mother. Fourth Sister and I would press our ears to the door, trying to figure out what was going on. Then Ma would take out her frustration on us, criticizing everything we did. After Fourth Sister started high school, things just got worse between them. When people bullied her at school, she'd come home angry and talk back to Mother. Once, Mother beat her so badly for it that she gave her a bloody nose."

She shook her head at the memory, and then she looked up at me with deep anger in her eyes. "You know, Little Six, just the fact that you exist means that no one in our family can ever walk down the street with head held high. Whatever we do, we always run in to people who say horrible things about you or Ma. Only Fourth Sister has the strength of character to stand up for this family's reputation and yell right back at them. She was sent down to the countryside after high school, and not only did she have to deal with people's prejudice against her for being one of the 'educated urban youth,' she got laughed at by the other educated youth who'd been sent down with her.

"When Ma retired, she was so worried that Fifth Brother would face the same problems if he got sent to the countryside that she let him have her job so he could stay in the city. Fourth Sister felt like Ma had completely failed her. She worked like crazy to get transferred back to the city as a construction worker. She was lugging heavy buckets of quicklime up and down those tall buildings every day. It was incredibly hard work, not to mention dangerous. When she started going out with her first husband, his parents were against the relationship. His family all worked in the shipyard, and Ma's bad reputation preceded her. Ma knew his family looked down on her, so she was scared that Fourth Sister would be picked on if she joined their family. Fourth Sister didn't listen to Ma's warnings, but things started to go wrong as soon they got married. Your poor sister's fate—such a bitter pill!"

At last, Second Sister paused. "I won't say any more. You know more than me about what happened next anyway."

She'd gotten herself so worked up that she was gasping for breath again, so I helped her put the oxygen mask back on.

2

I walked into the hallway to look for a bathroom. There was a very long line, so all I could do was wait patiently and take advantage of the moment to catch my breath and think about everything Second Sister had said.

I was pretty sure she'd made that little speech, as hostile as it had been, with the goal of getting me to help Fourth Sister.

I couldn't remember Fourth Sister ever speaking up when I was getting picked on by the neighbors. Maybe she had, and I'd simply forgotten. Or I hadn't been there when she defended me. Everyone has selective memory, remembering the bad things and forgetting the good.

What was harder to believe was that my mother had beaten her. Ma was so softhearted she couldn't even slaughter a chicken. My entire childhood and adolescence, I could only remember one occasion when my mother raised her hand against anyone. Once, Mother lost her temper and banged Elder Sister's head against the bed frame. Elder Sister threw a stool at her and, unable to get out of the way, Ma was knocked to the floor, injuring her knee. Then Elder Sister put a kitchen knife to her own throat and threatened to kill herself. My mother leapt to her feet and, after managing to wrestle the knife away, cuffed Elder Sister hard around the ear. Later, she was stricken with regret.

When we were growing up, Ma's words didn't count for much with us kids until my father repeated them. It had always been that way. If we were afraid of our mother, it was really because we were afraid of our father—or, more accurately, that we loved him very much. And because Second Sister was Father's favorite, she was really the head of the household, just like Elder Sister said.

Even now, Second Sister's word carried the weight of authority, and the speech she'd made to me resonated deeply. I knew she wanted to keep the family together, so she must have had her reasons for being so cruel.

When I got back, I found Second Sister sitting up in bed. The color had returned to her lips. Her cell phone rang, and she removed the oxygen mask to take the call, leaning away from me and speaking as quietly as she could. I was 80 percent sure that she was talking to Fourth Sister. Hanging up, she looked at her watch, climbed out of bed to put on her leather shoes, and muttered to herself, "We'd better get back. Where's that husband of mine, anyway?"

I was about to go and look for him, but Second Sister indicated that I should sit back down.

"Listen, Little Six, I'll give it to you straight: this time, you've got to be on Fourth Sister's side."

I thought for a moment, and then said, "Second Sister, when Tang gets here, all we can do is try and get the couple back together instead of urging them to go their separate ways."

"Of course."

"But there's something you're not telling me," I said. "You have something up your sleeve."

"Not at all," Second Sister replied. "No matter what you think you remember—like that story in your book about me supposedly beating you with firewood!—we've done right by you, Little Six. You have to stand by your own family."

"That depends."

"How dare you? So you'd just let someone do something horrible to us? It's like you're not really our sister at all." Second Sister's voice rose.

At that moment, her husband came back with apples, pears, and bananas. He handed me a banana and then peeled one for Second Sister. I thought she was lucky to have such a loyal and considerate husband.

Tang had been the same way once. He'd once waited seven hours at the airport when Fourth Sister's flight was late, and he didn't complain one bit when she finally arrived. When she had swollen gums and a terrible toothache, he went with her to the hospital, where he paced frantically without eating or drinking a thing. He didn't like to cook, but for Fourth Sister he would drive for an hour to an Indian supermarket just to buy chili peppers so that he could make superspicy brown-braised pork for her. And he was more dedicated to Tiantian than even most biological fathers are. He once flew to China in the heat of the summer just to get her a visa and bring her back to London.

Sadly, Tiantian hated Tang for breaking up her family, and Tang's trip halfway across the world only strained their relationship more. They stayed in my house in Beijing for two nights before flying to London. Tiantian's father came to see them off and take Tiantian out for hot pot. He accidentally spilled a whole cup of scalding water over her foot, and they had to go to the hospital. Far from being angry, Tiantian actually consoled him while he blamed himself and apologized. His hand, she insisted, had only slipped because he was so distracted by his sorrow at her impending departure.

Tiantian was sixteen and lovely—but about me she never had a kind word to say. She deliberately left her diary out where Tang would see it, and he told me she'd written that she blamed me for helping Tang and her mother get rid of her father. Fortunately, we got closer as time went by. Although she never apologized, she brought me a steady stream of little presents to alleviate her guilt. Youthful rebellion is both beautiful and brutal. The people we hurt most are the people nearest to us—our families.

Tang had truly loved Fourth Sister, just as Second Sister's husband loved Second Sister. In many ways, he had treated her with even more care and consideration.

Relationships between men and women are funny things. When they're good, the two want nothing more than to be together every single moment. When they're bad, there's more enmity between them than between the most dreaded of foes.

3

We called a taxi from the main gate of the hospital. The red Xiali started along a stretch of pavement before turning down a bumpy dirt road intermittently bordered by steep hillsides and bomb shelters. Some of the shelters had been converted to warehouses, but the vast majority lay abandoned. Grass grew waist high in the doorways, and moss covered the rock walls. Inside, insects, rats, and possibly even poisonous snakes lived a parasitic existence.

Everyone who's been to Chongqing knows the place is full of bomb shelters. The first of them were built during the War of Resistance as a defense against Japanese air strikes. In the 1970s, the old shelters were renovated, deepened, and reinforced against nuclear attacks, while a new round of shelters was collectively dug out to accommodate the growing population, making the mountain city even more like a beehive.

A large cluster of shelters sat alongside Alley Cat Stream. As a child, I was instinctively afraid of them, as young girls were often dragged into these man-made caves, raped, and strangled to death. The bodies were either left inside to rot or thrown into the river. When the Cultural Revolution broke out, both factions kidnapped people from all around. My neighbors hurried to shut their courtyard gates before dark had even fallen, reinforcing their doors with wooden bars. They stashed the metal implements issued by their various work units, everything from scissors to kitchen knives, in dark corners within easy reach, put out the lights as early as possible, and sat up nervously in bed, ready to defend themselves.

But in the daytime, children took no heed of such things, sneaking quietly out of their houses while the adults weren't looking. They stripped to their underwear and ran to the riverside, the bomb shelters, and the steepest cliffs, where they threw themselves into the water with total abandon. I was scared of the river, but even more scared of Third Brother. If I hadn't jumped in, he would have looked down on me from then on, so I shut my eyes and leapt. I was four and a half years old.

Worried about getting in trouble, Third Brother didn't tell Mother about any of this. However, a nosy neighbor said to her, "That girl of yours is a plucky little thing. I saw her in the river with the older boys. She could've drowned and ended up as a water nymph!"

That evening, mother's face was dark. I brought her a glass of water, but she told me it was too cold. I returned with a towel and began to mop the sweat from her brow, but my sluggishness brought her temper to a boil. Snatching the towel from my hands and throwing it over my head, she said, "So you went down into the river, did you? Does even the Dragon King, the evil spirit of the river, deserve better than I do? Why are you gawking at me with those horrid little eyes of yours?"

I stood in front of my mother, my eyes blurring with tears at the unfairness of it all. She ordered me to fetch the heavy washboard and kneel on it in the courtyard as a punishment. I knelt there for I don't know how long until darkness had descended completely, but nobody from the family came out to check on me. I suddenly heard footsteps in the street outside, and a group of Red Guards passed by, puffed up with aggression and arrogance. In the distance, the crack of gunshots resounded like firecrackers.

Only then did my mother bolt outside, scoop me up with the washboard, and hustle me back inside.

The memories of my childhood made the traffic jam easy to endure. The taxi driver lit a cigarette, but I asked him to put it out. After a little while, the cars began to move again. Finally, our taxi came to a stop by the back gate of the plastics factory.

Second Sister, her husband, and I got out of the car and began the long climb down to Middle School Street.

Even all these years later, Middle School Street was still the best place for people watching. The locals loved to sit at their mildew-covered doors and windows, or even right out on the stoop, to watch people pass by.

I could hear them discussing us and saying nasty things as we walked down the steps.

I squinted toward the family house and could just make out a broad-shouldered man with glasses sitting on the balcony. Next to him was a woman wearing a hat. It had to be Fourth Sister and Tang. So he'd arrived and was having what looked like a very civil conversation with Fourth Sister. But how could that be?

By the time we reached the bottom of Middle School Street, we could hear the firecrackers going off like gunshots. Another relative from far away must have arrived to see Mother off. I turned back to look at Second Sister and her husband, and I quickened my pace.

As we entered the courtyard, I bypassed the newly arrived guests, walking over to Mother's coffin and lighting nine sticks of incense for her. Then I headed straight upstairs.

I was right. Tang and Fourth Sister were sitting side by side, seemingly on good terms. Perhaps I was worrying about nothing, imagining rain where there was only wind. But just last night I'd overheard my sisters saying they wanted to get even with Tang. Maybe, I speculated, when Fourth Sister had set eyes on Tang again, love had won out, and she'd changed her mind about revenge. Fourth Sister's expression looked very natural and her eyes revealed more than a hint of happiness. When she saw me walk out onto the balcony, she offered me her seat and asked, "Second Sister's all right, isn't she?"

"She's fine now. She's downstairs," I replied.

Tang patted me on the head before hugging me. He held me very tight, and before long, my eyes were wet. "Little Six," he said, "Don't cry!"

"I'm glad you came, Tang."

"I had to see Mother off. She was always so good to me!"

"Ma always said you must be from Rice Porridge County, since you liked her rice porridge so much!"

Fourth Sister walked inside and began tidying up, her face still a picture of tenderness and her eyes bright. Tang lowered his voice. "Looks like your fourth sister's had some work done?"

"Yes, she had her freckles removed."

"Sure, but haven't you noticed that she had her breasts done? They're bigger and higher."

I hadn't noticed, and I was taken aback by his words.

"Surely not," I mumbled.

Tang handed me a glass of water infused with red dates, which Fourth Sister had specially prepared for him.

"You should really try to help her find someone new, Little Six. Your sister's still quite beautiful, and she's kept her figure very trim. She doesn't need a rotten old codger like me. You know, we never did speak the same language. It was always a struggle to find things to say because we have nothing to talk about. She just wants to gossip about that restaurant she works in: who got the biggest tips, who's lazy, who's slacking off. She has no interest in books—when she gets home from work, she just watches TV all night. It's not as though I blame her. She never had any higher education. And really, there's no reason for her to go back to London when she could stay here in Chongqing and find someone who speaks her hometown dialect. Then she can play a little mah-jongg, watch her TV shows, visit her relatives, and have spicy hot pot every day. Wouldn't that life be more comfortable for her?"

We'd been talking for two minutes and already Tang was trying to recruit me to his side.

"You didn't think of her like that before," I replied. "The two of you used to talk and joke for hours. You'd go out to buy food together, you went to the seaside, you took her to Amsterdam. You photographed her naked and made love every day. You're only saying these mean things now because you've got someone new and you want to dump her. And on top of it, now you're asking me to betray her, to help you out of the mess you made."

"You're the most rational person in your family."

"She'd die for you, you know."

Fourth Sister bustled in and out, not interrupting our conversation, though it was obvious she was trying to eavesdrop. Her breasts did seem bigger, which made her waist look even slimmer. When it came to women, Tang had eyes like a hawk, as sharp as the Monkey King's. He must realize that Fourth Sister had gotten plastic surgery for him. If he still had feelings for her, he should be touched, but a man really trying to extricate himself would only feel pressure.

On his past trips to Chongqing, Tang had occasionally stayed with my mother, but mostly he stayed in hotels or at Fourth Sister's place. Once he'd even brought his wife with him. Embarrassed, Fourth Sister had felt like she was supposed to ask Tang's wife's permission to sleep with him.

But that wife had refused to say a word. And now, I thought with some satisfaction, Fourth Sister must know how his wife felt back then. I knew for a fact that she'd wanted to dig a hole in the ground, bury him alive with his mistress, and put up a sign above it that read, "This is what happens to cheaters!"

Fourth Sister despised Tang's new girlfriend with a passion, harboring hatred toward her that would last for several lifetimes. By comparison, his wife had handled the situation better. When Fourth Sister went to bed with Tang, his wife would leave the apartment and head for the busiest square in the city. The idyllic, sunny square was filled with children playing and couples walking hand in hand. Sitting on a bench, she would stick her fingers in her ears and bite her lip without making a sound.

"Are you hungry?" Fourth Sister asked, bringing over a plate of sticky rice cakes.

Tang shook his head.

"Aw, come on. Try some." Fourth Sister affectionately passed him a piece. "They're your favorite."

"I'd love one," I said, reaching out and grabbing one.

Fourth Sister looked at me for a moment, before passing Tang another piece. She called me into the kitchen, closed the door, and said, "What do you think you're doing?"

"I don't want any trouble during Ma's period of mourning."

"You think I would actually hurt him? You're not right in the head."

"You're the one who's not right in the head. Why did you get a boob job? Is that the way to keep a man now?"

Fourth Sister shook with anger, but nevertheless lowered her voice as she spoke. "He's the one who gave me the money and asked me to do it. He said my breasts had sagged because I had a baby. I was going to do it for him before everything happened, but why would I want to put myself through an operation after he was so cruel to me?" She lifted up her top. "See? No surgery. I'm just wearing a push-up bra. That woman of his would get any surgery he asked her to. He used to say she looked like the back of a bus with her long face. He promised he'd give me a million dollars if he got together with someone like that. You can't trust a word this man says. But I can't help it—I love him, and I won't give him up. Do you understand?"

She told me how they'd dug a fishpond in their garden together and how the lotus flowers had bloomed. It all came pouring out, how happy they'd been, how when she had first arrived in London, Fourth Sister had planted cherry, pear, jujube, and peach trees, and all but the peach had borne fruit. Fourth Sister talked about the cocker spaniel she'd spotted online, black and white with long ears, barely a month old. They had driven out to the countryside near Swansea to pick the dog up, and Tang had named her Cosette, after the heroine of Victor Hugo's *Les Miserables*. When Cosette cried at night, Fourth Sister would go downstairs and sleep with her on the sofa. The puppy got bigger with each passing day, even learning to open the door. She would shoot outside like lightning to fetch her ball or swim in the nearby stream. One day, Cosette wandered a little too far. Unable to see Fourth Sister, the dog panicked, ran into the road, and was almost flattened by a speeding car. Fourth Sister was beside herself. Once the dog had recovered, Fourth Sister doted on her more than before, taking her down to the stream every day. Sometimes Tang would come along too.

She described an evening when Tiantian, Tiantian's boyfriend, and her younger cousin had sat around Tang while Cosette lay at his feet. It was a cozy family scene. After dinner, Tang went to Fourth Sister's room and told her that he would never leave her. They made love, and he told Fourth Sister he would take her to Italy and Greece. Fourth Sister believed him, as they had been to Paris only two months earlier, where he'd showered her with gifts. Tang said he had always wanted to be with her, and now his wish had come true.

She dropped her head. When she looked up, her eyes were cold. Now she realized, she said, that when he took her places and gave her things, he was just assuaging his guilty conscience. She said that once he'd actually come close to admitting it. He couldn't understand what sometimes came over him, he whined to her as they lay in bed together, or why he'd hurt so many innocent people in his life.

Fourth Sister began to cry.

I handed her a towel from the bathroom.

"It was all the fault of that cheap slut," she sobbed, "telling me off on the phone and saying I'm just an uncultured worker. When I told her to stay away from him, she said to me, 'If you got on a bus, it would crash; if you got on a plane, it would drop out of the sky; if you walked down the street, you'd be struck by lightning. I've decided I want him, and you just can't compete.' You tell me: What kind of intellectual behaves that way? Once, we got to Tang's office at the same time. She was so scared she tried to run, but I caught up and slapped her a couple of times. I said, 'You really want to steal a man? Then go ahead. You just try!' But Tang ran out to help her. I was flabbergasted. He held me back, and that disgusting woman bit my hand so hard that she took a chunk out of it and got blood all over her face. She was taken down to the police station, but she pretended not to know me. I went to her university to demand that she pay for my medical bills, but she hid. Considering all the shameful stuff she's done, I've been more than reasonable. For Tang's sake, I didn't try to press charges or denounce them. Otherwise, both their reputations would have been ruined."

Fourth Sister held up her hand to show me a bite wound that still hadn't healed. It seemed like her thumbs were inextricably tied to her romantic woes. One had been badly injured blocking the robber's knife aimed at her second husband, and now, the thumb on her other hand had almost been bitten off in broad daylight by Tang's mistress. I felt sorry for her because she was my sister, but at the same time, I thought she should have handled the situation a little more rationally.

So I did my best. I told her that if all this was true, she couldn't say Tang didn't love her. It was just that he'd made promises to that younger woman, and now he thought he had to honor them. He must have been suffering greatly. Tang was well over sixty, and the years are not kind to anyone. He must have been dyeing his hair black every couple weeks, terrified that white roots would show themselves and remind him that he was old, that the grim reaper was on his tail. He must have hoped that sleeping with a younger woman would stave off his own aging. The older some men got, the more often they changed women. It wasn't about the women but about the men's fear of death.

After listening to my words, Fourth Sister stopped crying. "Forget it," she said. "You've always taken his side. I'll tell you something. He only came to Chongqing to sort out Ma's condo on the condition that I never bother him ever again."

I was dumbstruck for a few moments, but then said, "If you agreed, then you can't go back on it."

Fourth Sister shook her head. "I wouldn't do him any harm."

"Has Tang been downstairs yet? He wouldn't leave without seeing the rest of the family, would he?"

"Don't worry, I'll handle it," Fourth Sister replied. She gazed downstairs nervously.

4

The cruelest wounds are caused by the people we love the most. What had Fourth Sister done wrong? If anything, her mistake was simply to love Tang with all her heart.

Our mother never actually told us that we had to marry the right person, but we could sometimes guess her feelings from the way she looked at us. Her relationships with men were like a light shining in the distance on a dark night: almost invisible, but if we had really looked, we would have seen them. Once Ma turned sixty, she stopped asking about her children's marriages. After Fourth Sister went to England, Mother missed her and would mumble to herself, "How's she doing? Is she coughing like she did when she was little? They say the winters in England are cold."

For my mother, Fourth Sister was like a sprite or fleeting shadow. After her love for Tang took her to England, she completely disappeared from our mother's sight until just before Mother died, a total of nine long years. Mother preferred to remember Fourth Sister as a child, always sick and needing to be cared for by her and Father. Back then, Fourth Sister was always by Ma's side. Her cough made it impossible for her to go to school, and Ma was constantly searching for folk remedies. Eventually, Father heard that using bat meat boiled in a young boy's urine would cure her. Bats would fly out of the courtyard late at night, so Father held the wooden ladder while Third Brother climbed up with a flashlight and grabbed two. The young boy's urine was harder to get, as all the neighbors thought mother was a bad woman and refused to give her any. With no other option, Father took Fourth Sister out on the street and begged passersby until some kindhearted person brought their two-year-old son over. After three months of assiduously taking this remedy, Fourth Sister finally recovered from her illness.

Once she was able to go to school, Fourth Sister was the best student in the family. She borrowed foreign novels to read and could recite whole passages from *Pride and Prejudice* and *Wuthering Heights*. She always got excellent marks on her essays, not to mention being the champion hurdler on school sports day. Those were the days when Deng Xiaoping briefly held the reins of power and focused on improving the quality of education and sending youth to university. When Deng was deposed in 1976, the bubble burst. All the middle-school and high-school graduates were sent down to the countryside. Fourth Sister went to a village designated for children whose parents worked in the shipyard. The village was in the Xuanhan area of Sichuan, where life was hard and the only produce was potatoes. There wasn't even rice to eat. Fourth Sister was desperate to get back home, and she was devastated when Mother gave her job at the shipyard to Fifth Brother, which meant she had to wait many more years for a chance to transfer to the city as a construction worker. She'd held it against Mother ever since.

Fourth Sister had long ago lost faith in the concept of family and placed all her hopes instead in romantic love, which she pursued with such devotion that she would have given her life for it. Ma could see this, and it broke her heart. Parents can always see the helplessness that lies behind their children's posturing—even when those children grow up.

I remember Mother once said to me with resentment, "Why do you have to live so far away? Or if you have to, fine, but did you have to take Fourth Sister with you? Your ma never gets to see either of you at all."

Mother knew I had always been rebellious, and she understood that the way I handled personal issues was always aimed squarely at her. One time, I tried to bring a boyfriend home, but on the ferry, the more I looked at the guy, the more he annoyed me. I decided I didn't want my mother to meet him. When the ferry docked on the south bank, I said, "I changed my mind. I don't want to go home anymore. Let's just head back." My boyfriend felt insulted and promptly got drunk in a little restaurant nearby.

Another time when I was incredibly stressed, I took the last ferry home across the river with a new boyfriend. Mother had already gone to sleep, but I knocked on her door, went in, and told her I'd gotten married. She gave us her room and bed, but first she asked my boyfriend to leave us alone for moment.

In a low voice, she said, "Marriage is a big thing—you should at least have told your ma first. And who is this man you chose? His right hand shakes—he must be ill. How is he ever going to take care of you?"

"That's my business," I snapped.

"Do you still hate me?" Mother asked.

"I hate the world," I replied.

"Coming home like this is like not coming home at all. I don't want to see you like this. You have to learn to love. If you can love, then you'll be happier."

"Then just pretend I never came home at all," I said.

My boyfriend and I left first thing in the morning. Mother didn't see us out. From the dark bags under her eyes, it was obvious she hadn't slept all night. I wanted desperately to tell her that I hadn't actually gotten married, that I didn't plan to go anywhere near marriage my whole life. But I wanted to make her angry, and I ignored her advice.

I was willful and impulsive in those days. Puffed up on my own talent and looks, I looked down on my mother. I was heartless and reckless. My life was a kaleidoscopic mess. I treated art as life and life as art, turning my days into a series of twists and turns on a high wire, performing acrobatic tricks that alarmed me as much as they did everyone else. Had I really brought a boyfriend with a bad hand home? I couldn't quite remember. Maybe I'd just been taking revenge on my mother in my dreams. After all, she always acted as though she didn't care whether I had a boyfriend or what kind of person he was. I told myself she didn't care about how I was doing, knowing all along this was self-deception and unfair.

It's dangerously easy for a daughter to hurt her mother, even if she doesn't mean to. For a rebellious brat like me, who fully intended to make her mother miserable, it was a walk in the park.

Before I left China, I went back to Chongqing to see my mother. She did her best to smile, but when I turned to go, Ma began to cry. The tears poured out of her as if she were crying for all the injustice and humiliation in my life. I knew, of course, that she was happy for me, happy that I could get far away from this country that had only ever hated and hurt me. But she was concerned that for someone like me—introverted, melancholy, scarred—being all alone in a unfamiliar place would bring even more hardship and pain. Plus, not knowing when she'd see me again left her feeling helpless and alone. In spite of all the suffering I'd brought her and the public humiliation I symbolized, or maybe because of it, she'd always had a special place hidden deep in her heart for me. That day, she cried and cried, as if nothing could ever make the tears stop.

In London, I got a letter from Second Sister saying that mother hadn't eaten or slept properly for days after I'd left, and had ended up getting very sick. I had almost no reaction to this news. My mother and everything in Chongqing already seemed so distant that they were scarcely real.

When I did finally walk down the aisle with the man I had chosen, I didn't tell my mother ahead of time—just sent photographs. That way, when I brought my husband back to Chongqing, it would be a done deal and my mother would have no choice but to accept him.

She'd have to be nice to him and keep a smile on her face in the hope that he would treat me well. Even when he treated me badly, Mother kept a smile on her face. Time crept by silently, and the world became increasingly wicked and unstable, while my mother learned not to let me see the hundred ways in which she worried about me.

Later, when I left my husband and went to live in Beijing alone, she never asked what had happened. Every now and then when we talked over the phone, she would simply say to me, "Don't worry, Little Six. When the sun sets, the moon rises. When the moon sets, the sun rises."

I wrote a fictionalized account of Virginia Woolf's nephew coming to teach in China and falling in love with a married woman. By the time a Chinese magazine serialized it in 2001, the book had already been published in Taiwan and quite a few foreign countries. An elderly Chinese lady sued me for damaging the reputation of her late mother, but British laws don't protect the deceased, so they threw out the case. The old lady then filed a lawsuit in the Haidian District of Beijing, which also refused to review the case. Finally, she filed a suit in Changchun, where the magazine was published. The Changchun Intermediate People's Court decreed that, in my novel, I was guilty of salacious, pornographic writing. Besides paying a heavy fine, I had to issue public apologies in national newspapers and magazines, and the book was banned for a hundred years.

The lawsuit dragged on for two years, consuming a great deal of my energy and financial resources. It was widely reported around the world, and set off a big debate in China about creative writing and the law. What responsibility did authors bear? How much room was there for re-creation in literary fiction?

Several newspapers branded me the "lawsuit author" and rumors and gossip ran rampant. A lot of people were surprised to find I was a far cry from their preconceived image and apologized for misreading me.

I appealed to the high court in Jilin. My husband pointed out that the plaintiff had a strong piece of evidence in that he'd published a letter naming her mother as the woman in my story. If he weren't my husband, then this piece of evidence wouldn't stand up in court. He said we should divorce as quickly as possible and, once the lawsuit was over, we could remarry.

But it wasn't on the strength of his letter that the court had ruled against me. The plaintiff enlisted the former head of some government department, who personally asked the court to find me guilty. What chance did I, the daughter of a poor family, have of winning, of escaping a lifetime of punishment? Moreover, my novel discussed the ancient Chinese sexual arts and argued that women should actively enjoy sex, breaking with convention in a way that no previous novel in Chinese literature had ever done. A completely male-dominated society like China naturally would not tolerate this. My novel was like a tree that had grown too tall above the forest, and it had to be destroyed by the wind. I was in a fight with a much stronger opponent, like an egg banging against a rock.

However, I'd become obsessed with the lawsuit, and I thought that if it might help me win, why shouldn't I agree to a temporary divorce? I agreed unconditionally, and we signed the papers.

The divorce came through very quickly, and my husband's letter was removed from the evidence. The high court in Jilin deliberated for two days and two nights, while three different TV channels camped out in front of the courthouse. The high court's verdict was that the hundred-year ban on the novel would stand and that I had to pay compensation to the woman and make a public apology in the magazine. However, they said, I could rewrite the book under a different title with the story set elsewhere.

After the lawsuit ended, my husband never seemed interested in reregistering our marriage. When I asked him about it, he replied that we had a common-law marriage whether or not we carried out the formalities. I didn't mention it again until a few years later when I found out he'd been sleeping around and lying about it instead of being open and honest like we'd always agreed.

I called him, crying, and he said scornfully, "What are you crying for? There's something I think I need to make clear to you. You have no right to criticize anything I do. We haven't been husband and wife for a long time. Just ask the court."

When I heard this, I froze. "But you said you only wanted to get divorced to help with my lawsuit."

"I can't remember what I said back then. In any case, that was then and this is now." His tone was firm.

I felt like the biggest fool on earth. How I had been so blind? In his heart, it had been over a long time ago, but he had never said so because he still needed me.

"You've never been an ordinary woman, and you're not going to be one now. De Beauvoir created the myth of polygamy with Sartre. Are you up to that or are you just less of a revolutionary woman?"

What he meant by that was that I shouldn't ever find another man—I should just be his living widow. I believe in straightforward breakups. If he'd said we should break up and had given me a reason, however much that reason might have hurt me, I would have accepted it. I'd never been one to cling to a man, even when my heart got broken.

I flew straight back to London and found him in the house I had bought for us seven years earlier and never really lived in. That evening, he chatted amiably with me as if nothing had happened.

The next morning, I inquired about my British bank accounts. He wrote down all the details in a very gentlemanly fashion. I went into my room and logged in. I panicked for a moment and almost changed my mind. Then I gritted my teeth and changed my password so he couldn't get in anymore. When I turned the computer off, I realized that my hands were shaking and my face was slick with sweat. I walked out of my room to find him standing in the hallway. I told him what I'd done.

He went pale and cried out, "That's my money. How dare you!"

"No, it's my money. I trusted you all these years in dealing with it, and I've never questioned you about it. Even when the stocks you bought tanked, I never made you feel bad about it. I should have taken the money back years ago, but I trusted you. Now that you're saying it's over between us, I should handle my finances myself."

He yelled and screamed. He said he should never have given me the logins, how hard it had been for him, how he'd put his savings into the account every month.

What savings? I replied. We both knew he'd just been draining my account all these years. I asked myself, *Am I finally ready to leave this man for good?* I could hear the sounds of dogs barking and children laughing from the neighbor's garden, the clock on the wall ticking. My heart gave me my answer.

"I'm leaving you."

"You can't treat me like this." He was so angry that his voice was unrecognizable.

I said to myself, *From now on, this person is dead to me. From now on, I will do everything that he used to do for me by myself—managing my British accounts, doing my UK taxes, writing checks, replying to letters from foreign publishers.* No matter how bad I was at these things, I would never allow this person to do them again. I had to free myself from him utterly. Whatever happened, I had to stand tall like the stone statue in the hallway. I hadn't been strong enough when I went back to China five years earlier. It seemed as though I was leaving him, but I hadn't really succeeded in doing so. I had still been living in his shadow, influenced by his happiness, anger, sorrow, and joy, even by the moods of his lovers. I might have covered up the wound, but it had never healed. No, I couldn't live like that. Even if it killed me, I had to reclaim my self-respect.

When he realized I was serious, he planned to get a lawyer and take me to court. He wrote out a list of all our respective properties, our savings accounts, and our investments. I told him I had always been intimidated by very paternalistic men like him, but I had faith that the British courts would be fair. His eyes filled with hatred, and it was suddenly clear that he'd only stayed connected to me all these years for my money. Now he was determined to cut all ties for good.

I flew to Munich and took up residence in a house borrowed from a girlfriend.

A week later, I got a letter from him saying that another man must have taken over my finances for me. I'd never have been able to do it on my own, he said, and I'd never have dared to. I shook my head. It was sad that he had lived with me for so long and never really understood me at all. My mother always said, "My Little Six was as timid as a mouse when she was a child, but if you push her too far, she's capable of anything. She could cut her own heart out and serve it to you, just to show her resolve."

As Christmas drew close, glittering Christmas trees lined the streets of Munich, filling them with festive cheer amid the heavy snow. I went to a little Turkish shop in the neighborhood to buy bread and watched the passersby carrying presents home through the whirling snowflakes.

And where was my home? I had always been homeless. I had thought that the house my husband lived in was my home. In reality, I had been a stranger wandering the earth for years now, lonely and alone, with no one to comfort me or care for me.

Late one night, I dreamt about the old family home at Compound No. 6 again, and saw my mother there. When I awoke, I looked at the bare branches of the snow-covered trees and thought of that poor house. It seemed more like home than anywhere else did because my mother was there. I wanted to call my mother and tell her what kind of person my husband had turned out to be. It wasn't that fate had been unfair, but rather that I had married the wrong person. When it came to men, I'd failed miserably. I wanted to tell my mother that the one time I'd met my biological father, he had warned me, but I simply hadn't listened. He'd said, "Whatever you do, never let anyone know that you were born out of wedlock—especially not your future husband. Otherwise, he and your in-laws will think you're beneath them and never respect you. You'll be badly mistreated."

My ex-husband was educated in the West and his head was full of Western liberalism, but beneath it all, he was very traditional and chauvinistic. From beginning to end, he never treated me as a husband treats a wife, or a friend treats a friend. He simply acted as a father figure—and sometimes an abusive one. More than anyone else, he hoped that I would thrive professionally, but when I actually did succeed, he couldn't stand it. He felt left behind—not just by me, but by the times. His resentment grew greater and greater as the years went by.

With tears in my eyes, I picked up the phone and called Chongqing. When I heard my mother's voice, though, I chickened out and said to her, "I'm fine, Ma. No, nothing's wrong. Just wanted to say hello. I should go. Actually, I'm with a bunch of people right now. We're going to have a big dinner, do some singing and dancing. Then we're going to ring in the New Year with fireworks."

Yet another missed opportunity to connect with my mother. In that moment, I'd wanted nothing more than to pour my heart out, to hear her tell me, "Don't worry, Little Six. When the sun sets, the moon rises. When the moon sets, the sun rises." But somehow, I still couldn't get any closer to her.

No, that wasn't altogether true. Since my move back to China in 2000, the time I brought my mother to stay with me in Beijing was the closest I had ever been to her. I remember one morning I took Ma to Yonghe Temple to light some incense. She knelt on the floor cushion and muttered prayers to herself. Then, I sat with her on a bench under the gingko trees, wishing I could break through the ice around my heart.

I ran to a nearby kiosk and bought us ice cream. My mother took one bite and said, "This is really good. It's just sweet enough. It's like someone who's been dealt a bad hand by fate finally getting a sweet reward."

Then, without looking at me, she asked cautiously, "Are you all right, my little sixth girl?"

"I'm fine, Ma. You don't need to worry about me," I replied.

As I spoke, tears welled up and began to run down my face. Afraid that my mother would see, I jumped up to buy more ice cream.

My mother took my hand and said very gently, "One is enough for me. Let's sit down. It's so peaceful here, isn't it?"

She sat on the bench in front of the temple with me for the longest time without saying a word.

5

Tang didn't want to go downstairs to greet our distant relatives. Fourth Sister said he was tired from the long journey and that he should lie down for a while. They still had to go and sort out the keys for Mother's condo. She shut the bedroom door.

Potbellied Cat had asked the chef to make noodles with shredded pork for the guests who hadn't made it in time for lunch. Fourth Sister nagged the chef to make a special bowl without chilies, which she carried upstairs for Tang.

When I went to the bathroom, I caught sight of myself in the mirror. I looked exhausted.

The sunlight had sunk slightly to the west, while a few dark clouds were suspended in the sky. A few more tables had been added in the courtyard, since the people who'd already had the rice boxes came back to eat pork noodles.

As I helped pour the tea, I noticed that the assembled friends and family weren't talking much about Mother. Instead, they were just chatting about normal things—how long it had been since they'd seen each other, how many children they had, what they did, who'd gotten married, and so on.

The feng shui here was good, they said. The house had a great view of the Yangtze River meeting the Jialing River. Surely, Chongqing would find a way to lift itself out of poverty. Then the conversation turned to spiteful gossip about which families had money. When you had no money, they asserted, you smoked fake Zhongnanhais. When you had no money, the first thing you looked at when you bought clothes was the price tag. When you had no money, you pretended to have money, and when you had money, you pretended not to.

Neighbors came and went as if they were attending a dinner party or participating in some festival. The wreaths were piled several layers deep all the way to the end of the street.

I noticed Tang looking down from the fifth-floor balcony, but this time, Fourth Sister wasn't with him. She, Second Sister, and Elder Sister were conspicuously absent. I made a circuit of the courtyard, but still couldn't find them.

Where could they all have gone?

Potbellied Cat cleared the disposable chopsticks and napkins from the table, while my two brothers collected the dirty bowls. A skinny, middle-aged man was wiping the tables with a cloth. I walked over and said, "Let me do it, Brother Shouli."

"There's no need to stand on ceremony, Little Six. I'm nearly done."

Shouli was one of my mother's godsons, and a chauffeur for the CEO of a big company. He said he hadn't slept much over the last couple of days, but luckily, he had been able to catch a little sleep that morning. We wiped the tables together and made small talk.

"I hear that the relationship between my ma and your uncle was a little out of the ordinary. Do you know anything about that?"

Shouli's eyes widened when he heard my question. He picked up a packet of Marlboros from the table, took one out, and lit it. We moved to a more discreet location, away from the others. He said he'd heard his mother say something had happened between them, but a good sixty years ago. Shouli's uncle had liked my mother very much. When my mother came to Chongqing to escape her arranged marriage, she found herself with new people in unfamiliar surroundings, and Shouli's grandmother had been very kind to her. Shouli's uncle began to pursue her, but she treated him like an older brother. Not long after that, my mother met and married the mob boss. Less than a year later, he found someone new and began to beat my mother. In a spur-of-the-moment decision, Mother took Elder Sister in her arms and snuck out of the house. She didn't go to Shouli's grandma, however, out of fear that the gangster would harm their family. When Shouli's uncle heard what had happened, he searched high and low for my mother. "If my uncle had found your mother, they might have gotten married, and you'd have to rewrite your whole family history."

"What happened after that?" I pressed.

Shouli seemed lost in memory for a moment before replying. "When my uncle couldn't find your ma, he thought she was dead, and he eventually got over her. He married a woman from downriver and left Chongqing. Later on, when he found out your ma was alive, he was always finding excuses to come back to Chongqing to see her."

"So did they rekindle the old flame?"

Shouli gave me a funny look.

"I just want to know what really happened. My sisters always assumed they were lovers—they were gossiping about it just last night."

"It's a shame that people talk like that. According to my ma, my uncle adopted your ma as his little sister in front of my grandmother that very year. He called your dad his brother-in-law."

I breathed a sigh of relief.

"Still, my uncle always kept your ma in his heart. She was his first love. He died suddenly of a heart attack in 1975, and his wife sent a telegram from Wuhan. When it arrived, a lot of relatives and friends were over at our house for dinner, and everyone was stunned. Your ma cried so hard she fainted, so people started talking, and the rumor replaced the truth. I remember your second sister was there too."

I had never met Shouli's uncle, but I'd seen his photograph at Shouli's house. The uncle was handsome, solid and imposing in a way that seemed more northeastern than like someone from Chongqing. I wondered why my mother hadn't been responsive when he'd courted her. Well, she must have kept him in her heart too. Otherwise, why would she have been so close to Shouli's grandmother, not to mention his parents? She'd treated Shouli like her own child. The bond between our families, untainted by even a drop of common blood, had lasted for decades! No wonder my sisters thought that Mother and this man had been lovers. As for the other lovers my sisters had mentioned, I asked myself, *Who could give me the real story?*

As I frowned in thought, Elder Sister appeared in my line of sight. She was dragging my second cousin away from the crowd.

Curious, I left Shouli and followed. Elder Sister and Second Cousin were whispering by the grain storehouse wall, their expressions very mysterious. Unless I was mistaken, Elder Sister was trying to borrow money from him.

I ran in to Xiaomi on my way back upstairs and told her what had just happened.

Xiaomi's eyes flashed. "So Ma really went to them?"

"Xiaomi, what's going on?"

Only then did she confess that she had written to her mother asking for help and admitting that she needed money. Her boyfriend had been harassed in prison until, unable to stand the bullying any longer, he fought back, snapping his opponent's neck in the process. Now he had to pay compensation. Her mother had yelled at her and told her she didn't have the money. Then, Elder Sister had told her that Second Cousin was in charge of administering various immigrant settlement allowances, and although it was a minor position, he had considerable power. These days, he thought everyone was beneath him and wouldn't even acknowledge his family connection to relatives from the countryside who came to seek his help.

Second Cousin didn't look to me like a corrupt official, but appearances can be deceiving.

6

There was fog that afternoon, a rare occurrence, and it was accompanied by high winds that noisily shook the plastic marquee. Fortunately, the marquee rested against the house at one end, while the other end was supported by the old courtyard walls. As I was checking to make sure it would hold, Second Sister and Fourth Sister came through the main entrance to the courtyard, closely followed by Third Sister-in-Law and Fifth Sister-in-Law. They asked me to go upstairs with them.

"Those people came, but I got rid of them already," announced Second Sister.

I guessed right away that they were talking about my biological father's family. It was my two half brothers and my two uncles. They'd come to pay their respects to my mother.

"Got rid of them by yelling, no doubt," I said, glaring at Second Sister.

"You should just thank God they didn't make it to the house and Elder Sister didn't see them. She would have thrown them out physically."

Fourth Sister explained that my relatives had stopped at Auntie Ma's little shop to ask directions. They were the spitting image of the man named Sun, so Auntie Ma had no doubt whose sons they were. She told them to wait in the shop while she ran over to get Second Sister.

"What, you think Elder Sister could beat up four men?" I was very annoyed.

Second Sister flew into a rage. "Did you see how many of Elder Sister's friends are here? Of course we'd win!" she snapped. "Still, there's no need for that as long as they stay away. I don't want anyone from the Sun family in this house, especially during Ma's period of mourning."

"They mean well, and besides, you know I've got Sun blood in my veins. Do you want me to get out as well?"

"We don't care whether they mean well. They cannot be here under any circumstances. You've seen the world, Little Six. But you don't understand us country bumpkins. At times like this, you have to let go and trust us to do what's right," Third Sister-in-Law said.

"Don't worry so much about it, Little Six," Fifth Sister-in-Law added. "The Suns must understand."

As I looked at them, I was overcome by a wave of fury, but I didn't say a word. Instead, I just walked down the hallway, headed downstairs, and after gazing at my mother's coffin for a moment, marched out the doorway of the courtyard. I followed the towering wall of the courtyard's grain storehouse down to the river.

I gradually calmed down as I watched the ferries coming across the river. Once my heart rate had slowed, I headed up the hillside. As I passed a bomb shelter, I heard female voices inside. One of them was very familiar.

I walked over and saw that it was Xiaomi and another young woman. The instant they saw me, they jumped apart in a panic. The girl quickly waved good-bye and took off.

"Xiaomi, you're not actually doing heroin, are you?"

"Of course not, Sixth Auntie." Xiaomi's tone was far from convincing.

"You've got a son to take care of," I said.

"Don't worry, even if I was dealing drugs, I wouldn't take them. Don't freak out, I wouldn't deal drugs either. I'm just saying. I know how serious that type of thing is, and I don't want to go to jail. Even if I had no other choice, if I was so poor there was no way to keep going, the most I would do is sell my blood, or my body."

"You must be hungry. Let's go back and get some noodles," I replied.

After the noodles, later that afternoon, the sun had begun to burn through the fog. I perched on the cliff over the river where I had sat before with my father. He had gazed at the boats, puffing at his pipe. He must have been very unhappy. My father loved boats, but hadn't been able to board one in decades. All he could do was sigh wistfully as he watched, and later, he was denied even this pleasure when he went completely blind. He kept a notebook in which he had recorded which sections of the Yangtze had submerged rocks and reefs, as well as what steps to take in case of an emergency. He'd left the notebook to Third Brother, who also loved boats and hoped to pilot ships like Father someday. When he transferred back from the countryside, he joined Father's old ferry company, but he was assigned to be a longshoreman because of our family's lack of clout. His childhood dreams destroyed, Third Brother was filled with despair not only toward the world but also toward his family.

Father, too blind to work, spent years as the "housewife" in the family. When Mother came home on weekends, it was rare to see much warmth between them. Mother never sat by the river with Father. She was always very tired, and her moods were strange. She often treated me like an eyesore, a thorn in her side. Father was taciturn and uncommunicative, so between the two of them, laughter was rare in our house. I wanted so badly to believe that they loved me.

When Elder Sister came back to Chongqing and gave birth to her child, she spent the traditional month of recuperation in the attic. Mother took extra shifts at night, working herself half to death to cover the cost of chicken and duck meat for the new mother.

Still, Elder Sister was not satisfied. She lay in bed complaining bitterly that she had only been able to endure hunger in dirt-poor Wushan by comforting herself with the thought of being able to get away from our family.

"Tell me, when has this family mistreated you?" Second Sister had asked her. "Even though she barely makes anything, Ma managed to send you money in the village whenever she could. And now look how hard she's working to take care of you. She's been doing it for years now! How could you repay her by saying such hurtful things?"

Mother interrupted the two sisters, saying, "What do we gain by raising children? Now you're a mother, so you'll find out sooner or later."

Now Elder Sister was a grandmother, but I wasn't sure she'd really grown up. Mother always told us you reap what you sow, even if it takes a long time. Elder Sister's first daughter rarely came to visit her, and she could hardly reach her son at all. Only her second daughter, Xiaomi, was with her now, and they were practically estranged.

As I walked back to the house, I took a deep breath and told myself that my brothers and sisters had their reasons for hating my biological father, for loathing everything to do with him. Of course they wouldn't let his sons or brothers pay their respects. It went against all their instincts even to allow me to say good-bye to Ma. In their eyes, I was the embodiment of Mother's betrayal, the source of all their misfortune, the cause of the whole family's unhappiness.

I was their scapegoat, but if I could ease the dissatisfaction and pain that had plagued them for so long, perhaps I wouldn't feel so aggrieved.

CHAPTER 8

1

Standing on the street in front of Compound No. 8, I could see everyone who walked up the narrow stone steps from the foot of the hill below. Even the handful of houses that had not yet been plastered with "Condemned Building" stickers looked like they might fall down at any moment. A mountain of garbage had been dumped along the riverside—rotting vegetables, dog shit, cat shit, plastic bags, broken glass, ashes, and tattered clothes. The whole place stank to high heaven. A man in a straw hat meticulously sifted through the piles for tin cans and glass jars, which he deposited in the bamboo basket on his back. From time to time, he would swat away the flies swarming around his face and hands.

I covered my nose with one hand and walked uphill.

Spectacles Wang was standing at the top of the stone steps in a pair of plastic flip-flops. Seeing me approaching, she cackled, "The great writer! So some earthly things still reach you, eh?" She seemed excited, almost drunk with glee.

She was the last person I wanted to see, so I pretended not to hear her and walked on by.

"Hah! You're scared of me. Your ma was scared of me too. She's dead now, but she's still scared of me."

When I looked back at her in shock, she started in again. "You little piece of shit, don't ever think you're better than anyone else. Your ma was just like that beggar. Did you know that? You don't know how much pleasure it gave me to stand up here and watch her."

"She's not even with us anymore. Why don't we call it a truce?" I replied.

"Truth?" Spectacles Wang asked, mishearing. "Listen, you little wretch. If you don't even know the truth about your own family, how can you talk about what goes on in other people's families, let alone make a living writing about it? Everyone for miles around knows about your ma and the garbage pits down by the river, it's not just me."

It was just like when I was a kid, as though she was still director of the local neighborhood committee, harassing me on my way home, spittle flying out of her mouth as she spoke. I turned back to look at the man in the straw hat. Did Spectacles Wang mean that Ma had done that, picked through garbage in broad daylight? It couldn't be, but Spectacles Wang had always known how to hurt me for her own pleasure. I realized with a start that she'd only appeared at the gate last night to humiliate my mother one last time.

Then again, Spectacles Wang had bullied me all her life, but there was always some truth to what she said. I was devastated to think that what she was saying now about Mother might not be entirely false.

Spectacles Wang continued her diatribe, but I hurried away, unable to stand another word.

2

An ocean of monks dressed in yellow kasaya robes stretched from the courtyard at Compound No. 6 all the way to Compound No. 7 at the foot of the stone steps. There must have been more than a hundred of them sitting on the ground, facing my mother's coffin and chanting Buddhist scripture.

The mist suddenly cleared from the peak of the mountain, staining the sky pink for a few moments. The sound of voices receded, and even the sparrows in the eaves sat perfectly motionless. The rows of houses on both sides of the river seemed almost to leap into view.

It was as if I'd entered another world. When at last I pushed my way through the crowd into No. 6, Potbellied Cat hurriedly waved me into the hallway.

"Impressive, isn't it, Little Six?" he whispered.

"Is this all from your 'one-stop' funeral service?" I retorted.

"That's right."

It turned out that the traditional red envelope of money sent by Uncle Jian's son had also contained a short note. The note said that the hundred thousand yuan inside was to fulfill his filial duty to Mother as her godson and also to pay for monks from the temple to perform the proper rites, chant the scriptures, and release Mother's soul by expiating her sins. He had arranged everything with Ciyun Monastery on Lion Mountain, so all we had to do was let them know when to come.

Third Brother hadn't noticed the note at first. He'd talked it over with his wife and Fifth Brother, as well as Potbellied Cat, who was delighted by the news. People already spoke highly of his funerals, and this could only be good for business.

Second Sister broke her own rule about not getting involved in the affairs of the funeral committee. She said having all those monks was too flashy and ostentatious and that I wouldn't approve. The Jian family's money had come with this string attached, so there was no other way to use it. The only option was to return the money.

Elder Sister disagreed. Her opinion was that if someone was willing to splurge on a grand funeral, why not give them what they wanted. Mother would definitely be pleased as she lay there in her coffin.

Fourth Sister went back and forth between agreeing with Second Sister and sympathizing with Elder Sister. Tang knew that no one wanted his opinion anyway, so he left with Second Sister's younger son to sort out the paperwork for the new condo.

None of them could make up their minds, so they asked Younger Uncle to decide. Younger Uncle, who'd never had much of a backbone, inevitably nodded his agreement as soon as they explained the situation to him.

Potbellied Cat told them that the monks would have to perform the rites today, as the funeral procession would be held tomorrow. So Third Brother made the call. The administrator at the monastery said that they had been waiting and would be there right away.

The ancient Ciyun Monastery sits at the foot of Lion Mountain, to the right of the pier in Wildcat Creek. The only monastery in the traditional "ten directions" monastic system to allow monks and nuns to practice together, the site also houses a large collection of priceless artifacts, as well as a Bodhi tree transplanted from India, which had been allowed to wither and die during the Cultural Revolution. Ten years later, to everyone's surprise, the tree miraculously sprang back to life. A steady stream of people came to worship at the monastery's temple, and the air was always thick with the scent of incense.

No wonder Spectacles Wang had blocked my path and said such nasty things. The sight of all those monks in their beautiful robes praying for my mother must have unleashed a tidal wave of righteous fury inside of her.

I walked up to my mother's coffin and kowtowed three times to ask her forgiveness. She'd endured more than her share of suffering and sin in this world, and her soul would struggle more than most to find peace in the next. Mother's adopted son understood this better than any of her natural children. It hadn't even occurred to us to have monks come to chant scripture.

Elder Sister's husband and a woman with wavy hair climbed up the stairs together. There was something so familiar and intimate about the way they walked that it caught my attention. Even though I'd been back a day already, this was the first I'd seen of him. At sixty, he was still one of those truly handsome men who look well dressed even in the most ordinary clothes. He wore a pair of rimless glasses, making him stand out from the crowd even more. The woman at his side seemed pleasantly surprised and nodded when she saw me. I nodded back in reply. She was meticulously turned out. Her necklace, handbag, and shoes were all very pretty, and her heavy foundation and powder made her face so pale that she didn't look Chinese at all. I felt as if I had seen her before, but I couldn't recall where.

I followed them inside. Mother's apartment on the fifth floor was filled with relatives, who crowded around the windows and the railings of the hallway to watch the monks chanting. Elder Sister's husband ushered the woman in and ceremoniously poured her a glass of water.

"Little Six, you probably don't remember me. I'm Cousin Chun. I carried you on my back over the mountain by the old shipyard when you were little." The woman spoke in deliberate, soft tones.

I held out my hand, and she clasped it between both of hers. I still couldn't quite place her.

Elder Sister's husband said that Cousin Chun was a friend of Ma's from the shipyard and that, coincidentally, Cousin Chun's younger sister was his ex-wife.

In 1953, the government had decreed that all Japanese people were to be driven out of Chongqing. Cousin Chun's family—which consisted of Cousin Chun, her two sisters, and their father—clung tightly to their Japanese mother, refusing to let the government agents take her away. Even nosy onlookers were in tears at such a sad scene. After the government restored friendly relations with Japan in 1973, their mother wanted to take the three girls out of China. At the same time, Cousin

Chun's younger sister was getting divorced from this man, now Elder Sister's husband, so the girls all joined their mother in Japan.

Years later, Cousin Chun returned and opened a Japanese restaurant in downtown Chongqing. People from Chongqing didn't like Japanese cuisine much, but Cousin Chun tailored her menu to local tastes and business flourished. She'd always stayed on good terms with Elder Sister's husband, and when she heard he'd lost his mother-in-law, she rushed over to pay her respects, hoping to see me while she was there.

"You used to really like me when you were a kid, Little Six. I was the only one you wanted to carry you. You didn't even want your ma to do it," Cousin Chun recalled.

"I think I remember that," I replied.

Cousin Chun's eyes moistened as she looked at me. She sat very close, and her scent reminded me of the way my mother smelled before she got old. Perhaps I had wanted her to carry me as a child precisely because she smelled like my mother, but she was nicer to me.

The monks had finished chanting the Bodhisattva Ksitigarbha Vow Sutra and moved on to the Diamond Sutra.

Listening, the tension in my chest seemed to ease a little. I felt rays of light illuminating the spot where I stood, and then came the recurring vision I sometimes had of a man on stilts, a crown of mandala flowers perched on his head. The man walked over, inclining his head in obedience and gazed at me attentively—

"The time has come!" Potbellied Cat's voice rang out.

Snapping out of my vision, I leaned over the railing and looked down at the scene below. Third Brother said something to the monk in charge, after which the monks bowed and began to withdraw from the courtyard and move down the stone steps. They put their hands together and called out the blessing "Amitabha!" as they went.

Third Brother, Fifth Brother, and Younger Uncle put their hands together and bowed in return.

3

After the monks left, my sisters set about dissecting the event. Fifth Sister-in-Law said that her legs and her back didn't ache one bit while the monks were chanting. It was as if a breeze had passed through her whole body, leaving a sweet taste on her tongue. Second Sister said that people were bound to imagine experiences like that if they believed in that sort of thing. Fourth Sister was distracted, sending text messages.

Elder Sister's husband said the whole thing had opened his eyes. In the whole South Bank District, Mother was the only one ever to have had such a lavish send-off. No matter how many sins our mother might have carried with her, her soul was sure to be blessed by the spirits now, and she would receive salvation and cross over to the other side.

He said he regretted that he hadn't done the same when his father died, even if it had bankrupted the family. In any case, it was bound to help their descendants. He was even more superstitious than Elder Sister was. Cousin Chun remarked that the Japanese were also very superstitious people. When someone in the family died, they always had to pay priests from the temple to come. Even though the trend today was toward simplicity, important families would still never hold a funeral without having rites performed.

Cousin Chun said she wanted to go downstairs and burn some incense for Mother, and as we all walked down, I heard Elder Sister say to her husband, "So? Are you going to talk to her or not?" He seemed reluctant to do whatever she was suggesting.

Cousin Chun knelt down before Mother's coffin. She lit three sticks of incense and then burned some paper money. When she had finished paying her respects, she handed me a red envelope. I thanked her and passed it to Third Brother.

Elder Sister tugged at Cousin Chun's arm and said that her daughter Xiaomi wanted to see her for a moment, but Elder Sister's husband interrupted, saying to me, "Little Six, why don't you keep Cousin Chun company?"

I walked with Cousin Chun to go see her old wood-framed house on Middle School Street. The door was locked, but two windows on the upper floor were open. Clothing hung between them on metal wires. We inquired at the corner shop and the clerk told us that three generations of the same family lived there, the elderly couple on the ground floor and the younger couple with small children above. Overhearing our conversation, several neighbors came out to see what was going on. Not one of them recognized Cousin Chun, although they did look curiously at this elegant woman.

When I asked Cousin Chun about the time when she had known my mother at the shipyard, she was more than willing to reminisce about the old days.

Like my siblings, Cousin Chun had been sent down to the countryside as an educated urban youth, but she had been allowed to return to Chongqing after she contracted pneumonia. Once she recovered, she was lucky enough to find a temporary job at the shipyard and stay in the city. That was in early 1972. She worked as a carrier on the same transport team as my mother and was also assigned to the same dormitory.

With a key in one hand and a bedroll in the other, she walked into the room. No more than a minute passed before a bespectacled woman shot out from the mosquito net–shrouded bed opposite and punched her, throwing her bedroll down the stairs. She just stood there clutching her bruised face in shock until Mother ran in and stopped things from going any further. Mother took her straight to the housing department and got her reassigned, to a different room on the same floor.

They told her that the woman, Yueyun, was a lunatic who wouldn't talk to anyone. Nobody dared to sleep in that room with her, and anyone who went in ended up being beaten until they went out again.

My mother was the only exception.

Mother had already gained a reputation as a mysterious, colorful character in the eyes of the other female workers. Not only could she get along with loonies like that but there were also dark rumors about her. My mother took Cousin Chun under her wing, taking extra care of her when she learned that Cousin Chun was the daughter of the Japanese woman who'd been torn away from Middle School Street.

My mother told her that Yueyun had once been a university student, very plain, but very polite. She'd started seeing someone, and the two of them were serious enough that there was talk of marriage. Then, one day, the man suddenly announced that his family wouldn't agree to it. Yueyun had been devastated. From that day on, she refused to pay any attention to men. Not long afterward, the Cultural Revolution began, and Yueyun threw herself into making defamatory posters and arguing in public debates. She was like a vicious dog that would bite anyone. The shipyard leader made it onto one of her posters, as did my mother, because she'd once been married to the executed boss of the Chongqing mob. No one ever found out where she got her information, but she also managed to dredge up my mother's resistance to Elder Sister being sent down to the countryside, as well as the fact that she had an illegitimate child. During the "struggle sessions" for the shipyard bosses, they hauled my mother up for criticism too. They shaved half her hair off in front of the assembled crowd, cracking her head open when she tried to resist.

Even back in the dormitory, Yueyun didn't ease up on the revolution one bit, at least when it came to my mother. She made Mother memorize and recite whole books by heart, as well as making her write endless self-criticisms. She imposed corporal punishment on my mother for the slightest infraction, or made her go hungry.

In recognition of her zeal, Yueyun became a group leader in one of the rebel factions at the shipyard, where she wielded her power as ruthlessly and ostentatiously as she could. Perhaps she went too far, because somebody exposed the fact that her father had fled to Taiwan when the Communist Party liberated Chongqing in 1949. She was immediately arrested and subjected to a struggle session as the offspring of a counterrevolutionary. Exactly how high up Yueyun's father had been in the Nationalist administration, or exactly when he had run off to Taiwan, she didn't know. Ever since she was a little girl, her mother had told her he was dead.

Unable to get over the horror and shame of having a counterrevolutionary father, Yueyun threw herself out a fifth-floor window, hoping to end her life. Instead, she landed not only alive but essentially unharmed, on the paddy field below, her sanity the only lasting damage of the incident. While Yueyun lay in bed recovering, my mother brought her food and took care of her every day. After a several weeks, Yueyun got out of bed and went back to the shipyard. When she wasn't working, she spent all her time writing long letters to the local party leadership trying to prove her and her father's innocence in the hope of getting a reprieve from her sentence. From time to time, she would request a short leave of absence, ostensibly to go and apply for help from higher authorities elsewhere in the province. They never granted it, and she never bullied my mother again.

4

Now I remembered hearing about Yueyun once before, from my mother. It was the year I turned eighteen, around the time I wanted to take university entrance exams. She'd just said that she knew a university student to whom fate had been cruel. She didn't mention Yueyun's name or that she'd shared a room with a madwoman, let alone that they'd both been subjected to struggle sessions. That long-ago Chinese

New Year's Eve when I had insisted on accompanying my mother on her night shift at the shipyard, I hadn't seen anyone else in her dorm room. Perhaps Yueyun had been asleep.

The Cultural Revolution was a terrifying experience for me. At two schools on Middle School Street that had been converted from old temples, Red Guards stuck pointed hats on the teachers' heads and hauled them up onto a makeshift stage for struggle sessions. Each subject's chest was hung with a heavy wooden board bearing his or her name, below which the most awful accusations had been daubed. With my own eyes, I saw them grab one teacher by the hair and smash his head into the ground, not stopping until it was raw meat. Not one person shouted at them to stop, busy as everyone was chanting slogans. Every few days, I would see someone tear past the main gate of our compound and hurl themselves into the Yangtze. The bomb shelters became places to pile up unclaimed corpses. The revolutionary rebel factions drove amphibious landing craft up and down the riverbanks, and tanks appeared on the docks at Chaotianmen. Shells whizzed past as Third Brother, Fifth Brother, and I, all of us just children, climbed up the rocky cliffs beyond the compound to watch the big battle on the river.

Our father came looking for us and nearly got hit by a shell. Covering his head with his hands, he rolled on the ground as a big hole appeared in the brick wall of the building behind him. Everyone said the bodhisattvas must have been looking out for Father, as he was a good—and apparently very lucky—man.

Revolution swept the country. Third Brother joined a Red Guard unit and hopped a train to Beijing. He rushed to the Tiananmen gate tower, where he was in the first group to be received by Chairman Mao. Second Sister joined Chongqing's infamous August 15 Red Guard faction, while Elder Sister came back to the city from a village near the Three Gorges, where she'd gone to "carry out revolution to the end." Mother didn't join any group. One night, Second Sister had a heated discussion with her, telling her that she was not proactive about revolution and that she should "fight selfishness and repudiate revisionism." She fluently recited whole passages of *Quotations from Chairman Mao Zedong*, lecturing her own mother, saying that revolution wasn't about buying people dinner or writing articles. Elder Sister stepped in to argue several points with Second Sister until Mother could stand no more and yelled at them both, "Revolution? What do you two know about revolution? By the time you figure it out, your own mother'll be dead and gone!"

Mother had never been so fierce. She ordered Elder Sister straight back to the Three Gorges village and told Second Sister to go with her.

Elder Sister listened to Ma for the first time in her life and went back the next day. If she hadn't, she probably would have caused such a stink in Chongqing that her own "revolution" might have ended in tragedy. Second Sister, though, took no notice and walked back to Chongqing Normal University the same night. That summer was so hot that even the mosquitoes couldn't stand it, and smashed themselves suicidally at the walls. Second Sister refused to come home for several years, looking down on Mother because she supposedly lacked revolutionary consciousness.

Nobody noticed that Mother had taken to wearing a hat because she didn't want her children to see the wounds on her head from when the mob had shaved her. She didn't even tell Father what had happened. She trimmed her hair as neatly as she could and told him that short hair was quicker to wash. Not even I, the daughter who memorized her every move, noticed. The world outside was filled with the bloody ferocity of revolution. What could a tiny change in my mother's appearance mean in the midst of all that?

That summer, the river swelled to bursting, reaching so high up both banks that the ferries couldn't cross. Mother took the mountain road home every weekend. Much of the route was flooded, adding an extra hour to the trip. By the time she got home, she'd be angry, impossible to please. She wouldn't eat. Every day, Father went to the riverside at the crack of dawn to see if the floodwaters had receded, then slowly made his way home, where he would sit wordlessly, smoking his pipe. In those days, menacing thunderclouds enveloped the inside of our home as surely as they did the world outside. I lived in fear, terrified of doing something wrong.

Cousin Chun and I stood on the stone steps at the junction of Middle School Street, looking down at the crowds of people milling about with their heads held high, as natural and normal as before. But my mother hadn't walked like that. I remembered one time before I started primary school, how I'd sat right here on these stone steps, waiting for my mother to get home for the weekend. I waited for what seemed like an eternity, but she still didn't come. I watched the man at the knife-grinder's stall. His sleeves rolled up, he ground each blade a dozen times or so before holding it in front of his eyes for inspection. I suddenly caught sight of my mother. She hurried along anxiously, seeming distressed and unusually cautious, as if she were navigating a minefield. But when she saw me, she burst into a smile. But now, in my vision of her, a platform appeared and my mother was pushed roughly up onto it for a struggle session.

I shook off my trance, and then lowered my head again sadly.

"Now it's all in the past," Cousin Chun said.

Tears in her eyes, she spoke as much for her own benefit as mine. Everyone lives in the past. People want to forget, but it's easier said than done.

"Let's go back," I replied.

Cousin Chun and I walked slowly back to Compound No. 6. She told me that she had been transferred off my mother's work team after just a few months, and she didn't see as much of my mother after that. Later, she went to Japan.

"I miss those times, and I miss your ma even more. I wish I'd come to see her earlier." She sighed regretfully.

Cousin Chun couldn't remember anything about Uncle Jian, but she told me, "You should ask Wang Guixiang. She held the other end of your ma's carrying pole at the shipyard. I'm sure she'll know."

So it was back to Wang Guixiang. She seemed like the key to unlocking quite a few riddles about Mother, but she hadn't come to pay her respects, and Elder Sister said she hadn't been able to get in touch with her. The trail was cold.

5

Cousin Chun had to head home, and as soon as she was gone, Elder Sister and her husband began to argue. Elder Sister said he should have asked Cousin Chun to give Xiaomi a job at her restaurant. Her husband explained that, unlike Xiaomi, all the waitresses had graduated from culinary school. Most of them were university students.

Elder Sister hit the roof. "What a horrible thing to say! You're choosing your ex-wife's family over my daughter. You already married one sister, and now you want to marry this one too!"

Third Brother rushed over to break up the fight. "This is neither the time nor the place. If you want to fight, go home and do it!"

The pair fell silent.

Just then, Tang returned to a warm welcome from Fourth Sister. She accompanied him upstairs.

"Did you get the paperwork taken care of?" she asked.

"All sorted. It just needed a signature," Tang replied.

The three of us went into my mother's room. Tang paused for a moment before he announced with a grave expression, "I'm an honorable person, and I've done my part. It was convenient for you for put Ma's house in my name to get around the laws. Now that you've got the keys, I hope you'll be true to your word."

The message was more for Fourth Sister than for me, but I reassured him.

"Fourth Sister told me about your agreement," I said. "Don't worry."

"I'll never go to campus again unless you invite me," Fourth Sister added coldly.

"You know," added Tang, "I was thinking the whole way here about how hard things were for your mother all her life."

"Have you seen her?" I asked.

"Yes, she looks very peaceful," Tang replied.

"Would you believe that, before her death, she was rummaging through garbage heaps?"

"Who told you that?" Fourth Sister asked in surprise.

"Do you believe it?"

"That depends who said it."

Tang didn't say anything, but he looked shocked.

I said that it didn't matter who'd told me. The important thing was that, if it was true, why had Mother been so desperate, and why had none of our relatives told either of us? For that matter, why hadn't her sons and daughters done anything about it? If she had really been reduced to this, what possible explanation could there be?

Second Sister and Third Sister-in-Law walked in. They looked as if they had been listening in the hallway for some time.

"I didn't want to say anything, Little Six, but you've got a lot of nerve coming here and complaining about us when you didn't even come back for our father's funeral," Second Sister said.

I was so angry I could hardly speak. "You know I couldn't get a plane ticket! I tried everything. Father brought me up. It would have meant the world to me to be there for him."

"Yes, it was our father who brought you up. As long as you admit that. Ma always made excuses for you."

I asked her as sincerely as I could, "Please tell me what happened with Ma, Second Sister."

"Tell you what, exactly?" Second Sister snapped. "People get old and start acting strange. What were we supposed to do about it? If we told her not to do something, she was only more determined to do it. If we wanted her to do something, she refused. She just went back to being a child!"

"Second Sister, how can you sneer at our mother like that?" I said.

Fourth Sister cut in. "Hang on, you still haven't said who told you all this."

"Spectacles Wang. She said Ma was rummaging through trash like a beggar."

"Look at her, believing someone like that!" Fourth Sister was furious.

"You know Spectacles Wang would do anything to get at us," Second Sister said.

"That's what I assumed at first," I replied. "But then I thought about it some more."

"It's obvious she's just spreading rumors!" Second Sister retorted.

Third Sister-in-Law pulled me away. "Calm down, Little Six. This is Mother's funeral. It's not the time for fighting."

Tang gave me a look to indicate that I should drop it for now. I followed him into the hallway outside. As we stood in front of the railings, he told me he'd taken a look at the condos I'd bought for Ma, and I'd made a good investment. They were located at the crest of the hill on South Bank Road with great views of the Yangtze, not far from the city center and right near lots of shopping and easy access to buses. They'd shot up in price as soon as construction was completed.

I looked at him for a moment.

"I'm not trying to imply anything. It's just such a shame your ma died before she could enjoy this good fortune."

My eyes reddened, and I hurriedly turned my face away.

"I'm not very good with words," Tang said.

Only one month earlier, I had come back from Italy to see Ma and told her that I planned to move her into a brand new place. She had said, "You really are a loyal daughter, Little Six. I didn't take good care of you when you were little, but of all the birds in the nest, you always flew the highest and loved your ma the most. You never forgot your old ma for a second. If I did anything to deserve this good fortune, it wasn't in this lifetime."

What she hadn't said was whether she wanted to move. And when I thought about it now, I realized that our family had always lived here, in Compound No. 6 off Alley Cat Stream. We children had all left at various points, but Father had lived here for forty-nine years, and Mother had lived here for fifty-six. Perhaps Death had chosen this time to take her, just as she was about to leave behind this hurtful place.

The more I thought about it, the sadder I felt.

6

The sun dipped down to the west, leaving an intense gloom behind it. The oil-drum stoves were burning bright, the chef putting on an impressive show as he threw his arms about, flash-frying the double-cooked pork with an enormous spatula. Various family members were helping to set the tables and rounding up extra chairs.

Before long, Potbellied Cat announced that dinner was served, and Third Brother and Third Sister-in-Law steered the assembled relatives and friends to their places. Tang nodded to me from a table by the stairs. I pulled up a chair and squeezed in next to him. Second Cousin, Fourth Sister, and various other people were sitting there as well.

Potbellied Cat and two of his assistants served the food: cold bean-flour noodles with seaweed, spicy beef with star anise and pigs' ears, roast duck with konjac, white chopped chicken, sliced beef with celery . . . eight dishes in total, plus soup. It looked very clean and tasted pretty good.

Fourth Sister said to Tang, "Your stomach isn't strong enough for all this spicy food. Let me get you a bowl of soup."

She got up and walked out through the doorway of the courtyard, returning a moment later with a bowl filled with piping hot bone and radish soup.

"Little Six, I know how you love soup. Why don't you have mine?" Tang suggested, placing the bowl in front of me.

Fourth Sister said she was going to get another bowl of soup for Tang. She seemed very angry with me when I followed her.

"What are you doing?" I said.

"Do you really think I would put poison in his soup?"

"You said it, not me."

"The worst I would do is give that heartless jerk a stomachache," Fourth Sister laughed. "Though that would be letting him off too easily. Eat your soup, Little Six. I honestly didn't put anything in it."

"I hope not," I said.

"Listen, this is my business. You'd do well not to poke your nose into it." At that, she strode off. I felt a weight descend on me as I watched her retreating back.

I forced myself to finish a whole bowl of rice before I started on the bone and radish soup.

"Your ma always said she didn't want her funeral to be a gloomy affair," my uncle said as he looked around. "There are twenty-something tables going out past the courtyard gateway. I think she'd be pleased!"

"Everyone who should have come is here. All the younger generation came, except the granddaughters back in London who couldn't make it," said Second Brother-in-Law, who was usually loath to say anything at all.

Second Cousin made a face, but continued eating without a word. Seeing me glaring at him, he gave me a strained smile.

I stood up and went out through the courtyard gate, followed by Second Cousin's wife. "Little Six, is that all you're going to eat? You're so thin—you need to eat more!"

Telling you to fatten up was village people's way of showing they cared.

"You're not exactly plump yourself," I replied.

"I'm one of those people who can't put on weight no matter how much I eat. It just proves I'm not blessed."

I wandered over to where the chef was cooking. He stood on a seven- or eight-foot patch of dirt outside the courtyard. Piles of washed vegetables lay around the stove, along with a wicker basket of tinder and coal bricks.

Second Cousin's wife continued, "Maybe you know that Elder Sister wanted to borrow money from us, but we don't have any. I know my husband's a minor government official and she thinks he can help, but to be honest with you, he doesn't know how to do anything. Even when it came to moving the ancestral grave for your ma, he just stuck to the rules and refused to help. I pushed him about it, but he just lost his temper with me. He said that if you opened the floodgates to that sort of thing, it never stopped. I asked him whether he cared at all and reminded him that it was his grandparents' graves, but he just said he was an atheist."

I wasn't sure exactly what Second Cousin did for work. Something to do with immigrant settlement allowances, Xiaomi had said. This was the first time I'd met his wife, but the way she spoke made me feel close to her. Second Cousin had read all my books, and I was curious what he thought of the novel criticizing the Three Gorges Dam project.

She said he was incredibly busy most of the time, but they had taken two days off to come to the funeral. She said he was grateful to my mother, because she had been very good to him when he was stationed in Chongqing on his military service, and he felt guilty for not letting them move the graves.

I had always been concerned about the Three Gorges Dam, and about my mother's home area of Zhongxian County in particular.

"How are things back home now?" I asked.

Second Cousin's wife told me that there were major problems with fresh drinking water for people, never mind water for livestock and irrigation. Most of the places villagers had been relocated to were on drought-stricken mountainsides. The rising water had destroyed bridges and roads, so the new villages were barely accessible to vehicles, which obviously had a serious effect on production and on life in general. Yangdu Village used to subsist by growing tangerines and sweet oranges, with each household producing a thousand pounds a year. All that ended after the move. In other places, whenever the villagers went to sell their vegetables or the children went to school, they had to take a tortuous route around the mountains. If someone was seriously ill or having a baby, it was even more problematic. When the villagers complained, Second Cousin had personally joined the team sent to investigate. They offered apologies but were unable to improve the situation.

Just then, I noticed Second Cousin walking out of the courtyard doorway and talking on a cell phone. He frowned as he listened, before ending the call with a couple of words and putting the phone away. He walked over to us. "I'm sorry, Little Six. It looks as if I'll have to rush back to sort out some problems."

"Do you want me to go with you?" his wife asked.

"There's no need," Second Cousin replied.

He asked me to apologize to Uncle, Third Brother, and Elder Sister for him, and his wife and I escorted him to the edge of Compound No. 8, where he took a taxi and quickly disappeared up Binjiang Road.

"I hope it's nothing serious," I said worriedly.

His wife said that it was common for him to be called away like this. Some more junior officials were taking liberties, and even the village cadres weren't above extorting money from ordinary people. Some didn't even care if people's lives were on the line.

"I'm really sorry we can't help Elder Sister. Even if your second cousin tried to do something about it, he couldn't. He's not corrupt, but there are some people he just wouldn't want to tangle with. To be honest with you, Little Six, I'm really scared."

I didn't know what to say. Just at that moment, I heard a commotion coming from the direction of Compound No. 6, so I grabbed Second Cousin's wife and hurried back to see what was wrong.

7

Two beggars had appeared at the doorway to the courtyard. One was twelve or thirteen, the other maybe fifteen or sixteen. They had the same round faces, looking like brothers. Both were filthy from head to toe and gave off a foul stench. They weren't after food, but instead kept calling out, "Come on, give us some money! Give us some wine!" The neighbors gathered to watch the spectacle.

"Somebody must have told them to come," Xiaomi muttered behind me.

Elder Sister's husband bolted across the courtyard. He was irritable at the best of times and was even more unforgiving at a time like this.

"What kind of beggar asks for wine?" he shouted, shooing them away.

But clearly the beggars weren't going anywhere until they got something. The older one took hold of Elder Sister's husband's hand with a creepy smile on his face. He angrily pushed the boy, at which the younger brother leapt toward him.

Elder Sister pulled the younger beggar off her husband, while some relatives helped the older beggar stand back up.

Younger Uncle stuffed twenty yuan into the older boy's hand and yelled, "Get out of here!"

The two beggars beat a hasty retreat.

Elder Sister shrieked, "What did you give them money for? We shouldn't be taken advantage of by people like that."

"Young woman, just look at it as a good deed. Averting misfortune and bringing good luck. Let's just leave it at that."

Potbellied Cat raised his hand and called out at the top of his voice, "It's six forty now. At seven o'clock sharp, the mourning ceremony will begin. Ladies and gentlemen, friends and family members, I beg your indulgence one more time. We need to clear the tables, so please step aside!"

8

The sky darkened and the last of the lamps were lit. A group of men and women assembled in the center of the courtyard, carrying speakers and musical instruments. Fifth Brother rushed to help them plug in their equipment.

When seven o'clock came, the speakers gave off a terrible humming and cracking sound. Potbellied Cat said the amplifier wasn't connected properly, and the band was trying to find out why. Apparently, it wouldn't be possible to start the mourning service at seven sharp after all. I made my way upstairs, and found everyone crawling on the floor, searching for something in the gaps between the bed and the chairs. Xiaomi's brow was slick with sweat, her face flushed.

"What's going on?" I asked.

Elder Sister sat up to respond. "This unlucky creature lost her gold wedding ring."

I couldn't help but laugh. Elder Sister had always insisted that Xiaomi was a wife and not a mistress.

"Have a little compassion, would you?"

"Elder Sister, she was never in a legal relationship with that man from Hong Kong."

"He'll come back to Xiaomi someday. They have a son."

"If he comes back, then they can get married for real. Get another ring and start again."

Only when Elder Sister wiped her face with her hands did I realize that tears were streaming down her cheeks because of what I had said. "It says in the Bible, 'Man that is born of a woman is of few days, and full of trouble. He cometh forth like a flower, and is cut down: he fleeth also as a shadow, and continueth not.' Little Six, we women are fated to suffer!"

In that instant, my impression of Elder Sister was transformed. She had said before that she believed in God and went to church, but I never bought it. Now it seemed as if she really did believe. Not only did she believe, but she could quote from the Bible and even use it to gain a greater understanding of life. For the first time ever, I felt for Elder Sister and thought that the distance between us had closed a bit.

Xiaomi was still searching everywhere for the ring—under the sofa, in the cracks in the chairs, under the fridge. They moved the furniture to expose every dark corner it could possibly have fallen into.

"It's a bad sign, losing the ring. Maybe it means that man will never want Xiaomi and her son." Elder Sister's tears began to fall again as she spoke.

I handed her a tissue and told her about Second Cousin having to go attend to business for the county.

One year when I came back to see my mother, she'd told me that the gold necklace I'd given her had been stolen. She was taking a rickshaw back from a visit to Elder Sister, clutching the sausages her daughter had given her. There were normally a few people on the little road by Marble Rock and No. 5 Plastics Factory, but that evening, there was not a soul in sight. My mother got off the rickshaw and began to climb the stone steps. A fellow with a carrying pole and rope in his hands suddenly approached. He said, "Would you like some help, Madam? You must be carrying something good there. It looks very heavy."

"Thank you. There's no need," Mother replied.

When the man drew closer, she held on tight to the sausages, but to her horror, he pulled out a knife and grabbed roughly at the gold chain around her neck.

Mother cried, “Wait! Let me take the necklace off and give it to you.”

Only once the man was gone did Mother realize her hands were shaking. She said to me, “It was the necklace you gave me. I’m so sorry I ran into that horrible mugger.”

Seeing how upset my mother was, I took off my wedding ring and gave it to her. It was a gold band set with an amethyst. It was pretty nice, but I wasn’t crazy about it, and besides, it was a little small for my finger. My mother’s fingers were thicker than mine, so she could only wear it on her pinkie, but it still suited her better than it did me.

I called my husband and told him what had happened. He said that it was fine, and that he would get me another one. He never did, though. Now I can see that it must have been because he was angry, rather than because he forgot. How could I have given my wedding ring away? Losing a wedding ring means throwing away the marriage, and I gave mine away without a thought. Could I blame him for being upset?

CHAPTER 9

I

The funeral band consisted of four men and one woman. The four men, in traditional-style black funeral outfits, played instruments, including keyboards and drums, and the woman sang and doubled as host. In her midthirties, she wore heavy makeup, a white top, and white trousers, with long hair flowing over her shoulders. The freckles on her face gave her a flirtatious charm. At her signal, the band began to perform "Bidding Farewell to the Soul."

Potbellied Cat joined the performance. He took a suona and began to blow hard. He was instantly transformed into a different person. His eyes lit up, and he became one with his instrument, full of energy and life. The high-pitched sound of the suona was gripping and sorrowful. Everyone was pulled into the mourning mood. When the suona brought the opening tune to its climax, the whole band threw down their instruments in unison and kowtowed to Mother's tablet. They cried and they howled, making a clamorous and chaotic scene. Potbellied Cat then seamlessly switched from the wailing tune to the calmer and more melancholic "Remembering the Soul." His notes—now high, now low, now suppressed, now piercing through the air—were precise and flawless.

Human emotion is like a contagious disease. The lead singer tearfully asked the children of the deceased to form two rows in front of our mother's coffin. The sons and the daughters were placed in the first row, and their spouses stood right behind them in the second. The grandchildren, all wearing white ribbons with red polka dots, were farther back. My mother's brother and Tang were also standing with the rest of the family.

The singer announced, "All rise! Observe three minutes of silence!"

Accompanied by softer music, she began to recount my mother's life in heavily accented Mandarin. She used a version Elder Sister had given her. Mother was born in 1923 at Guankouzhai Village of Zhongxian County, she intoned. She ran away from an arranged marriage at seventeen to become a textile worker at No. 601 Textiles Factory in Chongqing. She was forced to leave her job and made a living doing laundry for sailors by the bank of the river. She met my father, and gave birth to six children. She was survived by them and her nine grandchildren. She died aged eighty-three.

This version of my mother's biography omits Elder Sister's biological father, the mob boss, and of course, my biological father. Elder Sister got most of her info from my memoir, but it turned out I had the age wrong. Mother had taken three years off in order to get work in the textile factory. When every household was required to register after the Liberation, she reported her real age, but then made herself two years younger to get temporary employment at the dock. She went back and forth several times, and in the end, she lost track of her real age. Sometimes she would say that she was born in 1927 and was ten years younger than my father. Other times, she was pretty certain that she was born in 1925. None of us knew exactly how old Mother was.

The only thing we could agree on was my mother's birthday, March 31. Eventually, I remembered that Mother had said she was born in the Year of the Pig. From this, we could work out that her birth year had been 1923.

"From ancient times until today, in the human world, be you an emperor, a king, a general, or a prime minister, no one can escape death. Alas, eastward flows the great river. Its waves have swept away a thousand years of gallant men! Our dear mother! Your virtuous name will leave fragrance for thousands of years to come, and you will be forever remembered in history! Mother's love is deeper than the ocean, and we children are like fish swimming in it. Our great mother was a pure and kind person, a person full of sympathies and high morals, a person respected and loved by people old and young, a person forever in our hearts. We are here to wish our mother a happy life in heaven with our father. There, she will wear silk, eat heavenly delicacies, sleep on Simmons mattresses, watch flat-screen TVs, play mah-jongg all day, and use toilets and bathtubs made of gold. When you are in heaven, don't forget to watch the 2008 Beijing Olympics with us, Mother, to cheer for the Chinese! Our dear mother, your children mournfully yell out your name for one last time. Dear Mother! Please, rest in peace!"

The singer's eulogy was so clichéd that it could have been used at anyone's funeral. The speech couldn't have been more melodramatic or more hyperbolic, but, accompanied by the music, it was fittingly tear-jerking. The air of sadness in the courtyard reached its climax. Elder Sister was first to howl, and everyone else followed. The sound of crying could be heard in every corner. Some pulled out their handkerchiefs, some blew their noses, while others quietly dabbed at their tears. Tang, standing across from me, also had damp eyes.

The hostess cleared her throat and announced that it was time for the sons and daughters to give speeches.

While we were still debating who should be the speaker, Elder Sister grabbed the microphone and went ahead to represent all of us. She said that Mother was the best mother in the world. She used to fight with Mother when she was young, but when she was sent down to the poor Jiapigou Village in the Three Gorges area, she'd realized that Mother was always right. Mother objected to her first marriage on the grounds that first cousins should not marry. Mother always had foresight and knew what was right for her.

"Please forgive this ungrateful daughter!" she pleaded, kneeling down in front of the coffin and kowtowing three times.

As soon as Elder Sister was finished, Potbellied Cat began to blow hard into his suona again.

The singer pulled out a pocket mirror to check her makeup and hairdo. She then adjusted the white band around her forehead and walked slowly toward my mother's coffin. "Mother, you shouldn't have died!" she wailed, leaning against the coffin, as if she were my mother's own daughter. Every cry was echoed in the heart of the mourners. "Mother, our dear mother. No matter how loud I call out, Mother can no longer respond. No matter how much I cry, Mother will never wake up again. Raining tears and crying out blood, we are here to remember our mother. Mother, you suffered poverty in your childhood and had to run away from the arranged marriage to this big city. Your life was full of unexpected storms, but you were blessed with your marriage to Father. Your six children were showered by your love, as you went to work as a laborer to support the whole family. How hard you have worked! How much love you have given! Mother, our dear mother. No matter how loud I call out, Mother can no longer respond. No matter how much I cry, Mother will never wake up again. We wear black scarves and white flowers in remembrance of you. You have gone to paradise, leaving us in pain!" She cried so hard that her body began to shake with spasms. She couldn't catch her breath and looked as though she was about to faint.

Third Brother and his wife helped her up. With their two-hundred-yuan tip in her hand, she reluctantly moved away from my mother's coffin.

Tang remarked to me, "Her crying was sincere."

"Yes. Sometimes when people shed tears, you can tell instantly whether they're fake or not."

Potbellied Cat heard me and thought it was a good chance to show his professional pride. "My writer sister, don't be surprised. She's a real professional. She was sincerely sad, though she won't really faint from the sorrow. Folks in my line of work must understand psychology. If they make too much of a scene, the neighbors will complain about the noise. If they're not loud enough, then the families of the deceased won't be satisfied."

By then, the singer had quickly changed into a red dress, and she began to guide the funeral into the party stage. She happily passed around song lists. Elder Sister took the list and ordered a song for my mother with the title "Mother's Love." The band began to sing the song in a very high pitch.

Elder Sister took the lead, and then the relatives all began to request songs for the deceased. The price was twenty yuan per song, and the band could play any popular tune you could think of. The singer just changed the lyrics on the fly to fit the occasion. Everybody was cheering.

Tang turned to Potbellied Cat, "How marvelous! The band turns the mourning ceremony into a party just like that."

Potbellied Cat nodded his agreement. "The singing always draws a crowd. Normally, relatives and the neighbors don't talk much, but the occasion promotes communication and connection."

"How long have you been playing the suona?"

Potbellied Cat said that musical skills were passed down in his family. His father had taught him how to play, and he had practiced and practiced until he could excite and move his audience in an actual performance. Playing the suona was not a humble trade in ancient times. Confucius was considered the founding father of this profession. All suona players had to display Confucius's tablet in their homes, treating him as one of their ancestors. Potbellied Cat said that his father had died young and that he had no other choice but to join a funeral band to support his mother.

2

Our neighbor "One-Eyed" Auntie Ma ordered five songs for my mother. Normally, several neighbors would chip in and order one song together. And they usually would debate about what song to pick for a long time. People in this neighborhood were all poor. They would rarely pull out a hundred-yuan bill unless they were at the mah-jongg table—and that's only because money spent on mah-jongg had a potential for returns. As for other expenses, every penny must be pinched. But Auntie Ma didn't care about the money. She seemed to be using this occasion to express a special feeling toward my mother. She'd been stopping at our neighbors' houses, pressing them to buy wreaths for my mother. She had also brought over her tables and chairs as if she were part of the immediate family. With her home and shop located at the narrow entrance to the neighborhood, she knew everything that went on here. It suddenly occurred to me that she would be the ideal person to tell me about what my mother had been doing before her death.

I walked up to Auntie Ma and asked her if I could buy some candles from her. She said there was one box left in her store, and she'd go get it for me. I insisted on going with her.

It took only two minutes for us to get to the store, which was being staffed by her youngest daughter. There was a pay phone right outside, and Auntie Ma's daughter was busy eavesdropping on people's conversations. I couldn't resist looking around. On the counter, there were several glass jars of candy and peanuts. Against the wall on the right were some wine bottles and cigarettes, as well as noodles, seaweed, and spices. The dim light made it hard to make out much more.

Auntie Ma said apologetically, "Little Six, you've been around the world. You wouldn't object if I give you a tour of my little doghouse, would you?"

I told her that my mother used to say, "Even golden and silver kennels cannot rival a little doghouse of one's own." It was nice of her to want to show me her place, even if it wasn't much to look at.

Auntie Ma turned on a fluorescent light and I noticed that a part of the floor close to the stairs appeared to have been newly patched up. Downstairs, behind the storefront, was a dining area and kitchen, which was marginally clean. There was a big round dining table with wooden benches, an armoire used as a cupboard, and a big vat of water. Upstairs were three bedrooms, one of which was equipped with a color TV. Judging from the piles of DVDs scattered all over and the dirty laundry on the floor, it must have been her daughter's room. When we went back down the stairs, Auntie Ma explained that the house had originally been only one shabby floor with two rooms. The wall was so thin you could see through to the street. But they liked that the house backed up to a small creek and so was a little apart from all the other houses.

"Little Six, make yourself at home."

I sat down by the dining table and asked her, "Auntie Ma, did my mother talk to you much?"

"Of course she did. She always liked to chat. She'd come here all the time. Sometimes she would take home some salt or soy sauce." Auntie Ma's tone turned cautious. "But that was some time ago. She stopped coming here long before she passed away."

I asked why.

"Your mother didn't say anything, but I figured it out for myself." She looked at me meaningfully.

Her tone made it obvious that a member of my family had stopped my mother coming to the store. Auntie Ma took a can of Coca-Cola from her refrigerator in the kitchen and handed it to me. I took it and thanked her. She said, "Little Six, your mother once told me, 'Our children are a kind of ransom. Paying that ransom is the sole purpose of our lives.'"

"Did she really say that?" I was stunned. The words had profound ramifications and could be interpreted in many ways.

"Your mother was the smartest person I have ever met. She had gone places and knew a lot of things." Auntie Ma sighed.

When she had moved into Compound No. 6 in 1963, it didn't take her long to realize that my mother was not welcome in our neighborhood because she was considered to be a "bad" woman—and a lot of that was just jealousy. She was both pretty and intelligent. Some of the neighbors shunned her because they were afraid of the residents' committee. In those years, people were scared to be associated with the widow of an executed mob boss, a woman daring enough to have extramarital affairs and give birth to an illegitimate child. In the eyes of our neighbors, my mother was rotten to the core. Auntie Ma, however, saw her differently.

"Although I couldn't be seen befriending her publicly, I would always secretly solicit your mother's advice about everything," she said, adding gratefully, "It was your mother who suggested that my son buy this house, including the shop. The price was ridiculously low back then, and the location is ideal. I really have to thank her. She was always one step ahead of everyone else. She kept saying that setting up a shop here would be good business."

I was even more surprised than Auntie Ma was.

Auntie Ma said that, even though she was fifteen years younger, her memory was not nearly as good as Ma's. They liked to commiserate about the common problems of aging—deteriorating eyesight, hearing loss, forgetfulness, incoherent utterances, and frequent health issues.

I nodded my agreement. If it was any consolation, I told her, everyone had to go through these indignities, without exception. Then I pleaded with her, "Auntie Ma, you know that I live far away. I have no idea how my mother got by during her final days. You must know . . . is it true that she rummaged through garbage?"

Auntie Ma stared straight at me, all color draining from her face. "I don't know anything about that! Who told you such a thing?"

I told her that it came from Spectacles Wang.

"Has that witch ever said anything good about anyone?"

"That's why I needed to ask you." I sighed heavily. "Please tell me the truth!"

"The truth? You pass through here like a puff of wind, but I have to live in this place till I die."

"I need to know what really happened. I promise I won't bring you any trouble." I held her hands. "Please, for the sake of my late mother . . ."

"OK, Little Six. But please don't be upset. Yes, she did rummage through garbage heaps."

My tears gushed out.

"Do you know anything else about it? Please."

"I didn't see it myself. Someone told me."

It was clear the old woman already regretted telling me. She made me promise not to betray her. If her son caught wind of this, he would never forgive her. "Forget about it, please. Now that your mother is gone, nothing we say can bring her back."

Auntie Ma opened a cupboard, took out a box of candles, and handed it to me. Refusing to take my money, she urged me to go back to the funeral. She was going to watch the shop and let her daughter get some sleep before school the next day. Understanding that it was time for me to leave, I thanked her, got up, and began to walk toward No. 6.

3

I had walked these steps countless times since I was little. My footprints, if they could have been piled up, would have been as thick as a horse's hoof. None of my previous climbs up the hill, however, was as hard as this. It felt like stepping on burning irons. *My mother must have taken a different route on her way to the garbage dumps,* I thought. There were stone steps going straight down to the riverbank. Along the bank, there was also a trail leading to the recycling centers at Slingshot Boulder and Alley Cat Stream. I could picture my mother selling those broken glass bottles, old newspapers, empty cigarette boxes, and plastic bags, and how she carefully put away the several small bills given to her before she went home. Her hands and face covered with dirt, she must've needed to wash up. Maybe she cleaned herself at the river before she went home.

Then I went into denial. No, I could never accept that my mother had become a beggar living off the garbage dumps.

What if Auntie Ma had been wrong? She had acknowledged that she'd only heard about it secondhand. She could have fallen for a story invented by my mother's enemies. I told myself I had to step back from this. Without hard evidence, what could I really believe?

What if I asked Fifth Sister-in-Law? She'd definitely know. She was born in the same year as me. Both her parents were farmers in the village next to the shipyard where my mother had worked. She returned to her village after graduating from high school, but couldn't find a job. Then she married Fifth Brother and started to live in our house, raising their son. But she soon had a change of heart. Disliking Fifth Brother's cleft palate, she ran away from home. Fifth Brother looked for her everywhere. He even took out ads in newspapers, but she had disappeared without a trace. One day, the police called and asked Fifth Brother whether he had a wife who'd gone missing. Fifth Brother said yes. The police told him that she'd been kidnapped and sold off to be the wife of someone in Henan Province. She had managed to escape and go to the police for protection.

Fifth Brother asked my mother what to do.

She said, "Poor girl! Let's bring her home."

Before she arrived, my mother gathered everyone to talk about Fifth Sister-in-Law. Ma asked that no one look down on her.

Second Sister said defiantly, "How can this piece of meat treat our home like a shop, coming and going as she pleases?"

Elder Sister jumped in, "Once a beggar, always a beggar. She probably tried to run off with a handsome man, and then he turned out to be a crook and sold her off. Henan was poor before the Liberation, and now it's even poorer. They say that brothers have to share one wife. She must have been a sex slave to the brothers and a servant to the entire family. When she made mistakes, she would have been beaten. Now she wants to come back. No way! She has lost her chastity and ruined Fifth Brother's reputation. She knew that Fifth Brother would be nice to her no matter what, but what about us sisters? Do we look like people to be messed with?"

Third Brother also objected to my mother's compassion. He said we shouldn't shield that kind of woman. His wife chimed in, "She tried to leave her husband for greener pastures, and now she wants to come back to the old yard. We need to be practical and find Fifth Brother a new wife. Let him start over."

Fourth Sister also joined in. "That's right. Find a new wife for Fifth Brother. She doesn't have to be pretty, like this one, as long as she treats Fifth Brother right. What use are good looks? Sooner or later, those good-looking ones will want to run away."

Mother responded, "What you say makes sense. But Fifth Brother and Fifth Sister-in-Law have a son who has the right to be with his mother. Can't you all be a little more tolerant? She wants to fix her mistake. What woman can guarantee that she won't ever make a mistake in her life?"

Father suddenly broke his silence to declare, "All of you, listen to your ma. This is settled."

Mother continued, "When she comes back, none of you are to mention Henan. Let her have what remains of her self-esteem. You all must treat her nicely!"

When Fifth Sister-in-Law came back, the family treated her as if nothing had happened. She was so moved that she was on her best behavior with her husband, her son, and in her filial duties. Unlike before, she no longer complained or talked behind people's backs. Whichever way you looked at it, my mother had done the right thing.

I never had any doubt that my mother would forgive Fifth Sister-in-Law. She had always treated people with kindness, and she never thought that losing chastity to bad men was the big deal that people made it out to be.

As for Fifth Sister-in-Law herself, I never really got to know her. She was pretty and unusually smart for a country girl, but beyond that, the only particular association I had was the Henan incident. That year, many Chongqing women had been trafficked to Henan. It was all over the news. Many never came back. I hoped they'd been lucky: married into good families, borne children, settled down. Fifth Sister-in-Law had not been that lucky.

Occasionally, when I went back to Chongqing, Elder Sister would gossip about Fifth Sister-in-Law, saying she didn't love Fifth Brother, and that she went out all dressed up in the hopes of meeting someone better. I knew how untrustworthy Elder Sister was, but in this case, I didn't know what to believe. I had no idea what kind of person Fifth Sister-in-Law was, although I was usually an excellent judge of character.

Now I realized I didn't know how to talk to Fifth Sister-in-Law about my mother's secret life as a beggar. Fifth Brother was never an assertive person, and he'd always let her have the upper hand in the relationship. I didn't want my questions to cause any trouble for him.

4

The band was still playing, and now the speakers had been turned way up. The keyboard player had stepped in as the lead singer. With his right hand holding the microphone and his left hand high in the air, he didn't seem tired at all.

"How much longer are they going to play?" I asked Third Sister-in-Law.

She said big cities like Beijing or Shanghai didn't allow music performances at funerals, but in Chongqing, they could go till midnight. After that, if someone called the police, there would be fines.

I peeked at my watch. It was just past nine.

Fourth Sister had found an erhu, a two-stringed fiddle, and plopped herself in front of the band. With a quick tuning and a clearing of her throat, she began to sing the ancient folk song from the south, "Midnight Song." *"Who could yearn without singing? Who could be hungry and yet not want to eat? If the heavens do not kill all wishes, please let me see my lover!"*

Her song was so moving that everybody, whatever their background, was joining in—even the ghosts.

How could Fourth Sister know this song? Maybe Father had taught her? He was from the south, but I'd never once heard him sing it. Before Fourth Sister moved to England, my father's niece once came over all the way from his hometown in Zhejiang to visit. Maybe she'd taught her?

Wherever she learned it, it sounded exceptional, especially since Fourth Sister sang in the Sichuan dialect. She went on singing, *"I will be the North Star, remaining unmoved for thousands of years. I will allow my heart to travel joyfully like the sun, from east to west."*

Fourth Sister had learned how to play the erhu when she was sent down to the countryside during the Cultural Revolution. She told me she'd been asked to give concerts, but I'd never seen her perform before. During all those years we spent in London, I'd never known just how good she was with the instrument. She moved the bow back and forth and sang one song after another. She was singing to her lover, trying to win his affection back. She was singing to our mother in the coffin, hoping Ma could understand how much she yearned for love.

Tang listened intently. His eyes lit up and stared at Fourth Sister, giving her the encouragement she needed. She sang tunes from one ancient dynasty after another, all about love's ups and downs, twists and turns, separations and reunions. Times changed, but the love in her songs never altered. She sang as if she'd waited her whole life for this moment. She poured her soul into her songs. *"Who would ascend the high tower with me now? I forever remember how we looked afar on one clear autumn day. The past is now all empty, and everything is only a dream."*

Someone tapped my elbow. It was Third Brother, who signaled for me to look up. Up on the balcony, Fifth Sister-in-Law gestured that I had a telephone call. I ran upstairs to answer.

"Sixth Auntie, it's me, Tiantian. I hear the mourning ceremony's going really well."

"Can you hear your ma singing? She's amazing!"

"She's a fool who'd do anything in the name of love," Tiantian said offhandedly, then apologized, saying that expensive airfare and classes had prevented her from coming back for Grandma's funeral.

She was calling to say that she was worried about her mother and to ask me to keep an eye on her. Before Tang left London, he gave Tiantian a thousand pounds as a reward for getting into London Business School. It was his way of telling Tiantian not to intervene in his relationship with her mother. Fourth Sister had been very upset with Tiantian for accepting it. Tiantian said that she was stuck in the middle and couldn't please anyone, but she couldn't bear the sight of her mother pining away. The day before the mourning ceremony, Fourth Sister had asked Tiantian to check her e-mail for her. In her inbox, Tiantian saw an e-mail from her mother's friend saying that Tang was getting remarried.

Tiantian decided to hide this news from her mother and deleted the e-mail. Now she was wondering whether she had done the right thing. She asked me not to tell her mother about our telephone conversation. I told Tiantian not to blame herself, since what she did was for her mother's sake.

So Tang was getting married yet again. Fourth Sister knew all along that this would happen. She'd warned Tang that if he didn't take care of her, he and that other woman wouldn't have one day of peace. She would turn his world upside down.

Tang once called me to complain about Fourth Sister after a fight. He said that she'd really underestimated him and that he wouldn't be intimidated. The more she tried to ruin his life, the more determined he was to leave her. He would do exactly the opposite of what she wanted.

I said to him, "Give me a break. You're not a teenager defying his mother."

He responded by recounting his sufferings. He was labeled a reactionary before the Cultural Revolution and was sent down to a farm. Then, during the Cultural Revolution, he was exiled to a remote mine near Lanzhou, where the head of the mine openly tortured him. After the fall of the Gang of Four, the college entrance examination was reinstated, and he wanted to apply to graduate school, but his boss wouldn't grant him any time off to do it. He decided to risk everything and snuck off by himself to take the exams. He placed first in his subject, but when the university in Beijing sent someone to the mine to investigate his political background, the boss said the worst possible things about him: that he had wrong thoughts about politics and revolution, that he hated society, that he was antisocial, that he looked down upon common laborers, and that he had never attended the movies screened by the mining company for its employees. But his boss's thorough trashing of him backfired. The investigator refused to believe that one person could be so very terrible and insisted that he be granted release from the mine.

It was experiences like these that shaped Tang. Because of the hardships he had suffered in the past, he would never back away from a challenge now, including the pressure put on him by Fourth Sister, who was painting herself as one of those abandoned, mistreated wives. If the Communist Party couldn't reform him, how could an ignorant shrew like Fourth Sister force him into submission? What a joke!

Tang had a selective memory. He chose not to remember how Fourth Sister's contractor ex-husband had refused to break up with his mistress, the country girl who worked for him. As soon as Fourth Sister agreed to the divorce, he had married the girl and never looked back. Fourth Sister was putting everything on the line, making a desperate, last attempt to get Tang back. It was a matter of life and death for her.

There was a period during which Fourth Sister could only get one hour of sleep each night. As a result, her eyes became completely bloodshot. One day she couldn't even open them. She called me in Rome, where I was accepting an Italian award for literature. I had been planning to use the opportunity to spend an entire summer traveling in Italy, but had to fly right back to London to take care of her.

The neighborhood doctor referred her to a special hospital, and since it was in a remote location, I had to borrow my husband's car and overcome my fear of driving to get her there. I only had a Chinese driver's license, so I was terrified of being pulled over and extremely careful not to speed. Sitting in the passenger seat with her eyes closed, tears streaming down her cheeks, she told me that Tang hadn't offered a single word of consolation when she told him about her eyes.

I handed her my handkerchief and kept on driving, white-knuckled. When we finally reached the hospital, the doctor's diagnosis was simply that she had overused her eyes.

Fourth Sister admitted she had been crying a lot. Could too many tears be the problem?

The doctor said, "Relax, get a smile back on your face. There's nothing a person can't overcome."

Fourth Sister agreed, "Yes, there is nothing I can't overcome." And more tears gushed out while she was speaking.

The doctor said, "Listen, you must take care of your eyes. Let me prescribe some eye drops for you. Apply them three times a day."

I held Fourth Sister's hand and led her to the parking lot. She was in so much discomfort that she wanted me to apply the medication to her eyes right away. Her pain subsided a little after we got in the car.

I started the car and then realized that the tank was nearly empty. It took me about ten minutes to find a gas station. I slowly let the car glide into the station, then spotted a car parked in front of me. Instead of braking, I mistakenly stepped on the accelerator. Although I realized my mistake right away, my car still rear-ended the other vehicle. My front bumper was damaged, and the license plate was dangling.

The other driver jumped out of the car and demanded my insurance information. Panicked, I told her I'd left my insurance card at home, but she could have my phone number. I tried to explain, "Take a look at my sister's eyes. You can see she desperately needed medical attention. I had to drive her to the hospital in a hurry, and I wasn't paying attention. Please accept my apologies."

"Apologies? You hit my car! You have to pay for the damage!" she yelled, pointing to dents and scratches, including what looked like suspiciously old ones.

I asked for her phone number and, with my hands still shaking, pumped and paid for the gas. I went back to the car and started driving again. Both of us were depressed. For the first time, Fourth Sister didn't talk about Tang. We passed the supermarket, but I didn't dare to stop, fearing another accident. Finally, we arrived home. I helped Fourth Sister to bed before dialing the woman's number. To my shock, she quoted me an unreasonably high price for the damage.

That infuriated me, and I told her to talk to my insurance company.

A few days later, my husband got back to London. He was upset when he saw the car and scolded Fourth Sister and me for being stupid. He called the insurance company and was told that it was OK for an uninsured driver to drive the car to the gas station or in certain other circumstances. They'd cover the damage. The other driver was contacted and had her car inspected. They only gave her five hundred pounds, not the astronomical amount she'd demanded.

Then my husband took our car to a garage, where the repair estimate was a thousand pounds. Instead of fixing it, he decided to get rid of the car, since we were leaving London anyway. The tow-truck driver who came over was drooling all over the vehicle. It was a Rover, with a 1.6-liter, four-cylinder engine, a walnut dashboard, immaculate leather seats, air conditioning, and a chrome strip gracing the exterior. It had a classic look and modern luxury. If we'd had it fixed, we could have easily sold it for three or four thousand.

My husband had always been stingy with money. Normally, he'd never have gotten rid of the car, but he was angry and wanted to show that he was determined to throw away everything connected with me. Not long after that, we broke up for good.

Around that time, my mother came down with an illness. She was hospitalized and put on an IV. But Fourth Sister and I were so distracted we didn't even call, exhausted by our unhappy marriages and very depressed. Fourth Sister tried to commit suicide, and I wanted to kill myself too. She tried everything: taking pills, jumping in front of cars, drowning herself in the bath, sticking her fingers into an outlet, and using a kitchen knife to scar her face before slitting her own throat. Once, when I was out grocery shopping, she carved several bloody lines on her thighs. She was about to slice her artery when I came home in the nick of time. I used up all the remaining Yunnan Baiyao, a traditional Chinese medicine, before I was able to stop the bleeding. I couldn't let her die in front of me. If I died too, who was going to bury Fourth Sister? Her daughter Tiantian? She probably wouldn't even come to claim the corpse. Fourth Sister held my hands and sobbed. I didn't understand until then that you can't expect anything back from the children you've raised. As soon as they grow up, they become total strangers the second you don't do what they want. Yes, in that remote country, my sister didn't even have someone to see her off if she died.

What was I doing the entire summer of 2005?

Let me think about it. Let me think hard.

If I asked Fourth Sister, she would say that May of that year was when her tragedy began to unfold.

My tragedy began long before that. As the saying goes, that summer was just the frost on the snow. On Mother's Day in early May, a reporter contacted me to set up an interview. I made up an excuse, saying that I had to go to Chongqing for my mother's birthday. But I hadn't gone back to Chongqing, nor had I sent a present. I hadn't even called to sing "Happy Birthday." My mother must have been waiting for my call, which I had never failed to make before. But that year, the war between my husband and me was reaching its climax. I was scorched by the pain in my heart. I was a completely different person, cold and apathetic, entrepreneurial and materialistic. Instead of calling on my mother's birthday, I flew to Shanghai to sign the contract with a film and television production company on the adaptation of one of my novels into a TV series. The company wanted to set up a personal media studio for me. I thought that contract was more important than my mother's birthday.

In May, several universities in the south of China invited me and my husband to give lectures, and he insisted I go. The media wanted to do stories about our relationship. In particular, a celebrity gossip columnist had obtained a couple of sketchy details from me and blew them out of proportion, into a rosy picture of our marriage. Other reporters were too lazy to do their own investigations, so they simply repeated that version and embellished it further. And when audiences inevitably asked, I told them how in love with my husband I was. I must have been really sick, mentally sick, to slap my own face like that. I was really the most worthless thing in the world. Why didn't I tell the truth?

After traveling through the south, I went to Seoul to promote several of my books that had been recently translated into Korean. My husband went to Chongqing by himself and, of course, didn't bother visiting my mother. After I returned to Beijing, he avoided me as much as he could, but still asked me to buy a cell phone for him. It's really pathetic for a grown man to ask a woman to buy him a phone, but I got him one nonetheless. I even spent time teaching him how to use it.

After May, it was June. What happened that month? And what about July?

Moving ahead to New Year's 2006, I was in either London or Munich. But where did I go after that? What had I been doing in all the time up until October 25, 2006, which was yesterday, the day my mother closed her eyes forever? It was terrifying. The period of time had become a complete blank. My mother had problems with her memory, and her mind returned to the past. What about me? I'd rather my clock sped forward, so I could skip parts of my life altogether.

5

After hanging up with Tiantian, I spotted Fifth Sister-in-Law in the hall and pulled her into a room to talk.

"What's the matter?"

"I might be a little blunt. Hope you won't mind. I heard that Mother was rummaging in the garbage dumps before she died."

She wasn't surprised at all, and told me that Second Sister had already mentioned it.

"There's no need to make a fuss," she said.

According to her, the story was simple. My mother had gotten obsessed with not wasting things, so she'd started to gather used newspapers to sell at the recycling center. The whole family talked to her about her behavior, and she promptly stopped.

Fifth Sister-in-Law didn't look like she was lying. Her story was plausible, and it was a relief to hear. I should've stopped there. But a voice inside me wasn't satisfied.

"Then why didn't you tell me?" I retorted. "Is there more you're hiding from me?"

"Little Six, I don't know what you're talking about," said Fifth Sister-in-Law in a trembling tone. She looked around before continuing. "Why would I hide anything from you? Better to ask who is spreading rumors. What stinking, rotten mouth do they come out of?"

I looked into her eyes and said, "In front of my mother's coffin, you have to tell me the truth."

"It's far easier to be a good daughter than a good daughter-in-law." With that, she spun and walked away.

I sat by myself for a long time. Obviously there was something going on, otherwise Fifth Sister-in-Law would've been angry at my accusation. I looked out the window, but didn't see her. In the courtyard, friends and family squeezed around tables, drinking tea, peeling melon seeds and fruits, listening attentively to the singing, and circling titles on the song menus. The somber ceremony had turned into a karaoke party. Cheers exploded at the climax of each song. Some in the audience, no longer able to restrain themselves, jumped onto the stage to sing a song or two.

Tang walked in and told me he'd been in the bathroom with a stomachache, and needed to rest.

"Let me find Fourth Sister for you."

"What for?" He was displeased.

"Couldn't you tell she sang 'Midnight Song' for you?"

He nodded. I could see that he'd been caught off guard by her performance. In all the years he'd been with her, he hadn't known about her extraordinary talent on the erhu.

"The true master never reveals him or herself. Everyone in this family of yours has secrets!" Tang sounded genuinely surprised.

"True. I should congratulate you," I said in a flat tone.

Tang was taken aback and asked me nervously, "What do you mean?"

"Nothing. Relax."

That made him even more nervous. He said, "After all, we can't live our lives entirely under women's control. Men should also be their own masters. Let me use an analogy. In a swift river current, there are a lot of things swirling around, and they all rush toward their separate destinations. Nothing can stop them, and yet they are each so helpless."

With all the noise outside, his voice sounded far away. But the analogy gave me a sense of the burden he was under and what a failure he was as a man. He used to tell me that women were ferocious creatures, one more aggressive than the last. Men escaped one set of claws only to find themselves in another.

"What are you thinking?" he asked.

I sighed and told him that whenever I came back here, I was flooded by memories, and that it overwhelmed me with melancholy.

He said, "Remember, you and I will always have a place in each other's hearts, and we will never turn away from each other." His eyes were twinkling with tears.

His words made my heart ache. After a few long moments, I said, "Dear Tang, your destiny is to live a colorful life."

Fourth Sister came in and interrupted us. "I knew the two of you would be here. Come on, let's get some rest at Second Sister's." But she barely made it two steps before turning back to me. "What did you say to Fifth Sister-in-Law? She's downstairs crying!"

6

Tang went inside to use the toilet again. I could still recall the look he gave me—pregnant with implications. As if he was saying to me, "Look out: You've really kicked the hornet's nest now."

I went downstairs, ready to be attacked by my sisters and sisters-in-law. The band was playing a song by Hong Kong pop star Xi Xiulan. Some members of the audience were singing along and others were dancing.

To my surprise, my sisters and sisters-in-law all pretended nothing had happened. They all sat around one table, telling people who had just arrived about the moment my mother died, how scared they were, how they were overwhelmed by grief. The listeners seemed deeply engrossed. Fifth Sister-in-Law said that, during that one- or two-hour span, she went up and down the five flights no less than fifty times, notifying everyone and fetching things, but she did not feel tired at all because the emergency had numbed her senses.

It looked like the storm had ended before it had even begun.

The night grew even noisier. Firecrackers were popping everywhere and the air was filled with the smell of gunpowder and incense. A peddler of pirated DVDs took advantage of the large gathering and arrived to hawk his goods. A cotton-candy machine made from an old oil drum was set up outside the front gate. Children ran around in all directions.

Then Spectacles Wang arrived, reeking of alcohol. She had a white handkerchief in her hands, pretending to be a mourner. Third Brother spotted her right away, but Potbellied Cat was even quicker and blocked her at the gate. She immediately began to howl, "I am here to cry for the dead. Do you know how to weep? If you don't, let me teach you." She targeted Third Sister-in-Law, saying, "When the procession starts, you as the eldest daughter-in-law must sing 'Open the Gate.' Otherwise, Auntie Shi will suffer in the underworld."

"She's so drunk that she thinks your mother is Auntie Shi," Potbellied Cat exclaimed to Third Sister-in-Law.

"Get her out of here!" Third Sister-in-Law said.

"I'm not going anywhere. I've been waiting for this day. My son, and my dead husband, I didn't even sing for you when you were gone. My dear Auntie Shi, my elder sister, please don't harbor resentment against me."

Auntie Ma told her daughter and daughter-in-law to carry Spectacles Wang out, but she wouldn't budge. Stiffening, she yelled, "I have the party behind me: its authority is marked on my forehead! Every member of the revolutionary masses must listen to the party! Who dares to disobey?"

By the time Fourth Sister and Tang came downstairs, Spectacles Wang had been dragged away. I told them I wanted to stay for the vigil, but Fourth Sister looked into my eyes and said, "Little Six, please, I beg you. You must keep us company tonight."

The three of us walked down to the Yorike Café by the river to wait for a taxi.

It was almost midnight. South Bank Road was very quiet. Lights from the other shore reflected on the river, and the noises from Compound No. 6 faded into the background, making the scene surreal. Tang, Fourth Sister, and I stood side by side. The streetlights threw our shadows onto the ground, where they leaned against each other. Tang's and Fourth Sister's were intimately entwined. Why couldn't they stay like this the rest of their lives? They had come so far.

We humans seem to like creating trouble for ourselves. No matter how miserable we are, we only have ourselves to blame.

Two relatives of Second Brother-in-Law drove down the hill. We didn't know them well, but they offered us a ride.

The young driver was playing a Jane Birkin song about being lonely. Everyone in the car listened intently.

The thick night seemed pasted against the car windows. The river waves were licking the bank. Before long, Fourth Sister asked the driver to stop. We stepped onto the sidewalk and waved good-bye.

A steep slope led to Second Sister's apartment. Fourth Sister and I climbed it easily, but Tang was out of breath. Spotting a lotus-root congee stall, Tang pleaded with us, "Let's stop and have a bowl of congee. The diarrhea emptied my stomach."

The peddler hurriedly sat us down on wooden benches. We watched as he poured lotus-root powder into boiling water inside an old-style copper pot atop a charcoal fire. Each of us got a bowl filled to the brim. Tang instructed us to blow gently to prevent burning our mouths.

After gulping down his congee, Tang began to reminisce about the special significance congee held for him. During his compulsory service in the countryside, he once snuck back to Shanghai to visit his mother on her birthday. It was late when he arrived, and his mother had made him lotus-root congee. The taste was so sweet! Later, she was thrown in prison during the Cultural Revolution before being diagnosed with inoperable breast cancer that soon killed her.

Whenever he thought of his mother, Tang would remember how she had read to him. He'd become an insomniac at the age of thirteen because he brooded so much. Frustrated with his inability to fall asleep, he banged his fist on the floor every night until his mother began sitting up long nights with him, reading aloud.

That wasn't long after the Communist Party seized Shanghai from the Nationalists. Shanghai's status as a special administrative unit did not spare it from suffering the same supply shortage and strict rationing as other cities. Even soap and toothpaste were hard to come by. Young Tang had a lung disease, which meant he qualified for a special ration of a pound of butter. To make it stretch, his mother would lightly oil the wok with butter so that all their dishes could have a buttery fragrance.

She often hummed southern folk songs while she cooked, and Tang would sing along. His mother would stop and laughingly tell him when he was out of tune.

Tang missed his mother's smiles and her lotus-root congee. That's why he always stopped at lotus-root congee stalls. But their congee could never compare to his mother's, and that made him miss her even more.

I'd heard Tang reminisce about his mother before, but he'd never told me the congee story. Fourth Sister said to Tang, "Have another bowl! This congee isn't half bad."

Tang said, "You're right, this congee is much closer to my mother's than most. Maybe it's because I'm here to say good-bye to your mother, and the heavens are rewarding me. You must do good deeds. If you don't, you'll be punished by the heavens."

Tears were streaming down my face. Fourth Sister turned her face away so we couldn't see her expression. I knew for certain that that night, at that moment, she was so utterly in love with Tang that she'd forgotten all the times he'd hurt her.

7

Tang took the first shower and headed to bed, and then it was my turn. Through the splashing sound of hot water, I could make out the apartment door opening and someone talking to Fourth Sister in the hallway. I left the water running while tiptoeing to the bathroom door to eavesdrop.

"No!" Fourth Sister was saying.

A gruff voice replied, "You should have notified us earlier if you want to change the plan."

"I couldn't get to a phone. Please go away."

Then I heard the door being locked. Fourth Sister went into the kitchen to get a drink, and I snuck back to the shower. So my sisters really were up to something. Now that Tang was in their clutches, inflicting a mere stomachache on him couldn't possibly be enough to sate their anger.

Was it possible that they really wanted to kill him?

Whatever they had planned, Fourth Sister was clearly wavering.

I put on my bathrobe and stepped out of the bathroom. Fourth Sister went in and closed the door behind her.

Second Sister's youngest son had bought this two-bedroom apartment with a bank loan. The area was nicely landscaped with fountains and hundred-year-old trees transplanted from the mountains. The government had been benevolent. It was the same area that I'd chosen for the new condo my mother would never get to live in. Second Sister's old place close to her school was being demolished, so she'd moved in here. The décor was simple and clean, with white ceramic tiles and white furniture, making it appear larger than it actually was. Tang had been surprised by how nice the apartment was. We thought it wasn't fair that a young person could afford a place like this, while Tang, a professor, had to settle for the shabby room his university had assigned him. He said he should seriously consider buying something.

Fourth Sister responded, "With all the money you have, you should buy a house."

Tang immediately backpedaled and said it was just a thought.

Tang was in one bedroom, and I decided to give Fourth Sister the other. I grabbed a blanket from the closet and brought it to the huge sofa in the living room. It was spacious and airy here, with a view of the river from the balcony.

Suddenly, Tang rushed out of the bedroom and knocked on the bathroom door. "Sorry, before you shower, I have to go again."

Fourth Sister darted out wrapped in a towel, and Tang vanished into the bathroom.

I said to her, "Why don't you get him some diarrhea medicine?"

"How should I know where Second Sister keeps her medicine?" she snapped.

I searched all the cabinets and cupboards and finally found a medicine box. I took out two berberine pills and, together with a glass of water, placed them on the nightstand by Tang's bed.

Fourth Sister watched me do all this with a long face. Then she went into the other bedroom and shut the door.

I turned off the lights, listening to the breeze coming from the balcony. The city quieted until only the crickets on the cliffs were still chirping. I closed my eyes and fell asleep almost immediately.

8

He pushed her away, and she fell hard onto the floor.

I opened my eyes with a start, thinking that it was a nightmare. But it wasn't. The light from the bedrooms bled into the living room. Fourth Sister was in Tang's room crying.

"I'll do anything to make you love me again. How can you be so heartless? We have to work things out, get to the bottom of it all!"

"God, I can't believe I fell into your trap by coming to Chongqing," Tang said.

"Right here, while we are mourning my mother's passing, you dared to call that tramp! You thought I was sleeping. You told me you'd never go back to her, even if she were the last woman left in the world. You promised me when you left London!"

Tang said he'd been moved by Fourth Sister's rendition of "Midnight Song," but he was furious about having his phone call interrupted. He said Fourth Sister shouldn't have chased him all over campus or cursed at him every time they talked on the phone. What's worse, Fourth Sister had revealed to his girlfriend that he was a polygamist. No matter how much he had once loved her, their relationship was beyond repair. Never in his whole life, even when he'd been labeled a "May 16

Counterrevolutionary" or during the Cultural Revolution, had he been so humiliated. There was nothing she could do now to change that.

Fourth Sister ran out of his room. As soon as she saw me, she asked, "Did you hear what he said?"

I sat up. "Can't you two keep it down? You might not want to sleep, but I do."

"How can you sleep?" Fourth Sister said. "That man will walk away tomorrow after Ma's cremation. Then it'll be impossible for either of us to find him." She turned around to face Tang's room, addressing him. "I only did those things because you pushed me into a corner. Now I know that you only wanted to come back to China for your own sake. You never cared in the least about what we were doing in London. At the very least you could have asked about Cosette!"

"Didn't you find a good family to adopt her?"

After Tang left, Fourth Sister's dog, Cosette, had searched everywhere for him. Once, she disappeared for a whole week, and Fourth Sister was beyond distraught. Just when she'd almost given up hope, Cosette barked at the front door, all skin and bones, with a wounded leg. She rushed out and took the dog into her arms, telling it they were going to China to find Tang. But it was impossible to bring the dog to China. Dogs had to be quarantined for a month outside the Beijing airport before being allowed through customs. And for a dog as big as Cosette, it would be impossible to get a permit in a Chinese city. So Cosette stayed put, barking day and night in her grief and infuriating the neighbors, who grew increasingly hostile.

One evening, Fourth Sister came back from grocery shopping and was stunned to find a message scrawled in red spray paint on her front door: "Get out, whore!"

Another time, early in the morning, a neighbor threw rocks through the big double-paned window in the living room, broken glass splashing all over the sofa and the floor. These acts of violence were humiliating and frightening for a single Chinese woman with a young daughter. The police came, but they couldn't do anything about it.

As the vandalism escalated, Fourth Sister began to fear for Cosette's safety, and since it was impossible for her to take the dog with her everywhere she went, she had no choice but to give her away. She and Tiantian went online to find a family for Cosette. But everyone was looking for younger dogs. Finally, a family with a farm near Chailey volunteered to take Cosette in. As Fourth Sister bathed Cosette for the last time, she couldn't stop crying. Cosette licked her, attempting to comfort her, but when Fourth Sister began to take photos, the dog began to run around the garden, howling to the skies.

The doorbell rang. The adopter was a strong, middle-aged English woman driving a Jeep. Fourth Sister wailed, and Cosette resisted so much that the two women could scarcely force her into the car.

Tang looked moved to hear that Cosette had searched for him. But he didn't say a word.

Fourth Sister said, "I swear I will never raise a dog again for the rest of my life. I can no longer be counted as a human being. I am not a human being. For you, I deserted my own mother. Because of you, I had to give Cosette away. I hate myself for loving you! These nine years in England, do you know how lonely I've been? I poured my heart and soul into our marriage, and all of a sudden, you leave me. Do you have any empathy at all? Put yourself in my shoes. I am already fifty years old! If you want to leave, at the very least, we should part on good terms, and you should give me something to live on. But it can't end like this! The heavens will help me punish you!"

Tang said, "All you're doing is making it worse."

I did not know how Fourth Sister managed to keep silent. Tang shut his door, and she went back to her room and turned off the light.

Darkness enveloped the living room. I sat on the sofa for what seemed an eternity, and then went to the balcony. To my surprise, I saw Fourth Sister leaning out her bedroom window and staring at the river.

I came back in and went to her room to tell her, "Fourth Sister, please, for the sake of Ma's reputation, don't do anything you'll regret."

"Don't worry, Little Six," she snarled defensively. "First, I won't have him killed. Second, I won't kill myself."

"Then who were you talking to when I was taking a shower?" I blurted out.

"What are you talking about? There must be something wrong with your ears, or else you were hallucinating." Fourth Sister angrily pointed to the bedroom door. "Get out."

"Boom! Boom!"

In my dream, the sound came from thunder rolling across the sky. I turned over and tried to go back to sleep.

"Boom! Boom!"

It wasn't thunder. It was someone banging on the front door. The apartment was eerily quiet, both bedroom doors shut. I pulled on my clothes and glanced at my watch. It was only five forty in the morning. Who could it be this early?

I opened the door to find Third Sister-in-Law standing there with soy milk and fried dough sticks. "I was afraid you all might oversleep."

I let her in then went to the bathroom to wash up. My instinct told me that she wasn't really here as a wake-up call. As I came out of the bathroom, she stopped whispering with Fourth Sister and told me to eat the fried dough on the table. Tang emerged, greeting Third Sister-in-Law and nodding at Fourth Sister as if nothing had happened.

My right eye started twitching. As the old saying goes, "Left eye twitching, a windfall awaits. Right eye twitching, it's dire straits."

CHAPTER 10

I

The sky was dark and gloomy, and the traffic was light. Our taxi pulled up by Yorike, the hip Italian café where we'd waited last night. As we climbed up the stone steps, Third Sister-in-Law said that today wasn't just the funeral procession, but also the Third-Day Farewell. Traditionally, on the third day after death, the soul officially gets registered in the underworld. If one goes to heaven, the soul is then received by Buddha's messengers. When Third Sister-in-Law's mother died, they didn't hold a Third-Day Farewell ceremony, and she was plagued by dreams of her mother accusing her of not being filial.

All was quiet in front of No. 8, but as soon as we turned the corner, we saw a large crowd gathering at Compounds No. 6 and 7. Many people were holding flower wreaths. I hurriedly followed Third Sister-in-Law through the crowd and into the courtyard, a little out of breath.

Members of my family were walking around the coffin, sprinkling shelled peanuts at every step. We rushed to join the circle. When I passed Potbellied Cat, I asked him, "Didn't you say that the procession wouldn't start until seven? You didn't wait for us."

"Don't be upset. You're right. We were supposed to start at seven. But with more careful calculation, I realized that five to seven would be the most propitious time for your mother. That's why we had to go ahead."

Third Brother handed the sacrificial-food jar to his wife, telling her to hold on tight. He then raised the basin for burning paper money and smashed it hard onto the ground. The basin shattered. People began to cheer, "Great! Thoroughly pulverized! Good fortune for eight generations!"

Potbellied Cat shouted, "Hoist up the coffin!"

The four pallbearers, two at each end, lifted up my mother's coffin and started to walk toward the compound gate. The sky was still dark, but firecrackers were popping, and mourners carrying wreaths swarmed behind the coffin. Pieces of paper money shaped like copper coins were flung into the air, falling onto the faces and clothes of my two brothers.

The procession reached Middle School Street and turned up a side street that led past the elementary school. After climbing up the steps, the procession reached the unpaved road by the No. 5 Plastics Factory. Day finally broke. Potbellied Cat and the four pallbearers started loading the coffin onto the hearse. Firecrackers popped nonstop for ten minutes. With smoke whirling around them, Third Brother and his wife directed people into a coach and several cars. My mother's godson, Shouli, invited me into his car. I was pleasantly surprised to find Auntie Mo and Xiaomao, Shouli's son, already inside.

"Little Six, so good to see you! You'd already left when I arrived last night," Auntie Mo said.

Elder Sister had called Auntie Mo's commune office about my mother's passing, and it had taken a day for the news to reach her. Auntie Mo was about my mother's age. Except for two missing teeth, she appeared in good health and was sharp as a tack. Lean and small, she wore her hair up in a bun and looked to be in her early seventies at most. With red eyes, she told me how sad she was that Ma had died before she could say good-bye.

Auntie Mo was like my mother's sister. They'd worked together at the textile factory after my mother ran away from her arranged marriage. Auntie Mo was later married to a villager in rural Chongqing, but she kept in touch with our family and came to see us at least once a year. Second Sister and Third Brother both resented her visits because they believed that my mother gave her money. My mother defended herself, saying, "Your Auntie Mo loves us. Every time she comes, she brings bags of dried sweet potato, pickled vegetables, salted duck eggs, and other delicious things." It was true. After an especially good harvest, she had even brought us sausages and seasoned pork. Sometimes, when she couldn't come herself, she would get her son to deliver gifts.

"Country bumpkins!" Third Brother replied in contempt. "It's not worth wasting breath on them."

My mother responded, "That's because you have nothing interesting to say to begin with."

Usually, Auntie Mo came shortly before or after the Lunar New Year and stayed for a couple of days. There was no extra bed, so my mother and I slept with her in one bed, while my father set up a bamboo board to sleep on. Auntie Mo was a talker. Her topics ranged from hogs and sows to her sons, Damao and Xiaomao, to which family in the village had given birth to a boy, to which seeds had been sown where, and even to how many eggs had been laid by her little chickens and ducks. She wouldn't stop talking even after my mother fell asleep. The walls in our house were thin as paper, and my brothers and sisters hated her endless chatter.

My father, however, was always a gracious host. Even when my mother was away working extra shifts, he treated Auntie Mo like family and forbade my brothers and sisters from offending her. Auntie Mo was especially kind to me, teaching me needlework and how to sew shoe bottoms.

My mother used to say, "Relatives, relatives—one has to visit often to be related." When I thought about it now, I saw the wisdom in her words. Of course, my mother and Auntie Mo would always have a sisterly bond, even if they didn't see each other all the time. I could feel that bond even now, as Auntie Mo held tight to my hands in the car.

"My darling Little Six, you've really grown since I saw you last! Now that your auntie is old and useless, I really should follow your ma to the grave."

"No, Auntie Mo, you'll surely live beyond a hundred!" I told her.

"I hope you know how proud you made your mother. Every time I saw her, she'd go on and on about you."

I was desperate to ask Auntie Mo all kinds of questions about my mother, but Shouli's presence made me bite my tongue.

2

Raindrops appeared on the windshield, but the drizzle only lasted a couple of minutes. Shortly thereafter, our cars rolled into the garage at Two Mile Crematorium. Two employees in white coats and gloves rolled the coffin out of the hearse. Just when they were about to enter the elevator, I jumped out of the car, yelling for them to stop.

I ran over and peered at my mother's gaunt face one last time. There was a bruise on her right eyelid I hadn't noticed before. I straightened her hat, arranged her white hair, smoothed her wrinkled clothes, and untied her shoelaces in accordance with tradition. I gently caressed Ma's face and neck, and pressed my face against her chest, as I'd always wanted to do every time we parted, but never did. Now, of course, it was too late. Her chest was cold; her heart had stopped beating. I tried not to let my tears gush out. "Ma, this time we are really saying good-bye. But I'm not ready for you to go. Ma, even though I know you're dead, you're still here—I can still see you. Once your body disappears, I don't know what I'm going to do."

The crematorium employees began to pace beside me impatiently.

I tried to ignore them. I wasn't finished talking to my mother. I wanted to tell her everything I'd experienced in the previous three days, but Potbellied Cat asked my brothers to drag me away.

I resisted with all my strength. "Ma, let me tell you everything hidden in my heart. Please don't go before I'm finished!"

Auntie Mo rushed over and joined me. Holding my mother's hands, she howled, "My dear old sister, you have died an unjust and pathetic death!"

I clung to my mother's body and wouldn't let it go. My brothers forcibly picked me up and pulled me and Auntie Mo away from my mother.

The employees wheeled my mother onto the elevator while shouting at us to wait upstairs. I kicked my brothers away and spun around, only to see the elevator door closing. It felt like I was going to choke on my tears.

Potbellied Cat was officially finished with Ma's funeral now, so it was time to go see the next family. He hopped in the hearse and roared away.

3

The crematorium had a large reception hall with clean floor and walls. The seven or eight rows of benches were full. Apparently, a lot of bodies were scheduled to be burned that day. A glass wall separated us from the furnace room. Several hydraulic lifts were busy ferrying bodies up from the morgue and sending them into the ovens. Through the glass, families of the deceased could watch the entire process, the bodies disappearing into the furnace and emerging again as white bones. The walls were covered with strange slogans, such as, "Decrease the number of the population, increase the quality of the population" and "Come in sadness and leave with satisfaction." Some were a little more comforting: "Respect the body, handle with care." Fourth Sister gave Tang pen and paper so he could copy down the slogans. Then he decided to walk around and see more of the crematorium. Fourth Sister followed close behind.

I asked an employee how long it would be before our number was called.

"If the bodies are going fast today, a little more than an hour. If slow, it's hard to say."

Auntie Mo needed to use the bathroom, so I took her. When we came out, I seized the opportunity to ask, "Auntie Mo, why did you say my mother died an unjust and pathetic death?"

"Don't you feel that your mother went through life suffering from the pain and unfairness of it all?" The old lady was too sharp to be led by my questions. "Your mother was never a small-minded person. She'd do whatever she felt was right, never even considering her own personal loss or gain. You've heard of Uncle Jian, haven't you?"

I nodded my head, and my heart started to beat fast. I didn't need to go hunting for Wang Guixiang when Auntie Mo was here to answer my questions!

"Next to your father and biological father," she said solemnly, "Uncle Jian was the most important man in your mother's life."

"Then what my sisters said about Uncle Jian being my mother's lover is true?"

"Little Six, listen to my story first before you pass judgment."

When Uncle Jian and my mother first met, he was chief engineer on a boat and she was a shoulder-pole carrier newly arrived at the dockyard. She never said anything during her breaks and always had a frown on her face. That left a deep impression on him. He tried to talk to her, but she gave him the cold shoulder. The coldness seemed to come from deep within her heart.

That was the winter of 1964, Auntie Mo said, just after my mother and my biological father had separated for the last time. The two of them had met by the disused cable car tracks at Chaotianmen. My biological father watched as my mother, holding me, still an infant, walked away. They'd had many stops and starts, but this time, they were both determined to suppress their feelings and part ways forever.

But soon, my biological father began to miss me and my mother. He gathered up his courage and went to look for my mother at the dockyard. She hid in the worker's lounge and refused to open the door. He asked my mother's friend Wang Guixiang for help, but my mother still refused to see him, biting her lips so hard they bled. Wang Guixiang could only ask him to leave. My mother was so heartsick that, later that day, she slipped and fell off the dock. Jian's boat happened to be moored nearby. He leapt into the water and rescued her.

After that, my mother began to spend time with Jian during her breaks. Wang Guixiang would jokingly ask him to invite them to dinner at his house, and he'd insist that they were welcome anytime, that his wife was a good cook. My mother and Wang Guixiang never accepted the invitation, but they often caught a lift to the south bank on his boat, bringing with them the leftover firewood given out to the transportation crew. Jian would help them carry the wood home.

Soon the Cultural Revolution began, and my mother's crazy roommate Yueyun exposed her past as the wife of a mob boss. As I mentioned earlier, this resulted in my mother being tortured at a public struggle session. Up on the platform with her were factory heads, engineers, and counterrevolutionaries—feudalists, capitalists, reactionaries—all with heavy wooden signs hung around their necks. As the audience shouted slogans nonstop, the Red Guards became increasingly violent. They bound an engineer's arms and feet behind him, wrapped the rope around his neck, and lifted him into the air. As if that weren't enough, they kept piling big earthen blocks on his back until his bones broke and his muscles tore. His eyes popping and his tongue sticking out, the engineer passed out. Then, several young revolutionaries in red armbands jumped up and down on the poor man's back to make him shit himself. He stopped breathing shortly thereafter.

My mother started screaming in horror, and to punish her for it, a young man picked up a massive board and threw it at her head. Fortunately, the board was so heavy her attacker nearly missed and the impact was mitigated. Still, it left an inch-long, gaping wound. My mother was knocked out cold, and no one dared or bothered to check whether she was still alive.

When his boat docked later that day, Uncle Jian heard of the incident and rushed over to my mother's dormitory, bringing a basketful of dried longan. He anxiously asked my mother if she was still in pain. He told her that eating longan helps replenish the blood. My mother was resting in bed with her forehead bandaged. She asked Uncle Jian not to worry about her.

Uncle Jian looked for a spot to put down the basket, but every inch of the floor was covered with ink and scraps of paper for Yueyun's inflammatory posters. Finally, he found a nail on the back of the door to hang the basket on.

Yueyun flew into a rage, pointing to a propaganda poster pasted on the back of the door and denouncing Uncle Jian for blocking it. The poster depicted soldiers, workers, and students standing side by side, waving Mao's little red book. Above them were red flags and a red sun, in its center a portrait of Chairman Mao in military dress. There were also two quotations from Mao: "The People's Liberation Army must support the leftist revolutionary masses" and "The army and the civilians are united as one. Together they will defeat all enemies."

Uncle Jian responded, "The nail on the door is meant for hanging things. That's no place to put a poster."

Yueyun hollered, "I can put my poster anywhere I want. That's none of your business."

Uncle Jian realized that the walls were entirely covered with Chairman Mao's portraits and revolutionary posters.

My mother sat up to go take the basket down, but Yueyun was a step ahead of her. She hurled the basket of longan into the hallway. Uncle Jian's anger erupted.

"Haven't you ruined enough lives?"

Yueyun was so startled that she didn't say a word. But she went to the authorities to slander Jian that very evening.

Uncle Jian was arrested first thing the next morning. He was accused of sabotaging the revolution by placing stinking fruit on top of Mao's portrait. Around noon, his wife and their thirteen-year-old son, their only child, came to consult my mother. His wife had already been to see the personnel director of the factory, a notorious man who said he'd only consider releasing Uncle Jian if my mother went to him to plead his case. Jian's wife and son were about to kneel down before my mother. She stopped them and promised that she would go to the personnel director.

Mother went to the director immediately, and for several days afterward, she was in a strange mood. Auntie Mo said all my mother would tell her about the meeting was that the director refused to release Uncle Jian. The only favor the man did for her was not making her a target at any more struggle sessions.

On her way back, my mother had run into Jian's wife, who accused her of being selfish. My mother swore there was nothing more she could've done. Uncle Jian's wife stomped on the ground and said, "Heaven knows what you've done!" She walked away, leaving my mother standing there dumbfounded.

In the summer of 1967, Chongqing was transformed from a beautiful hillside city into a bloody battlefield. Gun battles broke out at Red Boulder Diesel Engine Plant between two factions of the Red Guard, Fight to the End and August 15, and things escalated quickly after that. All kinds of weapons were involved: small-bore rifles, automatics, submachine guns, heavy machine guns, grenades, and even tanks, cannons, and gunships. From inner-city shoot-outs to field battles, the scale of these conflicts grew and grew, as did the number of casualties. Every factory had to support one or another faction, all of which purported to be the true followers of Chairman Mao.

On July 9, a firefight erupted outside the dockyard kindergarten where Uncle Jian's wife taught. One side was a Fight to the End group from a military defense plant downstream; the other side was an August 15 squad from a school. The kindergarten shut its door tight, and Jian's wife went outside to beg the factions to stop fighting for the sake of the children. The Fight to the End people not only didn't listen, they took long spikes and stabbed them through her stomach and chest. Some rushed into the kindergarten and terrorized every adult and child inside.

Uncle Jian's son hurried over as soon as he heard what was going on, as did my mother. Both factions were long gone, and Uncle Jian's wife was bleeding all over the street. My mother took the woman in her arms and saw that she was soaked in blood, her breasts cut into pieces, her intestines spilling out. She was gasping for air, staring straight into my mother's eyes. She grabbed her son's hand and placed it in my mother's, telling her son that Ma was now his godmother. Then she breathed her last.

On August 8 of 1967, militia and Red Guards in the Riverview Machinery Factory sailed a fleet of gunships down the river and shot at targets along the way, including the East Wind Shipyard, the Chaotianmen Administrative Building, and the boats nearby. The fleet sank three boats, heavily damaged twelve more, and killed or injured hundreds of people. On August 13, the two factions engaged in heavy fighting in the city center around the Liberation Monument. The Utilities Mansion and a building next to it were burned to the ground.

A few years later, on September 13, 1971, the plane carrying Lin Biao, Chairman Mao's heir apparent, crashed in Öndörhaan, Mongolia. There was no official announcement, but the news spread quickly by word of mouth. "Have you heard? Vice Chairman Lin turned out to be a hidden enemy! Otherwise, what did he fly to our enemy state Mongolia for? He's dead!"

Gossip about the incident ran wild. "That good-for-nothing Lin Biao was really rotten to the core, huh? Can you believe he was such a traitor? He betrayed Chairman Mao and went over to the Soviet Revisionist Imperialists! Who knows what other treason he committed?"

"Yes, but no matter how he schemed, he couldn't outscheme fate, could he? His airplane ran out of fuel and exploded during a crash landing. They got what they deserved! But do you believe that's really what happened?" Everybody was aware, of course, of the other version of the story in which the plane was shot down.

But everyone was happy. By then, Lin was widely considered to be chiefly responsible for the chaos and brutalities of the early stage of the Cultural Revolution. People who had ruined countless lives were finally getting their just deserts. Justice had been served. Premier Zhou Enlai, riding the momentum, pushed for reinstatement of officials who had previously been stripped of their posts. A large number of imprisoned and tortured party, government, and military leaders had the cases against them thrown out.

In 1973, Deng Xiaoping was reinstated as vice premier, which led to the release of many of those wrongly accused in the factional fights. My mother got wind of it and began to frequent the shipping company and the public safety bureau to plead for Uncle Jian and his late wife. Due to her relentless efforts, his wife was recognized as a martyr. Uncle Jian was set free and allowed to work on a tugboat, but he never recovered from his time in prison, where the Red Guards had deliberately and severely injured his legs and groin. Uncle Jian and my mother grew close again, but after she retired in 1980, they rarely saw each other except at the cemetery in Shapingba Park on the anniversary of his wife's death. My mother would always bring chilled noodles, apples, peaches, a small bottle of liquor, and a bouquet of white chrysanthemums. They'd sit and reminisce about the past that still haunted them. At Shapingba, the evidence of what had happened was buried all around . . .

Back in 1967, that terrible year, the August 15 group attached to the kindergarten had used Uncle Jian's wife's death to rouse themselves to greater acts of valor. They decided to bury her in a grand ceremony and to kill their captives from the Fight to the End faction as sacrifices. They chose a site in Shapingba Park and dug a hole in the ground. After her coffin was lowered, they ordered four captives to kneel down at the side, and then they fired from behind. But they really shot only one of them: a seventeen-year-old girl in a blue student uniform tied with a leather belt with a shiny copper buckle. She wore a pair of military-style, rubber-soled shoes, a beautiful face under her short hair. Her terrified eyes were wide open. Her body was pushed into the hole to keep Uncle Jian's wife company.

The other three captives had more work to do. They were forced to dig up the graves of several August 15 Red Guards who had been killed in the fighting a few days before. The weather was hot, and the bodies were already decomposing. The three prisoners were forced to kneel and beg forgiveness from the bodies, before cleaning them, one by one, injecting formaldehyde as they fanned away insects and flies. When they had finished, they dutifully lowered the bodies into the mass grave, but they did not fare better than the schoolgirl. All were sacrificed to the deceased.

Every year on the anniversary of the massacre, my mother spoke to the souls while scattering liquor in front of their tombstones. Uncle Jian would sit on a stone, chain-smoking. Once he told my mother that his wife had been jealous of her and had forbidden him from mentioning her name. My mother marveled at her change of heart as she died.

The year 1980 saw the rounding up of those responsible for the factional fights, those who had previously slipped through justice's net. The factory personnel director was thrown into prison. Yueyun was also tried for her persecution and torture of others during the early days of the Cultural Revolution. Though she had suffered the same fate later, when her father's identity had been uncovered, she was still held responsible for her wrongdoings. Because she was deemed mentally unstable, she escaped jail time and was eventually sent to an institution.

My mother and Uncle Jian would always arrive at Shapingba Park at two in the afternoon and leave around five. They would ride the bus together to Chaotianmen and then go their separate ways. My mother would take the ferry to Slingshot Boulder, and Uncle Jian to White Sand Dune. Rain or shine, they followed the same routine for years.

Then, in the fall of 1983, my mother prepared the food offerings and went to the cemetery as usual, but Uncle Jian did not come. Knowing that something must have happened to him, she went straight to Auntie Mo's house. It was raining that day, but while she had an umbrella, she didn't think to use it. Auntie Mo said she'd never seen my mother so rattled. She was beside herself with anxiety and could only murmur nonstop, "He's gone. He left without telling me."

Auntie Mo understood immediately. She dried my mother's face and hair with a towel, and then sat her down, poured her a cup of hot tea, and listened as my mother told her the whole story. Then she said, "Poor man! He never even thought about getting remarried because he had you in his heart."

"But I couldn't spare him even one hair, because my heart was so filled with love for my husband and my children. I had nothing to give him."

It was dark already, and Auntie Mo asked my mother to stay for the night. But my mother said, "I have to go home. Otherwise, my husband will worry, and he won't sleep well."

It turned out that, the day before the anniversary of his wife's death, Uncle Jian had had a stroke on his boat. His son used to visit Auntie Mo. According to her, Uncle Jian's son was ambitious. He'd left his job in Yunnan to go to college. After he worked for the government for several years, he quit to become an entrepreneur in Hainan. His company was big now, but he never forgot the help he'd received in his youth.

I told Auntie Mo that this godson of my mother's had just spent a hefty sum on monks for her burial ceremony.

Auntie Mo responded, "I knew he would. He said a long time ago that whether it's sunrise or sundown, everything has its time and its reason. What he owed your mother, he had to pay back."

4

There were a lot of nasty rumors about my mother and Uncle Jian, yet my father treated him like his own brother, which confused my brothers and sisters. My father was an open-minded man, and he knew that the only other man in my mother's heart was my biological father. Uncle Jian was like a big brother to her. Twenty years of friendship made them like family.

Did my mother bid Uncle Jian farewell when he died? When his son fulfilled his wish to have his ashes scattered in the Yangtze between Chaotianmen and White Sand Dune, was my mother there? He chose that part of the river because it was important in his relationship with her. He was from Ningbo and was an only son, and his own son was also an only son. They couldn't have cared less what the ancestors would have wanted.

Of course, my mother was already over forty years old when she met Uncle Jian in 1964. By the time he passed away, she had withered, bit by bit, into an old woman no different from any other on the street. But Uncle Jian's love never faltered. I remembered the way he looked at her, his yearning obvious even to me, just a young girl at the time. A lifetime of hard labor had taken away my mother's alluring curves, but in his eyes, she was still beautiful. What he loved about my mother was her heart. When he was gone, my mother must have gone to the temples to light candles for him. That was her way of expressing her grief.

Three years after my mother lost Uncle Jian, she also lost my biological father. On my eighteenth birthday, my mother had taken me downtown to meet the man, but I refused to even acknowledge him. I wanted to punish her for waiting eighteen years to tell me the truth. Everyone had known but me. They treated me like a fool!

That's when I ran away from home, cutting off contact. I eventually established sporadic correspondence with Second Sister, but didn't go back to my mother for years. In fact, I never truly went back—it was never really the same. How my mother survived, I don't know. She had lost her youngest daughter. My sister told me Ma couldn't close her eyes even when she was asleep. She aged rapidly, her teeth falling out, and her back growing ever more hunched.

Her unwillingness to talk about those years even after I began to return to Chongqing to see her was proof of how painful they had been. I saw how my mother watched TV till long after all the programs had ended and the screen showed nothing but static. And she always kept the light on in her room. Maybe she was afraid of the dark. Maybe she needed sound to fill her up inside so that other noises couldn't intrude. What exactly had she experienced? Deep down, she must have been trying to avoid something.

Auntie Mo said my mother had lived a life of bitter suffering.

She didn't need to tell me all this. After all, she was the only one who knew these secrets, and she could have been like my mother and taken them to the grave with her. Why had she been so open with me, I asked her.

Auntie Mo said she really couldn't stand people's attitude toward my mother, and someone needed to set the record straight.

Second Cousin's wife and Second Sister were on their way to the crematorium bathroom when they spotted us talking. They walked over, and I introduced Second Cousin's wife to Auntie Mo, but Auntie Mo said they'd known each other for a long time.

Second Sister pulled me aside. "Little Six, nothing good comes out of Auntie Mo's mouth. The last time she stayed at our house, there was a big fight."

"Over what?" I asked.

"She was blaming us for not feeding Ma well."

"Were you?"

"What right did she have to listen to our mother's biased words? Family business is family business, and she had no right to interfere."

"So you kicked her out?"

"I didn't kick her out. She stormed out herself. I was glad, though. I can't imagine why Elder Sister invited her to the funeral at all."

Now that Potbellied Cat was gone, Third Brother, as the eldest son, was supposed to be in charge, but he lacked organizational skills. That meant that things fell to Second Sister. She had to hurry back in to check whether our number had been called.

I held Auntie Mo's arm as we followed behind Second Sister. I could easily imagine the uproar she'd incited on her last visit. After my father died, no one at home listened to Mother. By standing up for Ma, Auntie Mo had kicked the hornet's nest. My siblings must have been apoplectic. How dare she come between children and their mother? As far as they were concerned, Auntie Mo was a hillbilly and not welcome in our home. They didn't care how Ma felt when her sworn sister was humiliated and shown the door. My poor mother lost her only companion in her lonely final days.

Auntie Mo broke a promise to Ma by telling me the truth about Uncle Jian. She did so because she couldn't stand my brothers' and sisters' disrespect toward my mother. If my siblings knew what Auntie Mo had told me, how would they have reacted? No matter what they might say, one thing is certain—my mother had too many secrets, and secrets are dirty laundry that cannot be aired and should never be mentioned.

5

The cremation hall was crowded. A young girl's body was next in line. Her face had been beautifully made up. Her younger sister wailed, and her mother cried, "My dearest daughter! A white-haired mother should not outlive her black-haired daughter!" She tried desperately to break into the furnace room, her family scrambling to stop her. After a few minutes, the girl's body had been reduced to ash, and the group retreated from the hall.

Third Brother returned to say we'd be lucky for them to get to our mother before noon. He had already bribed the furnace operators with two cartons of cigarettes, and they'd admitted it wasn't a particularly busy day. The delay was because we hadn't wanted the crematorium's all-inclusive package, with cremation, a farewell ceremony, a DVD, an urn, and appointments for future visits. Families that agreed to pay extra for the package were bumped to the front of the line. Third Brother said he'd tried, but couldn't talk his way around it. Our only choice was to pay for all the extra stuff we didn't want. He said there'd been a worker who died falling off a truck and was sent to the crematorium. The body had been left in the refrigerator for a week because no one came to buy the special package. Eventually, some journalists broke the story, which drew the public security bureau's attention. But the police simply ordered the worker's employer to pay so that he could finally be cremated.

Then Fifth Brother and Third Sister-in-Law arrived and told us the problem was solved. Fifth Brother had found out that the crematorium's associate director was a relative of one of his fishing buddies. The associate director decided that Ma should enjoy special treatment as the mother of an overseas Chinese. She would be next in line.

It was not the first time, after I had become a British citizen, that my family took advantage of having an overseas relative. Each of my siblings and each of their children had secured a special government certificate proving their status, which entitled them to favorable treatment, such as bonus grades on the children's school entrance examinations, points toward better government housing, and promotions.

But my family members didn't know how to use these benefits. For example, Fifth Brother was shy, and my mother had always been protective of him. After she retired, she chose to let Fifth Brother take her job at the dockyard. Before long, though, the dockyard laid off half of its employees, including Fifth Brother. If he had known how to make use of his overseas-Chinese-relative status, he wouldn't have lost his job. For the past few years, Fifth Brother had made a living fishing in the big river using just fishing poles and worms. When it became increasingly difficult to find fish in the river, he went into the surrounding valleys to fish in mountain streams, where he befriended a lot of wealthy fishing buddies, some of whom had good jobs and influence. Once, while selling his fish in the market, the other peddlers were accusing him of undercutting their prices. One of his fishing buddies happened to pass by and saved him from their bullying. When this man found out Fifth Brother had lost his job, he got him a position as a welder on the railroad. Now, another fishing contact was helping to expedite the cremation.

Third Brother patted Fifth Brother happily on the shoulder. "Well done! My baby brother has made himself useful by making the right kinds of friends."

Everyone breathed a sigh of relief.

The crematorium employees, in light-blue shirts and white gloves, were busy clearing away the remains of the body that had just been cremated. The family of the deceased had hired a full-service funeral company to take care of the entire process. All they needed to do was wait outside. As soon as the urn was handed to them, they got into a stretch limousine and drove away.

Then my mother's body was brought up in the elevator. Her head turned to the left and she was covered in a white sheet with her black cloth shoes exposed. The employees asked if we wanted a minute to say good-bye again. Fourth Sister and I went inside while the others stood by the glass window. I borrowed Fourth Sister's camera and asked one of the employees if I could take a picture.

He took a quick look at me and responded that only the crematorium was allowed to take photos, but maybe an exception could be made if I made it quick.

I told my mother, "Ma, I am now taking a picture of you." Her face appeared in my viewfinder. Had she just moved? Maybe she sensed that I was right in front of her? My hands trembling, I pressed down the shutter release.

I dabbed at my eyes and took another. Then the employee pushed me and Fourth Sister out the door.

I rushed toward the glass to look at my mother. They started the machinery, and my mother was slowly carried into the furnace.

A door closed automatically, making it impossible to see what was going on inside the furnace. Everybody quieted down, except for one curious person who asked an employee what exactly was taking place inside. The employee remained silent.

A man with a mustache, apparently one of our neighbors' friends, took it upon himself to answer. He said he'd seen the whole process before. "On the other end of the furnace, there's a small hole. The operator sticks a steel hook through the hole to shift the body to an ideal position. Just imagine how hot it is in there. The fire-resistant bricks glow bright red."

Seeing how attentive the listeners were, the man was encouraged. He stretched and continued, "Did you know that hair and clothes burn immediately? The whole body becomes naked and the skin tightens. Then it doesn't take long before the skin stretches and blows up like a balloon. The legs open up slightly and curl upward. The upper body rises, with the head coming several inches off the ground. The arms arc outward. Can you imagine? Dead bodies can actually stand straight up in the heat!"

Everyone shuddered at thought.

The man nodded. "Years ago, many old folks didn't want to be cremated precisely because they didn't want to stand up."

I was sitting in the first row of the benches, staring at my mother's last earthly image on the little camera screen. My heart was in such pain that I felt numb. I tried not to listen to the man, but his words buzzed around my ears like gnats. I couldn't bear to imagine my mother being deformed and destroyed by fire the way he described. Would she be afraid? No one can escape fear, and my mother wouldn't be an exception. But she could hold on to my hands.

I felt her hands in mine. We held on tight to each other. My mother deserved my love and care, the kind I hadn't gotten enough of from her. I'd gotten a taste of it when I was little, but when I got older, those hazy memories of love were blotted out by her anger and indifference. She was especially cruel when I was planning to go to college. Sometimes she cursed me with the same dirty words the neighbors used to curse their children, making me suspect that she wasn't my real mother.

Sitting on the bench, I thought I heard my mother let out a heart-wrenching wail, as if she wanted to make it all up to me. Then my mother let go of my hands. I knew this time she was gone forever, nothing more than ash.

6

I had never really believed that my mother would die. Ten years before, a British psychiatrist had asked me if I'd ever watched a loved one die.

I shook my head. He said that he'd first seen his father die and, five years later, his mother. He made it sound as though I had some kind of deficiency. As though, because I'd never experienced the death of a loved one, my life somehow didn't count.

But, I had witnessed strangers dying. During my childhood, when I was only four and a half, I saw a ferry capsize in the river. The passengers' heads bobbed like rubber balls. In the blink of an eye, half of them disappeared. When I was five, I went to struggle sessions held by the two schools on Middle School Street. Red Guards armed with bricks knocked down a schoolteacher. A trace of blood appeared at the corner of his mouth, and then his brain spilled out. That summer, bodies washed ashore every day and were left there to rot, unclaimed. After I grew up, one of my artist friends came down with cancer. I went to see him in the hospital. He clutched my hands tightly as he breathed his last. He'd been harassed for years by the public safety bureau and arrested several times on charges of "sexual indecency" because his paintings were considered politically subversive and showed a lot of nudity.

"Doesn't all that count?" I asked the psychiatrist.

"Yes, but it's different with the death of an immediate family member."

I hadn't agreed with him back then, but now I understood what he meant. When your closest family member dies, parts of your own body die with them. Even the relevant memories die. Who says that memories of family live on forever?

My mother was reduced to a skull and a pile of ashes, which were sent back by the conveyor belt. The cremation and cooling process took one hour. The operator used an iron spatula to crush the skull and then invited the sons and daughters in to pick up the ashes. I looked at the face of the operator and was disgusted by his ugliness. Who gave him the right to hammer like that on my mother's head? How could he disregard the banner hanging above his head that read "Care for the body"? He reminded me of that Red Guard who threw a wooden board at her. The Red Guard militant and the operator were the same—both reckless with the human body. China has too many people, and they're treated worse than things. This disregard for human life has been constant throughout our history.

Neither the operator nor the Red Guard knew that they had crushed not only my mother but also me. I felt confusion and extreme pain. If I could have died in place of my mother, I wouldn't have hesitated. I picked up what remained of my mother's feet before Third Sister-in-Law took away my tongs.

I numbly watched my two brothers and three sisters picking at my mother's bones. More people entered the room: Elder Sister's daughter, Elder Brother-in-Law, Second Brother-in-Law, Fifth Sister-in-Law, Second Cousin's wife, Auntie Mo, my mother's youngest brother. They used iron tongs to transfer my mother's bones into a small iron basket. The operator ushered us out. They poured the ashes from the iron basket onto a piece of silk before rolling up the cloth and placing it into the urn we had chosen, white jade decorated with a pair of fish.

"Care for an urn placement ceremony?" an employee asked.

Elder Sister said, "Is that what people are doing outside? Looks interesting. Sure." She turned to Third Brother, who turned to Third Sister-in-Law and Second Sister.

Fourth Sister gave her vote of approval. Third Brother asked the price and decided it was reasonable.

We followed the employees to the solemn ceremonial hall decorated with blue silk and white flowers. Four young men, apparently selected for their good looks, were waiting at the entrance. In black uniforms, white gloves, black ties, and black shoes, they tied a piece of red brocade around the urn before putting it down on a sideboard.

In the middle of the hall, there was a traditional-style longevity sedan chair. One of the attendants instructed Third Brother first to wash his hands in a basin, and then kneel down in front of the urn, pick it up, and walk to the front of the chair. Third Brother handed the urn to another attendant, who placed it in the center of the chair.

The rest of us clustered by the entrance. Music started and a man walked up. He held a piece of paper in his hands and read a eulogy in standard Mandarin with a heavy Chongqing accent. I remember these sentences:

> All lives have an extraordinary history of their own. Only at the final moment when the loved one bids the world farewell do we realize how precious they are and how unwilling we are to part with them. There is no unjustified birth or death, and there is no regret for the deceased, because we will forever remember them.

The reading lasted just two minutes, but it made the ceremony more like a funeral than Potbellied Cat's circus had. Although the eulogy was universal, each sentence was pitch-perfect. Everybody cried.

They then invited the immediate family into the hall to bow three times to the deceased. The four young men walked in unison like soldiers in a military parade. Carefully, they took down my mother's portrait and handed it to Fifth Brother, the youngest son. With Fifth Brother leading the way, they lifted up the chair, followed by Third Brother and then everyone else. Once they'd descended the steps outside the hall, they placed the sedan poles onto their shoulders. They wore solemn expressions, and the respectful and ceremonial air was further enhanced by the three-person band performing ancient funeral tunes behind them.

They handed the urn to Third Brother, and a man holding a black umbrella escorted him onto the bus.

7

Tang left Fourth Sister behind and followed me into Shouli's car. As soon as he sat down, he said angrily, "Why didn't you ask me to ride with you? I am older than you, and you're still supposed to look after me."

I answered, "Sorry, it was Shouli who invited me."

Elder Sister shouted at me, "Why aren't you riding in the coach with us?"

Second Sister told her, "It's none of your business. Little Sister isn't feeling well. Hurry, get in. We have to get to our father's tomb at Lotus Mountain to tell him about Mother."

Elder Sister boarded unhappily, muttering under her breath.

The unpaved road leading out of the crematorium was significantly narrowed by the cars parked on both sides, and several rickshaws made things even more congested. Once we'd reached the main road, though, the ride to Lotus Mountain didn't take long. The cemetery office confirmed that my father's tomb was a double and registered my mother's urn in the same space.

My brain was still numb, and trying to think hurt. I didn't remember to hug my mother's urn one last time or say anything to her. I mechanically followed my siblings and simply mimicked whatever they were doing.

My father's tomb was on the left side of Lotus Mountain Cemetery, halfway up the hill. He had passed away on June 15, 1999, but his ashes hadn't been properly buried until October 21 due to disagreements between my mother and siblings about his tomb site. My father's nephew from Zhejiang wanted to take the ashes, arguing that my father had always wanted to go back to his hometown. Fifth Brother, despite his reluctance to express an opinion, pointed out how prohibitive that would make it to visit Father's tomb during the Qingming Festival. My mother was more vehement in her objection, but she didn't say a word about sharing a tomb with my father. That made the whole family furious. Elder Sister was her typical blunt self, asking my mother if she wanted to share her tomb with another man. My mother answered that she just wanted to be alone. Maybe scattering the ashes in the Yangtze River was a solution? But after several days, she gave in and said, "Fine, let's get a double tomb so that your father won't be lonely. He's already so far away from his home."

Having heard good things about Lotus Mountain Cemetery on Southern Mountain, my mother went with my siblings to visit the site. She was impressed.

Elder Sister and Second Sister returned on their own and picked a spot near the top of the mountain overlooking the Yangtze River. From there, my father's soul could drift downstream all the way to his hometown. The cemetery watchman complimented their choice, saying, "This site will bring prosperity to the daughters of the deceased."

"Does that mean the sons won't prosper?" Second Sister asked.

"Well, it's good for you!" the watchman responded.

"No, no." Elder Sister was displeased. "Our family also has two sons who need prosperity as well."

The watchman said, "You daughters are not selfish and should be rewarded." He helped them choose a space halfway up the hill that still faced the river, a location deemed good for both sons and daughters. Finally, they settled on an auspicious date, and I flew back to Chongqing for the burial ceremony.

The morning of the ceremony, we hired the same watchman to be our ceremony leader. He began by saying that humans have lingering qi even after death and that the qi circulates underground to impact the surviving descendants. Everything he said after that was unintelligible. After a two-minute monologue, he magically produced a rooster from behind his back, plucked its neck feathers, used a knife to slit its throat, and spilled its blood as a sacrifice to the soul, all the while chanting incantations. Then he set the dying rooster in front of the tomb. The rooster made a last attempt to flap its wings and died to the north of the tomb. That meant that the descendants who lived to the north of the tomb would be prosperous. The ceremony leader cleaned away the feathers and picked the bird up to let the blood drip all around the tomb to ward off evil spirits.

Before lowering my father's urn, he asked Third Brother to place into the tomb a basket containing the five cereals, which was topped with a small pancake. Then we each threw in a handful of earth. We turned around, facing away from the tomb, while the ceremony leader sealed it. He then instructed us to stretch out our clothes to catch the rice he threw at us. Whoever caught the largest amount of rice would be bestowed the largest fortune by our father. I happened to be the lucky one, which triggered my sisters' protests at our father's favoritism. Before departing, we had to circle the tomb three times, and we were admonished not to look back as we walked away. If we looked back, we would have spied on the journey of the soul to the underworld, and that would have been profoundly inauspicious to both the deceased and the living.

When we returned to my mother's house, the first thing we did was to wash our hands and rub them with alcohol. According to the ceremony leader, that would prevent our family from suffering another untimely death. We also followed the traditional practice from my father's hometown of drinking longevity soup and eating longevity beans. The soup was regular pork bone soup, and the beans ordinary soybeans, but they represented happiness and long life.

The banyan tree planted that year had now grown to be three feet tall, sheltering the tomb like an umbrella. The tomb was nestled against the peaks of Southern Mountain, boasting a spectacular view. Over the previous couple of years, two storms had struck, triggering landslides that destroyed a lot of the nearby tombs. Only my father's was untouched. Even the cemetery workers were amazed, believing that this tomb indeed had great feng shui and was blessed by the immortals.

Before my mother's cremation, we had prepared some wine and fruit, and on the way up, we'd bought incense, fake money, and paper houses from vendors, as well as several bunches of chrysanthemums. In order to keep the air fresh, the cemetery did not allow firecrackers.

Everyone burned incense in front of the tomb. Elder Sister cried and knelt down to report to our father, "Father, Ma is here. We have temporarily left her urn with the cemetery administration. As soon as next week, or maybe in a few months—no later than next year's Qingming Festival—Ma will be reunited with you here. But you should feel free to go see her at night."

I also knelt down, lit three incense sticks, and held them up in the air. The wind rustled the leaves, as if my father was speaking to me from the tomb, saying, "Little Six, your mother was too lonely. So I had to take her with me."

My eyes were brimming with tears.

I remembered my father telling me before he passed away, "Little Six, my child, don't give your money to the others. They are not fair to you and your mother. You should take care of yourself."

My father had been warning me. At this memory, the pain in my head eased. The *Analects* of Confucius says, "When your father is alive, observe his will. When your father is deceased, observe his former actions."

My father had been hardworking and thrifty, and he'd treated people with generosity and tolerance throughout his life. He'd treated me and the men in my mother's life that way too. What about my biological father? He was a good man in his own right.

My father's tomb had plenty of regular visitors. His children and grandchildren came to burn incense and fake money. But what about my biological father's tomb? Ever since it was built, I had never been back. I had never dreamt of him, except once.

In the dream, I'd heard strange noises outside my door and hurried to get up and open it. But there was no one in the hallway. Suddenly, an old man appeared, looking as startled to see me as I was to see him. I tried to close the door, but it was almost impossible. When I finally got back inside, it struck me that the man resembled my biological father, except much older. There was something in my hand. I switched on the light and took a look. It was a piece of paper with my biological father's address at a plastics factory. I took a long bus ride, probably as long as a day and a night. The sky was pitch-black when I finally got there. I didn't need to ask anyone for directions, just walked straight to my biological father's room in the factory dormitory. I pushed open the door, but he wasn't there, so I waited on his bed. He came in, blanching at the sight of me. But in an instant, he turned cheerful. "You must be Little Six. No place to go, right? Thank you for coming to see me." He offered me the bed. I was exhausted and immediately fell asleep. In the morning, before the rooster crowed, I opened my eyes and saw him making egg noodles on a kerosene burner. He placed the noodles on a small table, and in his hand were several bamboo twigs. He told me to turn around. I lay on my stomach. His bamboo twigs whipped my back and legs, causing excruciating pain. I was surprised that, instead of crying, my heart was filled with joy and happiness. After he was done with the beating, he threw down the twigs, rubbed his hands, and said, "You don't owe me anything anymore. My dear daughter, hurry up and eat your noodles. Then leave here as fast as possible. This is not the place for you."

I quickly ate the noodles, walked to my biological father, and hugged him tightly, saying, "Father, forgive me."

Then I turned around and walked out the door, down a stretch of dark road, and back into the human world. The sun was rising over the horizon, shining warmly on me.

In my dream, I had attained reconciliation with my biological father. The beating had been punishment for how unfairly I had treated him and my mother. When he was alive, I'd never called him "Father." But in the dream, I'd walked into his arms. On that long bus ride, the cityscape and the clothing I saw wasn't from the '90s, but the '80s, my decade of drifting. And when he beat me, I'd been five or six years old again, then twelve or thirteen, when I was at my most mischievous and defiant.

My biological father and my father had one thing in common—neither had ever talked to me about my marriage. They must have believed that my mother would give me proper guidance. But she'd given up when she realized that I was far more rebellious than her other children. She did not discipline me according to her principles because she knew I would not succumb to fate the way she had.

Standing at my father's grave, I saw my ex-husband's name on the tombstone. His name was also next to mine on my mother's funeral wreath. The jarring image felt like a thorn stuck in my chest. What would my father have thought of this person? And how would my biological father have looked on him? The wreath would be disposed of soon, and maybe I should tell Third Brother to have the name on the stone erased by the mason. A blank space would be better.

On the way down the mountain, though, I had second thoughts. Was it really necessary? My husband's name was part of the family history. Would it be childish if I tried to have that part of history erased?

8

By custom, the funeral procession was supposed to change the white mourning flags to red flags after cremation or burial. The family members were also supposed to take off their mourning clothes and put on red hair bands. But the tradition was no longer strictly followed. What we had worn for the funeral procession was the same attire we wore on our way back home. Fifth Brother was in the front, holding my mother's portrait, followed by Third Brother and Third Sister-in-Law, and then everyone else. Since it was considered inauspicious to return via the same route we'd taken up to the tomb, Fifth Brother chose a winding road to go downhill.

When we got back to Alley Cat Stream, Little Brother Jiang was waiting at the top of the hill, offering to host the homecoming banquet at his hot pot restaurant.

Little Brother Jiang used to live by the ditch behind the middle school. His father also came from downstream and was first mate on my father's boat. When the reform era started, Little Brother Jiang became the first person in the neighborhood to open his own business. His hot pot restaurant quickly became a chain, and he accumulated a considerable fortune.

Second Sister muttered that Little Brother Jiang shouldn't try to cash in on our funeral. Still, it was hard to say no to an old neighbor, and Third Brother and Second Sister accepted.

Little Brother Jiang was all smiles when he saw me. He came over to shake my hand. "Little Six, I am so pleased to see you. Later, I will have to ask you to autograph a book for me. I really have to thank you for writing about our South Bank neighborhood. When you have time, I'd like to tell you about my life so you can write about people like me. I came to this side of the river today just for your mother's funeral. If you have the banquet at my place, I guarantee you will be satisfied."

He told the waiters to brew the best tea and to arrange the tables for a big group. The restaurant wasn't very big, but it was clean. The hot pot stoves were already lit. The walls were tastefully decorated with black-and-white photos of the old city gates of Chongqing.

I ducked out to go to the bathroom, and when I headed back, Tang was waiting for me in the hallway.

"You know I can't eat spicy food," he complained. "And I have to leave this afternoon."

"Fine. I'll take you to a different restaurant," I said.

I let Third Brother and Fourth Sister know we were leaving. This time, Fourth Sister didn't insist on going with us.

We left the hot pot restaurant and walked for a few minutes. We passed several noodle shops, but he rejected all of them. We continued to walk until we saw a decent-looking restaurant across the street and went in. From the windows, we could see the bus stop at Stone Bridge Square. Next to it were apartment buildings, airing out laundry of all colors.

Tang handed me the menu. "You order for us. You know what I like."

Almost all the dishes on the menu were spicy—spicy cabbage, spicy cucumber, spicy string beans, and of course, the pork, fish, and tofu dishes would be even spicier. But I knew the pickled dishes would be safe. So I ordered a dish of marinated sliced beef with dried tofu skin, a clear pea soup, and stir-fried pork with tomato. I asked the waitress not to put in any chili peppers or MSG.

After the waitress walked away, Tang said, "I don't hate Sichuan food, but I can't stand when it's superspicy or when it seems like someone just dumped in a whole container of salt. Sichuan natives have such a penchant for strong flavors that they don't seem to care how unhealthy it is."

"You know my family's not a typical Sichuan family," I replied. "Sure, my mother loved spice and tongue-numbing flower peppers. But my father was from the south, and he preferred plain-tasting, fresh food. That's why our family always made every dish both ways."

The restaurant was quiet, so our food came out in no time. Tang ordered a Coca-Cola, and I had a pot of chrysanthemum tea with rock sugar.

After eating for a while, Tang said that he had wanted to come for the funeral, but he was glad for the chance to see me and to sit down for a quiet meal together.

I said, "I appreciate your thoughtfulness in coming to Chongqing to bid my mother farewell and help with the new apartment. I won't forget this."

"Why are you suddenly so polite?" he asked.

"I've always been polite! You've just never noticed before."

He sighed and spent several long minutes telling me about the time when Fourth Sister chased him across the Nandu University campus.

I'd heard Fourth Sister's side of the story from Xiaomi, but in Tang's version, he was the victim, while Fourth Sister was a vengeful demon.

"When two women fight, I can't side with either one of them."

"Because they love you."

"It's not because they love me. It's because they're programmed to fight each other. Women! Why are they all so impossible?" he asked, taking a sip of his soda so he wouldn't have to look me in the eye. After we were done eating, he said, he wanted to hurry and get his luggage so he didn't have to see Fourth Sister again.

"You should at least say good-bye," I said.

"Why don't you say it for me? Tell her to give up on me."

"You'd better tell her yourself."

"She listens to you."

"You're wrong about that. My sister is an independent woman. I've been pushing her not to let things get out of control, but she'll do whatever she sees fit."

"Well. I just hope she doesn't try to blackmail me again. I have to live my own life, and she has to live hers. You can call me selfish, but I really only want to live for myself."

His eyes were filled with cold indifference.

"Who wouldn't want to live for themselves?" I asked. "Even Fourth Sister has to care for her own interests." I then proceeded to tell him a story I had read.

A herd of sheep is being chased by hunters to the edge of a cliff. They must either jump off the cliff to their deaths or try to jump over to the opposite mountain. Almost instantly, the sheep pair up, a strong ram taking a lamb or a weak ewe on its back. Each ram uses all its strength to jump out as far as possible. Before the ram falls, the lamb or the ewe jumps off its back to reach the other side. The ram dies, its body disappearing in the abyss below, but the lambs and the ewes escape and survive.

"You're mocking me," he responded angrily. "You can't compare a human to a ram. You hate me as much as she does!"

"No. You misunderstand me. What I meant was that I don't want you to treat Fourth Sister with a cold heart. Without you, she has nothing. You are her life. If you don't want her to die, you should say goodbye to her properly. You came into her life gracefully, and you should depart gracefully too."

He fell silent. I could've said some comforting words, or changed the subject to give Tang an out. But I decided not to budge and countered silence with silence. The air in the restaurant was stuffy, and I asked the waitress to open a window. Beautiful strains of music flew in on the breeze. It was the second movement of Beethoven's Symphony no. 7. The grim reaper was approaching, sickle on his shoulder. People in black were mourning, heads lowered. The trumpets' notes struck deeply into broken hearts, and the rose balsam flowers were scattered on the surface of the ocean-like Three Gorges reservoir.

Once upon a time at my home in London, Tang had played me his whole collection of classical records. That had been before Fourth Sister or anyone else had come along. The wind was gentle and the sun was shining. The streets were filled with the scent of jasmine. Although I was disillusioned and angry, haunted by the traumatic memories of my childhood, I still yearned for love and comfort, for peaceful, small-town life. Time would erase everything in the end.

I looked at Tang, but he averted his eyes and stared angrily at the front door.

"Maybe you're right," he said. "Maybe a better man would say good-bye. But no one is perfect."

9

The waitress handed me the bill for the meal. Embarrassed, Tang said, "I always let you foot the bill. It's not right." He pulled out his wallet.

I was surprised by this sudden change. He was right—I had always paid for everything, and Tang had been comfortable with it for many, many years.

We were walking down the street when my cell phone rang. It was an old friend of mine from school. I hadn't seen her for years, but we'd been in touch sporadically. In fact, I'd been wondering whether she'd heard about my mother's death and if I might see her at the funeral.

"Meihuizi!" I exclaimed. "Are you in Chongqing?"

"No," she said. "I'm sorry. I've been on business in Shanghai. I would have come to your mother's funeral, but"—she paused, then lowered her voice—"listen, is this a good time to talk? Are you alone?"

"I'm with Tang," I said.

"Tang?" Then brushing aside her surprise, she said, "I have something to tell you. When can we talk?"

Puzzled by the urgency in her tone, I turned to Tang.

He said, "I can see when I'm not wanted. I know how to get to your mother's house on my own. I'll let you take care of your business, whatever it is. Good-bye for now."

I told my friend to wait a minute, and stretched out my hand to shake Tang's. He didn't look me in the eye. Maybe he was still upset about what I had said earlier. Watching him walk away, I said to my friend, "Sorry. He came for the funeral. You know how it is . . . old friends."

"Is that what you two are?" She laughed. "Were you really alone together?"

"Yes, we had lunch. Of course, it wasn't a very pleasant meal since neither of us had anything pleasant to say to each other."

"Do you really want pleasant conversations with that man?" She laughed again.

I was embarrassed and upset. Sensing it wasn't a good time to joke around, she changed the topic. "I wanted to ask if you've been approached by a reporter."

"No."

"That's good."

"Wait, I remember now. A reporter wanted to interview me about returning to Chongqing. I declined. Maybe they heard the news about my mother?"

"Look," she said, "I have to tell you something right away in case anything unfortunate happens to me."

I gripped my phone as if it might fly away. "Something unfortunate? What's going on?" If she had something to tell me, I knew it must be important.

10

Meihuizi, a journalist herself, told me that she was friends with the boss of Journalist Y, and knew that Y was a fan of mine and had interviewed my mother.

I suddenly recalled an article in the *Chongqing Information Newspaper* by a reporter who'd come to the South Bank a few months ago to interview my mother. She'd used my memoir to locate many people from my book, including Spectacles Wang.

"I remember," I said, my heart racing. "She put in some nonsense about me having just come back to celebrate my mother's birthday, when I was actually in England."

"Better that than the truth," said Meihuizi solemnly.

"What truth?" I asked.

"That she went to visit your mother, but the neighbors told her that your mother was at the garbage dump."

My heart was pounding even faster. So Auntie Ma was telling the truth. In her heart, Spectacles Wang must have been laughing at me and my mother.

This journalist had been perplexed, Meihuizi said, so she made inquiries with several neighbors—each of whom told her a different version of the story. They said my mother was often hungry because her children didn't allow her to eat lunch. When she was allowed to eat, if she dropped food on the floor, she was ordered to pick it up and eat it anyway. If she tried to pick up fresh food instead, her chopsticks would be knocked away. After each meal, my mother was so hungry that she'd sneak into the kitchen to eat scraps. But she got caught and had her food dumped into the toilet.

They told the journalist that, once, my mother went to the convenience store and Auntie Ma gave her two buns. Fifth Sister-in-Law spent all night chiding my mother for begging and humiliating her.

My mother had responded with one word: "Hungry!"

That had made Fifth Sister-in-Law even more furious. She accused my mother of being a whore when she was young and an ingrate now that she was old. She forced my mother to do her own laundry and cooking and to eat at a separate table. Her excuse was that Mother only wanted to eat congee while she herself preferred solid food.

Another time, my mother found that some money was missing from her wallet. She mentioned it to Fifth Sister-in-Law, who cursed at her, "You useless old bag! You should've given us that money instead of waiting for your grandson to take it himself. This just proves you're no good to anyone!"

My mother had responded, "You have no right to curse me like this. My son has treated you well and so have I."

Fifth Sister-in-Law hurled the cup in her hand at my mother and hit her in the shoulder. My mother warned her not to get violent, but

Fifth Sister-in-Law retorted that she was in charge of the household now. Then she threw a plateful of food. The plate hit my mother in the head, making her scream in pain. Fifth Sister-in-Law threatened her, saying she'd better not go around telling people—and nobody would believe her, anyway.

One neighbor told the reporter that the whole family liked to complain that all their sixth sister was good at was airing dirty laundry and that she couldn't redeem the shame of her birth no matter how many books she wrote.

My mother couldn't take any more—her blood pressure spiked, and she had to be rushed to the hospital. After that, her mind started to go soft. She would chase after anyone on the streets who looked like my biological father and call out his name, Sun.

There was one occasion, a neighbor said, when my mother waited all day at the ferry, telling people that Sun had promised to bring food for her six children. She had to keep waiting, she said, because without the food, the kids would starve to death in the midst of the Great Chinese Famine.

"Have you seen Uncle Sun? I miss him!" My mother asked Second Sister when she came to the ferry to fetch her.

"He's dead!" Second Sister said.

"No," my mother replied, "he can't die. He promised he would wait for me. Sooner or later, we will live together."

As I listened to my friend's voice, so many of the questions and puzzles hidden in my heart began to unravel. I had a vision of my mother walking the way she always did, gingerly, as though she was afraid of stepping on a landmine. Her back was bent and her hair messy, but her eyes were expectant. She was waiting by the Alley Cat Stream ferry, scanning each group of passengers for my biological father. In her mind, he couldn't have died because he would never leave her to suffer alone.

In those days, I learned from Meihuizi, Ma had lived in the past. She would change her clothes over and over, looking at herself in the mirror, not satisfied with what she saw there. She would go frequently to the balcony to see whether he had arrived. She would pick up the telephone and urge him not to be late.

The family would take the telephone away from her. But when there was no one else in the house, she would talk on the phone to him for hours.

My mother's actions, of course, could not be tolerated. She already bore a scarlet letter—me, Little Six—the living proof of her adultery. Yet here she was, making her shame even more public, searching for Sun, talking to everyone about him. The siblings had a meeting and decided to send her to a nursing home, but my mother's mind suddenly became clear. She refused to go and demanded to call her youngest daughter. They were forced to change their plan.

To make it even worse, my mother had nightmares every night. She could be heard crying, "Please, don't go! You're my flesh and blood. Please don't treat your mother like this!" Sometimes she would get up and rearrange sofas and tables to block the door, saying that the Red Guards were coming to arrest them. "Yueyun, hurry and find a place to hide!"

"Poor mother of my godson, don't die on me!" she'd wail, mistaking Fifth Sister-in-Law for Uncle Jian's wife, holding her tightly in her arms with tears streaming down her cheeks.

Most often, my mother would wake up begging for mercy. "Please, I beg you, don't do this! Let him go!" There were also times when no one could make any sense of her incessant screams.

For I don't know how long—months, years?—my poor mother had lived like this.

That's when she started rummaging through garbage dumps. When she saw people she knew, she would turn away or lower her straw hat to block her face.

When my family heard about what she was doing, they rushed to the riverbank, snatched her fishnet sack, and trampled on it.

"You insatiable old hag, haven't we fed you enough? You never listen to us! You're too old to remember anything. Get her out of here!"

"No, don't take me away!" she yelled, scared by the sight of people coming at her. She scrambled backward, stumbling dangerously.

They stopped. My mother looked at the boats on the river and said to herself, "Things are getting more difficult now. There is little cabbage in the river, even rotten ones are hard to find. What should I do?"

"This crazy old lady! She doesn't even know that the famine years are long gone!"

My mother shook her head, bent over to pick up the fishnet bag, and put an empty glass bottle in it.

The stories Meihuizi relayed were as impossible for me to accept as Ma's death. But I understood: her faltering memory had returned to those hard times because she lived once again in extreme loneliness and deprivation. It was only her memory of surviving the dark years that could get her through the day. She'd always been more afraid of hunger than of anything else. During the famine, she was terrified her six children would starve. My father had been gone such a long time. She went to his company to ask when his boat would return to Chongqing, but received no answer. The memory of that uncertainty never stopped haunting her.

Even before the Great Famine began, my grandma had been sent to the hospital in Chongqing for malnutrition. She was too far gone for treatment and soon died. One after another, our relatives in the countryside had also starved to death. My third aunt and her two sons wasted away. When my aunt's husband came to her for help after he was released from prison, she couldn't do anything for him. He died in a public bathroom at Stone Slab Slope not long after. All this was a torment for my mother, who worried herself sick. She gave every morsel of food to her children and soon was little more than skin and bones herself. Eventually, she'd had to take all her children out with her to rummage through the garbage. Seeing how resentful those same children were about her going through the garbage now just as she'd done for them back then, she was baffled and hurt. And when the sun came up the next morning, she'd set out for the dumps along the river once again.

My mother had spent so much of her life with no sense of security. She was full of conflict, and she lived in conflict. When she was young, she was beautiful and easygoing, courageous and intelligent and perceptive, and nothing could change her mind once it was made up. But when she got old, Ma became weak and meek, irrational and antisocial. She would often lock herself up in her room and cry or stare blankly, refusing to talk to anyone.

Living with someone like that for an extended period would try anyone's patience. I could imagine how depressed and frustrated my siblings must have felt. My mother's forgetfulness—whether due to dementia or a deliberate effort to torment them—made her determined not to accept reality. She ran away several times. Once, she went to Elder Sister's house, begging to stay, because, in her words, her home had been taken over by fascists. Elder Sister let her stay there less than a day before kicking her out, fed up with Mother's constant declarations of how much she loved Sun. If she had appealed to Fifth Brother about his wife's treatment, it would only have gotten worse. If she had gone to Second Sister, Second Sister would have accused her of not acting her age and would have refused to help. Third Brother and his wife were out of the question—they'd always made it clear that they did not want to be involved. As for her own younger brother, my uncle, he'd never forgiven her, convinced that her coddling of Elder Sister was to blame for Elder Sister's terrible treatment of his wife and the woman's subsequent death.

My mother eventually fled to Auntie Mo, who took her in with open arms. But my mother hated imposing. She knew Auntie Mo's two daughters-in-law didn't want her to stay long even if they were too respectful to object openly. So she didn't linger. She probably also went to several of her old friends, including Shouli's mother. But she'd always been an independent woman and never wanted to burden anyone. She certainly must have gone to the cemetery at Shapingba and sat in front of the tomb of Uncle Jian's wife. Finally, she'd had no choice but to go back to her children. Fourth Sister was far away in London, and I was in Beijing. The rest couldn't stand her talking about Sun, having horrific nightmares, or picking through garbage.

The last trip she took by herself was to see my father's grave. She cried in front of the tomb, "Old man, you shouldn't have gone away. I am so lonely!" She also tried to find my biological father's burial site. She knew that his wife from the countryside wouldn't have allowed her to visit, but she decided to take a look at his tomb from a distance. She took a bus most of the way, but got lost on a bridge over the Yangtze River. She watched the rapid currents beneath the bridge, pacing back and forth, and finally held on to a rail and started to cry like a child who had been unfairly punished.

A kindhearted street sweeper noticed my mother's distress, and escorted Ma all the way home. The valiant woman even berated everyone in the house for their negligence. They bit their tongues and thanked her for returning the old woman safely, but once the sweeper left, they took out their anger and humiliation on Mother and cursed her in the worst possible way.

After that, my mother never tried to find refuge again. Her spirit was broken. Maybe, when she was standing on that bridge, she'd thought about jumping off and ending everything.

But my mother did not jump. She chose to live on in misery.

According to Meihuizi, Y had been to the garbage dump by the river and had a long, candid talk with my mother. Before she departed, she asked my mother, "Do you know how upset your youngest daughter would be if she knew that you rummage through garbage?"

"Please, please don't tell her," Ma begged. "And please don't take me to the public security bureau. I promise I'll stop." But she immediately had second thoughts, asking plaintively, "But what if I'm hungry again?"

The journalist was going to write about what she witnessed and heard that day. She could easily use this story to satisfy her monthly assignment and gain a hefty bonus. It would be a smash hit. The headline alone would grab everyone's attention: "Elderly Mother of Renowned Writer Picks through Garbage." But on the ferry home, Y kept picturing my mother's eyes, so full of fear, and hearing my mother's trembling tone when she reminisced about the famine years. Y felt a stabbing pain in her heart. When she got off the ferry, she decided not to write anything.

Sometime later, she was passing through the South Bank and wanted to pay my mother a visit. But the house was locked. A neighbor told her that my mother was in the hospital, having fallen down in the garbage dump and hurt herself.

After answering all my questions and breaking my heart, Meihuizi paused a moment, then asked if I wanted Y's number.

I couldn't say a word.

She said, "I can only imagine what you must be thinking right now. I was so reluctant to tell you all this. It feels like rubbing salt into your wound. Fortunately, your mother has passed on now. Her tormented soul is finally free."

I looked around and saw trees, mostly white figs. The mountains were hiding behind tall buildings, and clouds were hiding behind the mountains. The sky was unusually gloomy, the air full of dust. People were walking along the street and standing against walls plastered with ads.

No wonder Auntie Mo had said, "My dear sister, you have died an unjust and pathetic death!"

Across time and history, everything was clear to me now, leaving permanent imprints in my brain. It didn't matter how much of what she'd told me was precisely true. What was important was that it confirmed everything I'd pieced together these past three days in Chongqing. My mother's last years were nothing like what I'd been led to believe.

I don't remember how I ended the conversation with Meihuizi. I found myself standing in the middle of the street, clutching my phone and gasping for air. After about two minutes, I felt slightly better. I watched people coming out of stores—schoolchildren with backpacks, a mother and daughter walking hand in hand, peddlers hawking pickled vegetables.

I seemed to have come out of the trance I had been in since my mother's cremation.

All right, now, let me start over and tidy up my thoughts.

When my mother was injured from her fall off the garbage heap, I was in hiding at the old hotel in northern Italy, writing my tale of old Shanghai. I got the e-mail from Second Sister's son saying Ma wasn't eating, so I called. She promised me that she would eat and said she had things she needed to tell me.

I'm still here, but my mother is no longer with me.

Before I turned eighteen, I had been the only one who didn't know the truth about my own birth. Now, when it came to my mother's last years, I was still the only one who'd been kept in the dark. My anger toward the others was far less intense than the abhorrence and disgust I felt for myself. I had the urge to slit my own throat.

CHAPTER 11

I

I pressed onward, paying no attention to the time. I began to notice how different the streets were from what I remembered, especially the side street connecting Slingshot Boulder and Middle School Street. It wasn't just that there were more houses and existing buildings had sprouted extra stories. In fact, some places hadn't changed in more than forty years. But it was as if everything had slightly shifted or twisted in shape—it all looked very slightly unreal. I searched for the sites deeply ingrained in my memory. The public toilets were where they'd always been, as were the two big ponds, and the air-raid shelters. Garbage still covered every hill, and dirty water flowed in all directions. The shoulder-pole carriers, ropes in hand and wearing tattered clothes, still craned their necks looking for someone to hire them. The walls were covered with ads touting cures for gonorrhea, syphilis, and genital warts.

In just an hour, it felt like I'd passed through several centuries, but even aswim in unreality, some facts remained clear.

My mother had been cremated. The funeral had come to an end. My siblings were treating our neighbors, friends, and family to end-of-funeral hot pot. Everyone must still be there, soaking beef tripe, pork kidney, and bean sprouts in the spicy soup, gossiping for hours about the past, present, and future. But Tang had left. Perhaps I could still catch up with him to say a proper good-bye.

I walked toward my mother's home.

The courtyard inside Compound No. 6 had already been cleared—by Potbellied Cat's employees, I presumed. The tents were all taken down, the ground free of debris from firecrackers. All of the funeral decorations were gone: the eulogies pasted on the wall, the giant wreath facing the entrance, all the yellow and white flowers. They'd either been burned or carted off to be reused by the next family.

In fact, the place was so thoroughly clean that no one would have been able to tell a funeral had just taken place. It was more accurate to say everything was back to normal. It was as if nothing had changed since my last visit. And if that were true, my mother would still be waiting for me on the fifth floor. As soon as I climbed the stairs, stepped through the door on the left, and called out "Ma," I would hear her respond, would see her right in front of me. Maybe I had made everything else up. Maybe it had all been a dream. However, this dream had lasted longer than any other—three days and three nights. No, more actually. I had been dreaming for forty-three years. I had been dreaming since the moment I was born.

I went up to the fifth floor and pushed open the apartment door. I actually called out, "Ma," but no one answered.

It wasn't a dream after all. My mother was really gone, burned to ashes and sent to another world.

Tang wasn't there either. The apartment seemed empty. But when I pushed open the kitchen door, I saw a girl with a round face busily sorting out meat and vegetables from the market.

"Where are my sisters?" I asked.

She did not respond. Perhaps she was mute.

These people could linger around the hot pot for the length of time it took the Yangtze River to flow from the dry season to the high-water season. Well, that was no surprise. But pouring myself a cup of tea, I was hit by a thought that made me jump to my feet.

Impossible!

My mind tried to reject the idea, but it had too fiercely taken control of my senses. I immediately put down the teacup and ran out of the apartment.

The air-raid shelter where Xiaomi and I had talked the day before was completely empty, so I searched another. When I was little, I was so afraid of being raped and killed in one of these places. Even now, I had to force from my mind the tragic images of young girls' corpses lying here. Back then, the shelters had seemed menacing, with high ceilings, and as deep as they were long, like devil's caves. Now they still felt gloomy and damp, but the ceilings no longer seemed high nor the rooms particularly long or deep.

I walked out of the second shelter, tired out. Maybe I had been wrong?

The cacophonous honking of riverboats and cars made me even more agitated. I walked up to the edge of a cliff, and looked out at Turtle Rock, a small island in the middle of the river, about 300 feet south of where the Yangtze and Jialing Rivers merged. During the dry season, you could walk all the way there, but during the rainy season, it would peep above the water like the crown of a hat. Sailors not familiar with the treacherous water would often capsize their vessels on the boulder.

The Yangtze had been at its seasonal peak only two months before, so it should have been deep and wide with impressive waves. But the water level was unusually low, leaving Chongqing with a water shortage that affected both people and livestock. That summer, Chongqing and many other cities along the Yangtze had record-breaking high temperatures, making this the worst drought since 1949, when Communist rule began. People were saying that the unusually low water level and high heat were related to the Three Gorges Dam.

This month, the water level had risen a little, but the top of Turtle Rock was still exposed. I saw children were playing on it. They were trying to catch the small fish trapped in tide pools and collecting pretty pebbles.

There was smoke from a small fire down below on the beach and some people standing around it. They looked distinctly familiar.

I took a shortcut across South Bank Road and headed down to the beach. The people were indeed my sisters and sisters-in-law, squatting around the bonfire, burning some of my mother's things, including her bedding and her shit-soiled clothes, as well as the junk she'd piled up on her balcony.

"There you are." Elder Sister turned her head and spotted me. I was so mad that I didn't acknowledge her.

Her head lowered, Fourth Sister just kept throwing things into the flames. Xiaomi and several other young women were helping.

"Are you deaf?" Elder Sister snapped.

Had they deliberately excluded me from the traditional burning of my mother's clothing and wreaths? I wanted to confront them with everything I'd learned, tell them I knew how they'd neglected and abused Ma—and lied to me through their teeth. But before I could say any of this, I realized there was something fishy going on. Elder Sister aside, no one was paying any attention to me. Their minds must have been elsewhere. Of course! My earlier intuition had been right! Fourth Sister got up, averting her eyes. I charged toward her and grabbed one of her arms.

"Don't you walk away from me! What have you done to Tang?"

2

Human beings are strange creatures. When cornered, we turn into wild beasts. My pupils must have been unnaturally dilated, and my words were deadly. But Fourth Sister's reply was strangely calm.

"Yes, I did what I've wanted to do all along. Now I am finally satisfied."

I wanted to slap her hard, but clenched my fists instead. "He was my husband first. You had no right to harm him."

Fourth Sister was stunned by my words, by the fact that I'd finally spoken the truth out loud in front of everyone. She stood there, frozen. The others all stood up and looked at me strangely. I spat the words out one by one, "I have been so gracious about your relationship all these years, but now? How could you do such a terrible thing! None of you has any idea how disappointed I am in you. I despise being your sister!"

They looked at each other, unable to utter a word. I turned and stalked off.

I climbed up to South Bank Road, crossed the street, and continued to walk up the steep and winding stone steps.

A voice called from behind, but I ignored it.

The wall of the old grain depot was covered with weeds. Next to it was a path made by innumerable footprints. Stumbling forward, I could hear the panting of the person chasing me. She pleaded, "Little Six, please, listen to me. Don't make me chase you anymore. I'm going to have a heart attack."

Fourth Sister and I stood by the edge of the path, just a couple paces from the cliff's edge. The short chase seemed to have aged her. She looked helpless and pathetic. I wanted to say something to her, but couldn't.

Fourth Sister started to tell me what had happened. Tang had gone to get his luggage. Just as he was headed down to South Bank Road to hail a taxi, Fourth Sister intercepted him. She said she wanted to give him a farewell kiss to show that they were parting ways peaceably.

Tang was surprised by Fourth Sister's kind gesture. She waved him closer and, as he approached, he was struck on his head from behind and lost consciousness. When he came to, he found himself sitting on the ground of a dark air-raid shelter, his back against the slimy wall, his hands and feet bound. He was surrounded by women, and some men guarded the entrance.

"What are you going to do to me?" His voice cracked, revealing his distress.

"Sulfuric acid or rat poison—your choice," Fourth Sister said.

"You . . . you! Don't be crazy! Are you out of your fucking mind?"

"I went crazy long ago. I told you that if I couldn't have you, no one could!"

"Let me go!"

"Even if I wanted to, my family wouldn't let me."

Elder Sister cut in. "Shall we gouge out this Don Juan's eyeballs first or cut off his penis? He's hurt enough women—and in the same family! Bet you didn't imagine our revenge would look like this, huh?"

"You are breaking the law!" Tang howled.

Second Sister retorted, "Breaking the law? Look who's talking. When have you ever respected the law, you polygamist?"

"If you want to get out of here alive, you'd better swear not to go back to that woman." Fourth Sister paused briefly before continuing, "or else kneel down to beg my forgiveness. If I decide to grant it, you can leave."

Tang's courage suddenly came back. "Go ahead, I dare you! I'm not afraid. If your mother were still alive, she would never have allowed you to treat me like this."

"If my mother knew the terrible things you did to us sisters, she would never have forgiven you. She would've told us to chop you up into tiny pieces and feed them to the fish in the river."

"I was an idiot to come to Chongqing. You must have been planning your revenge for a long time. Fine, then. If you untie me now, I won't move a step away from here. I am a gentleman and a man of my word. Go ahead. Kill me or hurt me. I am all yours! But you shouldn't insult me by tying me up like this." He looked straight into Fourth Sister's eyes. "Untie me! This way both of us will have some dignity."

My sisters looked at him and then exchanged looks among themselves before untying him. The ropes dropped to the ground next to a black plastic bag, a container of gasoline, a bottle of sulfuric acid, a bag of rat poison, and a butcher knife. Tang grabbed the knife and yelled, "Don't come any closer!"

"The dirty liar! Let's cut off his limbs!" Elder Sister wielded a staff and yelled, "Think I can't knock that knife from your hand?"

Tang backed up against the wall, sweat dripping off his face. "I always do what I say. Here, I'll do it for you!" He turned around, pressing his left pinkie finger against the wall and swinging the knife.

Fourth Sister paused.

I gasped. "Then?"

"Don't worry, Little Six. We let him go."

Then she told me that if Tang had just been scared, the plan was to give him a beating to teach him a lesson. They'd even hired people to do it right—but Fourth Sister had turned them away the previous night at Second Sister's place. If, however, Tang had groveled and lied, showing that he was a worm rather than a regular coward, then they really would have cut off his penis so he could never mess with women again. As it turned out, he had proven to be tougher than anyone expected, and that had impressed her. After he cut off his finger, she'd let him go. The other sisters were annoyed they hadn't gotten to follow through with the original plan, and they took their disappointment out on Fourth Sister, who simply replied that she appreciated their help, but she could handle things on her own from now on.

I thanked the heavens and the earth: the Chinese Don Juan had not been fed to the Dragon King! I took out my cell phone and called his number. An automated voice replied, "The phone number you have dialed is out of service."

I looked at Fourth Sister with suspicion. "Are you sure you're not lying to me?"

"I don't care whether you believe me or not."

"Did he really lose a finger?"

"Oh, who cares about his stupid finger?" Fourth Sister said cruelly. "He gets to run off and live his happy life without me. Losing a little finger won't change anything. At worst, it'll be a minor nuisance when he wants to put on his new wedding ring."

Then Fourth Sister softened and said, "Forget him. It's all over. It's just family now. Come, Little Six. Let's go home and make dinner together in honor of Ma."

She grabbed my hand, and my tears gushed out without warning. It had been a long time since Fourth Sister had been so warm toward me. She had always treated me as her garbage dump, a place to pour out her complaints. Rarely had she acted like an older sister.

She handed me a handkerchief to dry my tears.

Then she led the way, and I trailed behind. The weeds on the path were tall enough to rub against our knees. Grasshoppers jumped occasionally. I looked toward Chaotianmen Dock, crowded with ferries. Tang, who had for so long come between Fourth Sister and me, must have already been on his way back to London.

At that moment, whether Fourth Sister had spoken the truth or not (I didn't believe he'd really lost a finger), the incident seemed absurd and almost funny. My sisters, after all, had set him free. When all was said and done, their violence was only verbal. Our parents had never done anyone physical harm, and neither would their children.

Stormy seas, no matter how big they were, would eventually calm. I felt that my moment of tranquility had at long last arrived. The man who had hurt me so badly and for so many years was suddenly and finally fading into the distance.

3

Xiaomi came in to tell us she was leaving. Two friends were waiting for her outside in the hallway. Elder Sister waved at them.

Xiaomi whispered in my ear, "Sixth Auntie, don't forget to find me that foreign boyfriend like you promised."

I nodded.

Third Brother and Fifth Brother returned from the dock, where they'd been seeing off some of our relatives.

"Auntie Mo asked that you to stop to visit her when you're free," Fifth Brother told me.

Third Brother let out a sigh, "Those old people. I tried to get them to stay for dinner, but they all insisted on leaving. At least they said they'd visit our parents' graves next Qingming Festival. One person got up to go, so they all followed. Anyway, I am really tired. I'm going to go take a nap."

By the time we four daughters had gathered in our mother's bedroom, it had begun to drizzle outside. I put mother's portrait on the top of the old dresser. Elder Sister made a proposal. "Since we're never all together like this, why don't we sort out the treasure in Mother's trunks?"

Third Sister-in-law and Fifth Sister-in-law heard her from the living room and eagerly agreed.

My mother had three old-fashioned trunks covered with a piece of red cloth. They'd always been off-limits. Only one member of the family had ever broken into them before.

Elder Sister said, "Wow. Finally I can justify opening Mother's trunks. I've waited so long that now I'm a grandma myself."

This was so close to an admission of guilt that everyone burst into laughter.

Third Brother produced Mother's big bunch of keys. I recognized the traditional-style, bronze key to our old house and the cute little key to the old attic. My mother had kept them long after the building had been demolished.

Elder Sister snatched the keys from him, but the locks were all from the 1950s and were rusted shut. Fifth Brother got some lubricant, and Elder Sister, after trying a few keys, managed to pry the trunks open. The first one contained scraps of fabric redolent of mothballs and an old scarf of my father's that Mother had knitted herself. Elder Sister opened the second trunk and found more cloth, some old family photos, several bedsheets, some red Mao badges, and a red hardcover notebook wrapped in a towel. The contents of the third trunk were much the same—fabric, pillowcases, and silk duvet covers.

The pieces of fabric were all different sizes, including whole uncut sections as well as small scraps big enough only for making baby clothes. All of them had beautiful floral patterns, most with green or blue backgrounds. These pieces of fabric were evidence of my mother's resourcefulness, as well as her impeccable taste. They were cheap but beautiful. For years, she had used pieces like these to make clothes for her grandchildren, often working well into the night. My nieces and nephews were often approached by people wanting to know where they could buy such charming floral-patterned outfits. Of course, garments like that weren't sold anywhere. Those patterns and colors used to be condemned as feudalist, capitalist, or revisionist, but my mother couldn't have cared less. She continued to dress her grandchildren in beautiful homemade clothes.

Elder Sister piled all the fabric pieces on the bed. She was most interested in the silk duvet covers. Having counted them, she concluded, "Enough for everyone!"

The pillowcases were hand sewn, with patterns ranging from the Tiananmen gate and Mao's red sun to plum blossoms and auspicious magpies. Second Sister confessed that she was the one who had sewn all the pillowcases. Elder Sister didn't believe her. "How come I never heard about that?"

Second Sister explained that her school roommate was obsessed with sewing, and she'd taught Second Sister quite a bit. Second Sister made a lot of pillowcases, intending to give them to Ma. However, she had a falling-out with Ma, so in anger, she hid the pillowcases in her dorm room. The two didn't talk to each other for two or three years. When Second Sister got married, she finally made up with Ma and gave her the pillowcases. Ma treasured them so much that she never actually used them.

Fourth Sister browsed through the red notebook before handing it to me. She knew I had been looking for this notebook, since it was a present from my biological father to my mother. I eagerly opened it, only to find that it was full of household info such as income and expenses or doctors' visits. Some of the characters were written incorrectly, but Ma was obviously a meticulous bookkeeper. The records grew less frequent in the late 1970s, and there were none for the 1980s, after she retired. Most of the pages in the second half had been torn out.

"Can I keep this?"

All three of my sisters replied in unison, "Of course."

I put the notebook into my bag.

Second Sister asked for the leftover pieces of cloth. She could use them to sew a patchwork quilt for her future grandchildren. The large pieces went to Elder Sister and Third Brother. Fifth Brother asked for the pillowcases, and Third Sister-in-Law wanted a few as well.

The old family photos were all laid out on the bed. Some were pictures of my mother and father. Only one featured the entire family after the Cultural Revolution. I was only five then, a skinny little girl hiding in a corner of the photo, barely visible. Several photos dated from before 1949, with my mother wearing a cheongsam and men's leather shoes that looked fashionable even today. One photo showed my youngest uncle and two of my cousins, looking incredibly young and handsome. In front of them stood my parents, with Fifth Brother, still a baby, in my mother's arms, and my three older sisters in braids and their best clothes, all grinning from ear to ear. I hadn't been born yet. The family looked poor, but happy.

There was also a photo of my father on a boat with his crew. He was wearing his uniform, and his eyes were sharp and bright. There was even a picture of my biological father, flanked by two boys. How had my mother gotten her hands on it? Most of the photos were of my mother's grandchildren. One showed Tiantian, not even two years old, standing in front of Compound No. 6 and looking up at a girl in red. That girl was me.

But looking again, I realized it wasn't—it was Fourth Sister. She looked very much like me when she was younger, especially from the side.

There were almost no photos from after I moved away, but back when the foreign television station followed me home, the director took several pictures of me with my mother. None of them turned out—one of us was always blinking. They did get one shot with the entire family. In it, my father squats in front of the door, as if he were still on a boat. My mother is smiling, and so is Elder Sister. Second Sister shows no emotion, but Fourth Sister is laughing and looking extremely fat. It must have been taken right after she caught her second husband sleeping with his employee. She dealt with her frustration through excessive eating.

Another photo is of Xiaomi, in a wedding dress with her groom. Xiaomi looks beautiful in the photo, and the scar on her face is well disguised by the makeup. The groom looks mature and charming and appears to be a responsible man. So Xiaomi hadn't lied after all. They did get married. The man was the one who'd lied. Maybe, I thought to myself, I should publish this photo in the Hong Kong newspapers so that Xiaomi could locate her son's father.

One photo had the date printed in the corner: March 31, 1996. I'm in the middle, leaning against my mother, and we're surrounded by many of our friends and relatives, though Uncle Jian is notably absent. It was my mother's birthday, and Shouli's mother, whose birthday was five days later, decided they should celebrate together. I flew back, unaccompanied by my husband, booked the restaurant inside Loquat Hill Park, and invited all of our relatives. My mother and Shouli's mother each hold a bouquet of flowers.

That day, a relative told me that once, when I was little, my mother had taken me to visit them and I'd wandered off by myself. My mother was beside herself and searched all over. Soon, everybody was combing the streets. Eventually, my mother found me sitting on the steps of the movie theater, studying the passersby. She grabbed me by my shoulders and shook me, yelling, "Go ahead! Run away! Run to a place where I can never find you!"

I was terrified and began to cry. "Ma, you're hurting me!"

She stopped. Seeing that my shoulders had turned red, she apologized with tears in her eyes. "I'm so sorry, Little Six. Ma didn't mean to hurt you."

I realized that none of my pictures from cities around the world were here. Whenever I traveled to a new place, I would send a photo to my mother. Sometimes, if I didn't have enough time to have the photos developed, I would just send her a picture postcard. Later, I e-mailed my pictures to my niece and nephews, but they couldn't be bothered to have them printed or take them to my mother's house, so I'd had to go back to sending pictures to her myself. Where did my mother put all those pictures and postcards?

Fourth Sister suddenly called everyone's attention to the fact that many of the photos were duplicates. There were, in fact, six sets of each.

I was shocked. Elder Sister said, "How considerate Ma was! If she had been rich, she would have left each of us a pile of gold!"

Second Sister said, "To give us photos is better than giving us money. Photos can be kept by generations to come so that the good times we have had together will be forever remembered."

4

Third Brother walked in. Sitting on the old wicker chair, he summarized the credits and debits of the past three days. "We received a large amount of red-envelope money for the funeral, so we won't need Sixth Sister's money."

Second Sister sighed in relief. She had been worried the funeral expenses would be more than we could afford. Third Brother cleared his throat before he continued, "There is a little over two thousand yuan left. What should we do with it?"

Second Sister thought before responding. "Let's give it to Fifth Sister-in-Law, who took care of Ma in her last years. She's more patient and loving than any of Mother's real daughters."

Fourth Sister seconded the proposal. "Yes, let Fifth Sister-in-Law use the money to buy herself a piece of jewelry."

Third Brother and Third Sister-in-Law said nothing. Fifth Sister-in-Law just beamed, but Fifth Brother nudged her before saying, "No, no, we can't accept it."

I thought back to everything I'd learned from my journalist friend, all the lies unmasked. I'd missed my chance to confront them with it at the bonfire, and now wasn't the right moment—besides, Fifth Sister-in-Law was far from the only one at fault. "Sure. That sounds like a good idea."

Hearing my words, Elder Sister jumped to her feet. "How can we give the money to this piece of shit? I wasn't going to say anything, but do you know how many times Ma came to me and complained about

Fifth Sister-in-Law's abuse? She wanted to come and live with me, she was being treated so badly. Ma died because of this selfish vixen."

Fifth Sister-in-Law's face turned white. "Elder Sister, stop your venomous slander!"

"You went to Stone Bridge Dance Hall every day for your own cheap pleasure, and so you could flirt with good-for-nothing men. You barely even fed Ma—a sick, helpless old woman! You thought I didn't know? I saw everything with my own eyes. Give you money? I'm not giving you shit!"

Fifth Sister-in-Law grabbed Fifth Brother by his shirt. "How can you sit there and let your family bully me?"

Fifth Brother pushed her away and walked out. Fifth Sister-in-Law was so upset that she collapsed into the old wicker chair.

Elder Sister continued, "You piece of garbage! Don't you dare treat Fifth Brother this way! Have you forgotten how you were abducted to Henan to become another man's wife? And don't you remember how we welcomed you back with open arms?"

I tried to intervene. "Elder Sister, Ma told us not to mention that. You are in the wrong here."

Elder Sister pointed her finger at me. "You have no right to criticize me. So what if you're a writer? Big deal! All it takes is a pen and some paper. I never wrote because I didn't want to. Today, I'm spilling out everything that has been boiling inside me."

"No, today is not the right day for it!"

Third Sister-in-Law said, "Sixth Sister is right!"

Second Sister stood up. "It's settled. Third Brother, go ahead and give the money to Fifth Sister-in-Law."

As Third Brother handed the red envelope to Fifth Sister-in-Law, Elder Sister let out a blood-curdling scream. "Ma, can't you see? All of them are ganging up on me. No matter how I cry out for you, you won't respond. You never cared for me, dead or alive!" Her crying turned into bawling. "And my poor son, little Color TV, you've also died on me!"

Everyone in the room was stunned. They all thought that Elder Sister had lost her mind, but then she began to tell the story. Although her narration was frequently interrupted by her sobbing, everyone got the gist.

Her previous husband, a miner, wouldn't agree to a divorce unless she gave him sole custody of their son, who was less than a year old. He was named "Color TV" because she hadn't received government approval for the birth, so the Family Planning Office at the mine fined them the equivalent of a color TV. When he got a little older, his father forbade him to visit his mother, and he beat the child regularly. When he turned thirteen, he found his mother's address in his father's papers and snuck out of the mine. He hitchhiked, walked, and begged his way to Chongqing. By the time he made it to the South Bank, found Elder Sister's old residence from thirteen years earlier, got help finding the new address, found his mother, and threw himself into her arms, he was already gravely ill. His dirty face was red with fever.

Elder Sister didn't even have time to take a good look at her son, whom she hadn't seen in thirteen years, before rushing him to the hospital. The hospital asked for a ten-thousand-yuan deposit before they'd admit him. Elder Sister had to take him home, where she tried desperately to treat him with traditional Chinese medicine. Less than a week went by before her ex-husband showed up and took the boy back. Soon afterward, she learned that the boy was dead.

"Of brain cancer! He was barely thirteen years old! It must have been the result of all the beatings that son of a bitch gave him. They wouldn't even tell me where they'd buried his ashes. Their hearts are more poisonous than the most venomous of snakes."

We were dumbfounded. I handed Elder Sister a towel to wipe the tears off her face. Fourth Sister brought her water. Elder Sister had hidden this thing deep in her heart for more than ten years, partly from guilt and partly from regret. She felt great remorse for leaving her infant son behind in pursuit of her happiness. She blamed herself for being a hopelessly selfish mother. She said that she still vividly remembered the smile Color TV managed to give her when he'd said good-bye. He said, "Ma, I don't regret coming to Chongqing to look for you. All I wanted was to see you."

She said that after his death, she'd converted to Christianity.

I apologized to Elder Sister for always being so hard on her. She replied that she would be happy as long as everyone thought kindly of her. Money wasn't important to her anymore. If everyone wanted so badly to give the money to that worthless sister-in-law of theirs, she wouldn't try to stop them.

Second Sister said, "Elder Sister, nothing is more important than saving a life. You should have come to us. In the worst case, we could've all sold our blood to pay the hospital fees for Color TV."

Elder Sister burst into a smile, but then immediately started to cry again. "Thank you, Second Sister. It warms my heart to hear you say that."

So blood was thicker than water after all. We had all come out of the same belly, we were as close as Ma's palm and the back of her hand, we were sisters. No matter how heated our quarrels were, we always worked things out. Not long before, I had been hurling hurtful words at my sisters by the riverside, and now everything was fine again, as if nothing had happened between us.

Elder Sister took a look at her watch. It was almost six. She proposed that, for dinner, each of us siblings make one dish Mother or Father used to make.

5

The kitchen seemed tiny with so many people trying to squeeze in at once, but we sisters didn't mind. Every little thing added to the fun: lending a hand, tidying up, cutting vegetables, slicing the pork, cleaning the fish. Second Sister was afraid of smoke from the cooking fire, and she couldn't help but bring up how our father didn't eat anything spicy and how he always drank black tea. She prepared yanduxian: chicken simmered with dried bamboo shoots and salted pork in a stone pot. Second Sister said our father taught her how to cook this classic southern dish.

Elder Sister was in the living room, adding starch, salt, minced ginger, and green onion to ground pork and rolling meatballs between her palms before pressing them into tofu squares. She boasted about her dish, telling Third Sister-in-Law and Fifth Sister-in-Law that it was Ma's secret recipe from her days in the countryside. Normally, this dish was only made during the New Year celebration. It was too bad, she said, there wasn't time to grind the soybeans on the spot and make the tofu fresh.

I remembered my family making fresh tofu once when I was a child. It was for my youngest uncle's birthday, and also for welcoming Third Brother back from the countryside. My mother and father had worked nonstop for a night and a day. My father did the grinding, walking in a circle, while my mother kept adding in beans. We borrowed the grinder from a neighbor in Compound No. 7, and when we were done with it, my mother gave the grinder's owner a bag of the bean paste she'd made. Ma had mixed it with greens, cooking oil, and salt, and it was delicious.

Elder Sister finished assembling a plateful of stuffed tofu and said, "The real way to make this is to add a lot of freshly minced hot peppers, but Ma always made it sweet and sour because Father couldn't eat spicy food. I'll respect family tradition and only add peppers to half of it."

Boats on the river blew their whistles. The window in the family room faced Chaotianmen Dock, letting in the last remaining rays of sun as it set over the river. We turned on the lights, moved the table to the middle of the family room, and arranged chairs and benches. Second Brother-in-Law set the table. Fifth Brother took out his pan-fried peanuts, Ma's favorite. Fourth Sister made steamed bass with pickled vegetables, a dish Ma made all the time since it suited Father's taste. I made the special dish of six cold appetizers Ma had taught me—daikon radish, seaweed, lettuce, mung bean noodles, green pepper, and dried tofu, all cut into thin slices that resemble silk threads, threading Ma's six children together.

Third Brother made chilled noodles with bean sprouts. It was everyone's favorite. We only got to enjoy it when guests came over.

We all sat down at the table and toasted with green tea. Elder Sister jumped up.

"Let me say a few words. Christianity and Buddhism are different. Christian songs are easier on the ear and more lyrical. They make you cry. Buddhist songs cause your mind to go blank. Another thing: Christian candles have a nice scent, while Buddhist candles have no smell. All right, I will stop there. I want to ask your forgiveness. My brothers, sisters-in-law, sisters, and brothers-in-law, please forgive me for not having treated you with kindness. Now that our mother is gone, I promise that I will be a proper eldest sister. Please say grace with me before you pick up your chopsticks." She closed her eyes and crossed herself. "Bless us, O Lord! And these thy gifts, which we are about to receive from thy bounty, through Christ our Lord. Amen! We give thee thanks for all thy benefits. Amen! May the souls of the faithful departed, through the mercy of God, rest in peace. Amen!"

We all followed her. I tried not to laugh when I realized Elder Sister had accidentally combined the pre- and post-meal prayers. It seemed unlikely that she'd been saying grace at every meal since she converted. Of course, how frequently she did it really wasn't important, as long as she believed it.

During dinner, everyone talked at once, sharing our news, our sorrows, and our triumphs. Third Brother mentioned his daughter, who was studying accounting in England and getting ready to marry a doctor. Fifth Sister-in-Law told everyone that her son was about to graduate from a vocational school and, with Shouli's help, had already landed a job as a salesperson for Haier Electronics. Second Sister said that Turtle Rock was slated to be destroyed in the next year or so to accommodate the widened river that would result from the completion of the Three Gorges Dam. That triggered a wave of nostalgia and anger. Third Brother was excited about the new train line between Chengdu and Tibet. Before, you had to take a long bus ride or fly to Tibet. The train would make it possible to get used to the high elevation and also to enjoy the scenery along the way.

Third Sister-in-Law revealed what was behind Third Brother's excitement. After their daughter's wedding, the two of them planned to take a trip to Tibet in celebration of their thirtieth wedding anniversary. During the Cultural Revolution, Third Brother had marched to every Tibetan location with his fellow Red Guards, except the Potala Palace. Third Brother wanted us to be his witnesses to the grand plan in case his wife changed her mind.

The soup was incredibly delicious, the bass magnificently tender, the chilled noodles numbingly spicy. Every dish was superb. I marveled at my siblings' cooking skills, but found I had no appetite, so I just sat there, silently drinking one cup of tea after another and listening to the chatter. Chongqing natives talk loud and fast. My family was no exception.

I went to the bathroom. Through the open window, I could see a sprinkling of lights on the ocean of darkness. I had seen the same view many times before, but this time it felt different. In this darkness, there was a coldness that crept right into my bones.

I washed my hands, and when I grabbed the towel by the sink, I was hit by an uncanny feeling. Many years before, when I came home for a visit, my mother had given me a dark-green towel. The same towel was still here. Putting the towel back, I noticed my mother's toothbrush in front of the mirror. It was so worn that all the bristles were bent to the left side. I took it in my hands and pushed the bristles to the right, imagining my mother standing in front of the mirror. First, she'd take out her dentures, thoroughly brush her teeth, and then clean her dentures before soaking them in a glass of water. I put her toothbrush back, straightening the other ones that leaned there.

As soon as I opened the door, I would see my mother sitting there eating dinner, listening to her children. Mother was still there. She had never left me!

Laughter came from the family room, far more moving than tears. I'd spent my whole life wishing that my family could have a happy dinner, my parents surrounded by their loving children. Ironically, not until both of my parents were gone had this moment finally arrived.

I looked around the tiny bathroom. Every inch of the tiles and every breath of air were imprinted with my mother's body, filled with her smells and sounds. Looking at myself in the mirror, I saw infinite sorrow and suppressed indignation. I was trying so hard to forgive my siblings, to play the happy family, but I could never truly get over the fact that, during the last phase of her life, my mother was no better off than an abused daughter-in-law. No wonder she ran away from reality and returned to the past, descending into the life of a beggar. When she fell down from the steep and stinking garbage mountain, she tumbled all the way to the riverbank. She was bruised all over, and the wound on her right eyelid left a permanent scar. My mother had lain there, unconscious, flies buzzing around her face, only to be spotted by passersby hours later.

Yes, my family had taken her to the hospital, but the doctors only gave her a perfunctory examination, quickly cleaning up her scratches before sending her home. My mother's neck and arms had hurt. Aching all over her body, she'd cried out loud when the pain became unbearable.

"What are you whining about? You deserve it!"

They blamed my mother for making them the laughingstock of the neighborhood. They took her garbage bags and threw them all away.

"The older you are, the more ignorant you get! You only care about yourself, you selfish old bat, not how your children feel."

My mother must have clenched her teeth, afraid to make any noise. She curled up into herself and avoided eye contact. Maybe she had hidden in a corner of this small bathroom and cried, her shoulders jerking and her hair covering her sad face. I saw the scene, every detail of it. She went to the ferry and tried to find the person she loved, but he had left this world long ago.

And even when she was at her most desperate, lost on the bridge across the big river, she didn't have the courage to ask for my help. I could imagine how low she must have felt. Maybe in her mind I hadn't even been born yet, still an embryo in her uterus. She was enduring all that suffering in order for me to come into this world.

That day, the reporter magically made my mother talk. My mother told the reporter that in those days of hunger, she was pregnant with her sixth child, a girl, and, due to the lack of nutrition, she had bled several times and almost miscarried. Gathering up her courage, she took the ferry across the river to check herself into the women's hospital downtown. The doctor told her there wasn't enough amniotic fluid because of her undernourishment and that any further delay would kill both mother and baby. They gave her a shot to induce labor.

"My sixth child did not come easily," Mother had told the reporter. "And she was such a pathetic little thing who didn't get much of my love when she was small. I am not a good mother, but I had to do the things I did. If there were a next life, and we became mother and daughter again, I would give her everything that in this life I could not give her."

And to think that these past few years, my duplicitous siblings had told me a fairy tale about Ma's happy golden years. Was this the moment to let them know I'd uncovered the truth about Ma's misery? Should I interrogate them all, put everything on the table, and express my indignation on my poor mother's behalf?

At the very least, I should walk into the family room and unleash my disgust and anger on each one of them.

But I couldn't. I had no right to blame the others, because while I might not have been actively abusive, I wasn't an attentive or filial daughter myself. After I left home to be on my own, I only spent a handful of my mother's birthdays with her, and I never celebrated my own birthday by her side, thanking her for giving me my life and for bringing me up. I may have used my income from writing to help support my mother and siblings, but I wasn't actually there. Where was I when my mother needed me? All she'd wanted was for me to sit next to her, chat with her, give her a back rub, take her out for a nice meal, go to a play, sit in a park, walk around interesting places, or simply read her a book.

With a little effort, I could imagine how my siblings looked on my contribution to the family. I may have given money, but I was actually more selfish than they were because I hoarded all my time for myself. I used that money to buy my freedom, to assuage my guilt, to get out of dealing with my mother's illnesses, aging, and personality changes. She was hospitalized numerous times. Only once, when she was diagnosed with lung cancer, did I sit by her bed to care for her. I bathed her just one time, and realized I knew her body as well as she knew mine. I helped her to the toilet, washed her, and massaged her back. I ate with her, slept in the same bed with her, filled prescriptions for her, and listened to her talk about the past. That my mother was able to beat the cancer had a lot to do with me being there with her. But after that one time, I left her to the others.

I couldn't sit in judgment of my family. If anyone should be put on trial, that person should be me.

I thought back to one of my infrequent visits to Chongqing, sometime around October 2005. I flew in for a symposium held by a city-planning magazine and stayed in a hotel on the north bank. As soon as the symposium was over, I was heading to a nearby city. Ostensibly, I needed to go there to deliver a lecture, but really I was going to take a look at my husband's new lover. Since I didn't have time to get home,

Second Sister suggested that Third Brother bring Ma downtown to see me. I waited in Second Sister's apartment for what seemed like an eternity. Finally, Third Brother and his wife brought Ma over, panting and sweating. I complained about their lateness. Third Brother explained that the bridge on the big river was blocked by a protest. They had to get out of their cab and walk the whole way, taking frequent breaks for Ma to catch her breath.

My mother looked me over, commenting that I had lost too much weight and chiding me for not eating enough.

Third Brother explained the reason behind the protest. The city government had announced that they were about to demolish the old city to make way for new developments. The residents were unhappy with the compensation offer and wanted to negotiate a better deal. But compulsory evictions had already begun. Anyone who resisted had been beaten. One family was beaten so badly that the mother suffered a miscarriage, the father's kidney ruptured, and the ten-year-old son's legs were broken. The residents were so angry that they staged the demonstration on the bridge.

My mother spoke up, saying she felt terrible for the family and would pray for Buddha to help them.

Impatient with the story, I told her not to worry. I looked at my watch and said that it was time for me to catch my flight. Ma immediately became uneasy and apologetic, standing up from the sofa. "My dear Little Six, no matter how far I had to walk, I was glad to get a look at you. Next time you come back to Chongqing, please be sure to tell Mama."

I said I would.

Then I just left. I did not so much as shake her hands, let alone apologize. I could very well have postponed my flight and gone to see my mother instead of spying on that other woman. I could at least have stayed a little longer, been a little kinder. But all I wanted right then was to be alone because I had been hurt by a stupid man. But my mother was not the person who hurt me. Why couldn't I get over myself and be a better daughter to her? I didn't even pay attention to how skinny she was! She was eighty-two, and in just one year, she would leave me forever.

Out in the living room, Eldest Brother-in-Law was telling a joke. The whole room burst into laughter. *I should force myself out of this bathroom and rejoin them—pretend to be as happy as they are.*

But perhaps they weren't so different from me after all, trying their best to suppress the deep sorrow in their hearts. They laughed like that so that they could forget that Ma had passed away.

My brothers and sisters all loved our mother, although they did so in their own ways. But all of us were selfish. We were all the same kind of person. How could our love match our mother's? She gave us her entire heart, her entire body, and finally, her life, without a shred of regret. As the old saying goes, there are three thousand rivers in the distance, but not a single spoonful of water at hand to quench your thirst.

6

The next morning, I got dressed, packed my bag, and got ready to leave before I even realized that Fourth Sister was not in her bed. I searched all over for her. Fifth Brother's wife told me he'd left to go fishing with his friends at Cuntan. It was his way of thanking them for their help with Ma's funeral. The previous night, Elder Sister, Second Sister, and Third Brother had all gone back to their own homes, leaving only me and Fourth Sister in Ma's room. I was beginning to worry.

I opened the front door and there she was, standing in the empty hallway, looking out on the river. I was relieved. It was another overcast day. There were boats moving slowly on the water.

Fourth Sister said, "No need to say good-bye to me again. We already did that last night."

"Why are you up so early?"

"I was up all night."

Looking at her, I was overcome by a memory from four years earlier, when I'd come back to Chongqing to sweep my father's tomb for Qingming Festival. My mother stood next to me and stared mournfully at the river just like Fourth Sister was staring now. She looked so lonely. I wanted to embrace her, but didn't. I had always been shy with my mother, and she was just as shy with me, except maybe when I was too little to remember. I saw her kiss other children, but never me. She hid all her love for me deep inside her heart, inadvertently teaching me how to hide my own feelings.

"I thought I could forget him," Fourth Sister said, "but the pain is too deep. I shouldn't have let him go."

I tried to change the topic. "How long are you planning to stay here?"

"As soon as Ma's ashes are properly buried, I'll go back to London."

"You're too lonely over there by yourself. Why don't you stay in China?"

"I need to be in London. His shadows are everywhere there." Fourth Sister turned around. "I'm a lost cause. I just can't make myself hate him enough. It's karma, I guess. I have no choice but to spend the rest of my life waiting for him. Sooner or later, he'll remember that I'm the only one who truly loves him, and he'll come back to me. I will wait for him until I die."

My eyes turned red.

"Why are you crying? Stop it. You're going to miss your flight." She grabbed my bag and insisted on walking me to the top of Middle School Street.

7

After saying good-bye to Fourth Sister, I stood at the intersection, feeling unsettled. I decided not to go to the airport right away.

I took a shortcut and climbed toward the hilltop behind No. 38 Middle School. Halfway up the hill was a kindergarten. I could hear children singing to the accompaniment of a keyboard. I continued uphill.

My mother's best friend, Auntie Wang Guixiang, was supposed to live there, among several rows of bungalows. Junk was piled up everywhere as always, and the two neem trees seemed the same height as ever, even several decades after I'd last seen them. My feet remembered the way to her door, but it was locked. Maybe Elder Sister really had called, but I was sure she hadn't tried harder than that. I was determined to find Wang Guixiang myself. A fat man in slippers shuffled out of a unit several doors down and began to pee on the ground with his back to me. I knocked on the next door down. A woman in her fifties told me that Auntie Wang had gone to live with her daughter in Suining. I asked her for the address, but she refused to give it out.

I explained who I was and that I needed to talk to Auntie Wang about my mother. To my surprise, the neighbor said she'd known my mother well and even remembered me from when I was little. She cried to hear about my mother passing away, saying what a great person my mother was. She told me to wait a moment, and then she came out with a slip of paper bearing the address of Auntie Wang's daughter in Suining.

I hurried over to North Chongqing Railway Station. There was an 8:55 train from Guilin to Chengdu that made a stop at Suining. My watch showed 8:30. I bought a second-class ticket for twenty-five yuan and rushed to catch the train. The train was far nicer than the ones I remembered from the 1980s, much cleaner and better furnished. The first-class cars even had flat-screen TVs.

No sooner had I sat down than the whistle sounded and the train began to move. We were due to arrive at Suining in just under two and a half hours.

The rhythmic movement of the train rocked me to sleep.

"Now arriving at Suining Station!"

I woke with a start. Already? It felt like I'd just dozed off. I left the railway station and hailed a cab. Giving the driver the address, I asked him if it was far. He said it wasn't, and he asked where I was from.

I said Chongqing.

He responded, "Compared to Chongqing, Suining is a tiny place. If you look behind you, you can see Guangde Temple. It was built in the Tang dynasty! And it's filled with antiques."

I turned around and saw a corner of the mountain and the temple. The cabbie told me that we'd also pass Lingquan Mountain, which was dotted with ancient trees, hot springs, a temple from the Sui dynasty, and stone sculptures from the Tang. He was even prouder of the celebrities Suining had produced.

"Chen Zi'ang, the Tang poet; Huang E, the female poet from the Ming dynasty; Zhang Penghe, the famous Qing judge; and Zhang Chuanshan, the Qing poet. Suining is a beautiful place! You should take a good look around."

The taxi was driving east. I looked out of the window. The streets were neat, there were no high-rises, people on the street looked happy, and the girls were all fashionably and sensibly dressed. The small city was flat, but it was surrounded by mountains. Local legend had it that Guanyin was actually three sisters, bodhisattvas from Suining, who had decided to each pursue their own paths to enlightenment. The eldest sister had her temple built at Lingquan, the middle sister had hers built at Guangde, while the youngest sister went far down south and had her temple built on Mount Putuo Island in the South China Sea. There was another story testifying to the sacredness of this place. During the Japanese invasion, a Japanese airplane tried to bomb Guangde Temple. The bombs all missed the temple and dropped harmlessly into a river.

The taxi continued north over the Fujiang Bridge and, after winding up some mountain paths, dropped me off at the entrance to a village. I walked the entire main street, but couldn't find the house number of Wang Guixiang's daughter. A shopkeeper told me the person I was looking for lived up the hill. He sent his daughter to take me there, and we soon knocked at the door of a wooden bungalow.

The door creaked open, revealing an old lady in her seventies with a pair of reading glasses hanging around her neck. She took a good look at me and, before I could open my mouth, said, "Little Six, come on in."

I recognized her instantly as well. She was none other than Auntie Wang Guixiang, my mother's shoulder-pole partner at the dockyard, and her best friend.

8

I sat at the table, a cup of chrysanthemum tea in my hand. Auntie Wang put her glasses down on the table by several home-and-garden magazines. She said to me, "I knew you would come."

"Auntie Wang, you mean you . . . ?" I was speechless.

Auntie Wang wore a dark-blue cotton shirt beneath a sweater, with her white hair tied into a bun behind her ears, exposing her round face and wrinkled neck.

"It wasn't me who foretold it."

"Who was it?"

Auntie Wang did not answer me directly, but calmly proceeded. "By now you'll have found out almost everything about your mother, and you've come to tell me about her passing."

"But I still have a lot of questions!"

She stood up. "There's no hurry, Little Six. Let me show you around first."

I was almost certain I saw a glint of tears in her eyes. She didn't really care about showing me the house—she just needed a moment to collect herself. My mother used to say, "Your Auntie Wang's parents were highly educated, and she herself went to school. It's really tragic that she had to become a shoulder-pole carrier." Auntie Wang's education showed in her poised demeanor.

The house didn't look like much at first. The rectangular dining area was a little dark, but the two rooms on the right were perfectly square. One was her bedroom, but it was full of children's toys. A big mottled cat was passed out in a baby stroller. She said that she was now a great-grandma. Sometimes she babysat her granddaughter's three-year-old son, but he was at daycare today. The other bedroom belonged to her granddaughter, who owned a flower shop in town and was married to a middle-school teacher. Auntie Wang's daughter lived in the town center, making a living selling herbs. There was a smaller room next to the kitchen that her granddaughter's husband used as a study. Laundry hung in the hallway to dry.

Auntie Wang opened the back door, and the view suddenly opened up. The big yard backed up to the mountain, and a creek ran through bamboo groves and fruit trees. What a beautiful spot! Although the house wasn't that high up, the air was fresh, and Auntie Wang had planted mint, *Tribulus*, *Ophiopogon*, safflower, and chrysanthemums. She also grew some vegetables.

There was a small shed, one corner decorated with rose balsam, my mother's favorite. I walked over to squat down by the flowerpots. Auntie Wang put her hand on my head, caressing me.

"Yes, Little Six. It was your mother who told me that you would come looking for me after she died."

I lifted my head, tears pouring down my cheeks. My mother was like a part of me, knowing me through and through, even after her death.

Auntie Wang said, "Rose Balsam, your mother's favorite flower, also her nickname."

"My grandma liked to call her by that name."

"The flower is very hardy and easy to grow. It's also called 'phoenix-immortal,' and a lot of people like to call it the 'fingernail flower.' In the Song dynasty, there was an emperor whose queen's name was 'Phoenix.'

To avoid uttering a name used by the royal family, people of the court renamed the plant 'Good Children of the Flower,' because it looked like children playing around their mother's lap."

I gazed at the flower and saw what she meant. The petals did look like children around their mother. My siblings and I were like those petals, but there was no longer a mother to huddle around. I found myself envying a flower.

Auntie Wang took out two bamboo chairs and a bamboo card table from the storage shed and invited me to sit down. On the table, she placed a plate of pickled vegetables, a plate of peanuts roasted with salted beans and dried tofu, and some mung bean congee.

"Just a simple lunch! I made it myself this morning. Stay for a couple of days. I can take you to the temples," she said.

I thanked her, but said, "I'm afraid I have to hurry back to Beijing."

"Then I won't keep you. But you must let me show you around next time you come."

The cat approached us apprehensively. Auntie Wang mixed some rice with fish bones and set it on the ground for her. The cat happily dug in.

I was starving and polished off the congee in no time. Auntie Wang gave me another bowl, and I quickly finished that too. I waved her off, refusing to eat more. She poured me some chrysanthemum tea. I took out my camera, scooted my chair closer to hers, and showed her the photos I'd taken. They began four days earlier, when I arrived at Chongqing, and showed my mother's coffin, which was surrounded by eulogy banners, flowers, and wreaths. I pressed the forward button, showing her the scenes of each of the past several days. The last batch of photos was taken in the crematorium.

"She was so skinny!" Auntie Wang sobbed. "Much skinnier than when I saw her last month."

"You saw her?"

Auntie Wang explained that she'd had a bad feeling. She had been having recurring dreams about her life with my mother at the dockyard, so she took a bus to Chongqing and went straight to Compound No. 6. Her sobbing now turned into a wail.

"Your mother and I were closer than sisters. As soon as I saw her, I realized her spirit was gone. She told me her time was running out, but she had to hang on until her two daughters in England could make it back."

That must have been just before I flew from Italy to Beijing and on to Chongqing in September. After I visited Ma, Fourth Sister also came back to China. After trying and failing to find Tang, she'd gone to see Ma in Chongqing, but she soon took off again to track down Tang. More failure sent her back to Ma, and she'd stayed till Ma passed away on October 25.

Auntie Wang said that on that visit, she'd bade my mother goodbye and gone down to the courtyard, but then went back up again. She couldn't leave. My mother held her hands, saying that she knew that Auntie Wang would turn around.

"We controlled ourselves well. Neither of us wept. You know what, Little Six? Your mother and I never once ran out of words to say to each other."

Auntie Wang took out her handkerchief to wipe away her tears and told me this was only the third time in her life she'd allowed herself to cry.

I placed a cup of chrysanthemum tea into her hands. A breeze carried to us the fragrance of rose balsam.

It was 1960 when she first met my mother, and they'd remained friends for forty-six years. Almost half a century! Both had to rely on the strength of their bodies to feed themselves and their families. Working side by side, day in and out, Auntie Wang had spent more time with my mother than anyone.

"Little Six, you said you still have a lot of questions?"

I nodded. "My sisters believe that my mother had a lot of lovers."

"You must already know the truth about that. You are the only one of her children who truly understood her."

"Yes, but what about the personnel director at the shipyard, the former faction head?"

"Do not mention that animal!" Auntie Wang's face turned ashen. "Oh, Little Six," she sighed, "He was no lover. At his hand, your mother experienced the most unforgettable humiliation and abuse. And she endured it to save—"

"Uncle Jian?"

"Yes, to save him, but it didn't do any good. He threatened to torture Jian unless she came back to him. But then Jian was thrown into prison anyway, and she said she'd rather die than go near the man again. I had to stay with her, protect her from that bastard. Your mother never told me the exact details, but I could feel her humiliation. Her eyes were lifeless, like a zombie. It took her a long time to recover. Neither Jian nor your father ever knew what she'd done."

I had prepared myself for something like this, but the horror of it still knocked the wind out of me. A girlfriend of mine had once been raped at knifepoint, and after that, she couldn't even let her husband touch her. She would get depressed and smash things in the house. I went to see her, but she refused to open the door, cursing me from the other side of it. In some ways, my mother must have been even more psychologically torn up about what happened, because she'd had to make herself submit to the rape to save her friend. I could imagine her going limp and dead when the faction head climbed on top of her, and how this would have infuriated him. I could see him stopping to berate her, brutally abuse her, treat her like an animal. I started to cry.

Auntie Wang wiped away my tears and said, "If one day you are going to write about your mother, you must write with utter truthfulness. You should let your sisters know that there was nothing shameful about her love for Uncle Jian. Your mother always appreciated kindness—and returned kindness. All through her life, she was filled with love and loyalty to her friends. It's who she was."

I didn't know whether I should write about my mother, nor how to do it. Mother had spent her life drowning in disaster, never able to find a way to the surface. She struggled bitterly with her innermost fears and darkness, and she passed those fears and that darkness down to me. Like mother, like daughter.

People say that when you lose the person dearest to you, the sorrow can change your life completely. If you're not careful, it pushes you into the depths of despair, never to be happy again. I wondered what it would do to me.

Taking a sip of tea, I remembered Second Sister telling me that Ma had used unpaid child support money as an excuse to go see my biological father. I asked Auntie Wang if that was true.

She responded, "Your second sister became bitter when your mother forbade her from joining any of the factions during the Cultural Revolution. She complained that your mother didn't love her as much as she loved Elder Sister. Since the child support was sent to the school where your second sister taught, she took revenge by preventing your mother from receiving it."

"So, if she couldn't get the money through my sister, does this mean that my mother went to see Sun all the way up to my eighteenth birthday?"

"No. If she'd been able to see him, she wouldn't have been in so much pain."

"But what did they do once he couldn't get the money to her?"

"He came to me for help."

"Really?"

"Until you turned eighteen, he would either mail the money or deliver it to me in person." The cat jumped onto Auntie Wang's lap.

She caressed it, and said, "Your mother was afraid to see him, explaining that she'd lose control if they were to see each other again. How could she do that with a big family counting on her?"

Our conversation was interrupted by the arrival of the propane deliveryman. He'd tried the front door, then come around the house to find us in the back. Auntie Wang apologized for having forgotten the appointment, and the young man replaced the empty tank in the kitchen with a new one.

It was almost two o'clock, so I got up to make my departure.

"Stay just a few more minutes. I have something to show you."

She disappeared into the bedroom and quickly came out with a bundle of things wrapped in a scarf.

I opened it. It was a bagful of plastic pouches I'd used to organize my research materials when I'd come back to Chongqing in 1996 to work on my memoir. My mother had kept the leftovers and filled them with the photos I sent her and newspaper clippings about me. "Did my mother leave this for me?"

"Yes, when I said good-bye to her, she told me to give this to you when you came to see me."

The articles started around the year 2000, covering books I had published, promotional events I had been to, which of my books had been adapted for film or TV, where I'd traveled, and so on. There were clippings about my memoir being turned into a TV series, the court case and subsequent banning of my novel, and my winning the Rome Prize for literature.

There was also a sheaf of torn-out pages. Without a doubt, these were the ones missing from my mother's red notebook. They contained the records of child support from my biological father. There was also a note saying, "His wife's in the hospital, and they need the money."

Not only did my mother refuse to take money from him for three consecutive months, Auntie Wang told me, she also gave Auntie Wang one hundred yuan for him.

There were also loose scraps of paper with writing I couldn't decipher. Perhaps she hadn't wanted anyone to know what they said.

I had always thought that my mother didn't care very much about me or about my career. But I had completely misjudged her. She'd followed me every step of the way. She must have been as depressed as I was during the legal battle over my book. That's why she'd told me over the phone, "Little Six, don't be afraid! When the sun sets, the moon rises. When the moon sets, the sun rises."

There were photos of me from 1989, one taken when I arrived at Luxun Literature Academy that February. Two of the photos showed me in Tiananmen Square, and some showed me with my classmates. I couldn't recall when I'd sent these to her. It must have been after I left the country.

Auntie Wang said that she and my mother both went to downtown Chongqing to join the student protests that year. They made a lot of chilled noodles for the students. The two of them watched the news every day and read the papers together. In fact, my mother read so much about the protests that she learned a lot of new characters, and soon she could read an article all by herself.

Then, on the night of the third of June, 1989, my mother couldn't sleep, so she walked to Auntie Wang's house in the dark. She said, "I wish I knew my Little Six was safe. Knowing her, she must have been in the square." The next day, she grew even more anxious after hearing that many poets in Chongqing had been arrested. She and Auntie Wang went to pray for my safety, and she bought a lot of white chrysanthemums to appease the souls of those who were killed. She told Second Sister to find a way to contact me, to send word not to come back to Chongqing so I wouldn't get arrested. She even talked about flying to Beijing to look for me, even if she might only find my body! Auntie Wang said that it was my father who talked sense into her, pointing out that Beijing was now under military control. It would be futile to go looking for me now. My father was worried too, sitting glued to his radio all day, and asking Mother whether she had heard from me. Not until I left for England six months later did my family hear from me and know that I was safe. How terrified Ma must have been!

Hearing all this from Auntie Wang, I was speechless. I thought I would drown in my own tears. And to think—when I went back to Chongqing years later, my mother never even mentioned the hell she had gone through, not knowing whether her youngest child was dead or alive.

In fact, I only narrowly escaped from the grip of death that night in 1989. After several close calls, I managed to find a place to hide in a dorm at a research institute near Jingshun Road. As a poet who'd participated in the student movement, I knew I'd be thrown in jail if I went back to Chongqing. I didn't even dare to move about openly in Beijing for fear of being interrogated or detained, as many of my classmates were. I hid in the dorm at Jingshun Road until that fall. And somehow, in all that time, it never occurred to me to let my mother know that I was safe. My mind was filled with thoughts about the future of the country and selfish worries for myself. There was no space left for my mother or my family.

I thought about how nervous my mother had seemed when I went to visit just a month before her death. She'd refused to let me throw away the drawer of my old junk, but I did it anyway when she wasn't looking. Why? Why couldn't I just make her happy for once?

Thinking about her now, I could still sense that tension. It had nothing to do with the junk, but with the secrets she hid in her heart. I shared these thoughts with Auntie.

"Little Six, I think I should tell you now. Your mother knew what was going on between you and Fourth Sister."

"No, that's impossible!" Fourth Sister and I had worked diligently to keep the secret from the rest of our family so that Ma would never know. My hands were trembling. My brain froze.

"'Two sisters sharing one man. What a hardship for both of my daughters!'" Auntie Wang said. "Those were your mother's exact words."

Tang had accompanied me back to Chongqing in 1992, staying in the old Compound No. 6, and again in 1996, in my mother's new apartment. My mother always kept her distance from him. I didn't bring him with me again until the funeral. My mother's heart was as clear as a mirror, one that could reflect a man's true nature. She had long had a premonition that this man would be the major misfortune of my life.

I remembered once, when Fourth Sister and I were cooking dinner together in the kitchen, he had said, "You are both such incredible women! You would amaze the whole world if people knew about you."

That was shortly after Fourth Sister had arrived in London—but before things changed. The night was still, the trees serene, and the clouds few. The last rays of the sunset illuminated our faces. Everything was beautiful and perfect.

His eyes had been damp at the funeral. All sorts of feelings must have welled up in his heart. I had asked myself more than once, where did it go wrong between him and me? On the one hand, he was a highly respected scholar. On the other, he was so vulnerable that the thought of him could make my heart ache. Both of his parents had died violent deaths during the Cultural Revolution. His brother also died, leaving just one sister to keep him company. Other than her, he barely had any friends. He said he'd realized quite early that the Communist Party would never have a use for him. And he was right: they banished him to a coal mine. For ten long years, he toiled in endless darkness, under constant scrutiny and discrimination, his tail between his legs. The darkness in the mine was like the darkness in his entire life. The experience twisted his personality. A victim of the Communist Party, he unconsciously turned the people around him into his victims.

But how did my mother know that both of us had become his women? Auntie Wang didn't tell me, and I couldn't bring myself to ask.

Of course, my mother wasn't stupid. I'd come back to live in China without my husband, while Fourth Sister had stayed behind in London, never even coming back to visit. Mother knew that Fourth Sister had always been in the habit of taking things away from me, ever since we were children. She must have done something incredibly hurtful to her younger sister if she was too ashamed to see our mother.

That the two of us shared one man was impossible to justify, no matter how it had started or what the circumstances were. I was as used to suffering as my mother was. My own sister getting mixed up in my marriage? It was just one more thing to endure, that's all. My mother was in an impossible position. This wasn't the traditional polygamous culture of the old years, but the new China in which women were supposed to enjoy political and social equality. So we kept it from her, which meant that neither of us could talk to her about our heartache when that man left us each in turn. But somehow, she just knew.

Two of her daughters had deserted her, and Ma hated herself for it. She blamed herself for everything that had gone wrong, adding these new wounds to her endless regrets and sorrows.

This earth had been her hell, and the life she'd had to lead these last few years was its deepest pit. We would never know how much anger, hurt, and shame was bottled up inside her. The last few years before her death, whenever I called, she would always use the excuse that international calls were too expensive and hang up on me. Behind the feigned pragmatism, there must have been an incredible amount of injury. It broke my heart to think about it.

Thanks to that man, all my achievements in London had withered away. Only failures remained. I looked out as far as I could, and all I could see was a wasteland.

"Your mother wanted you not to hate him," Auntie Wang said.

"I don't hate him," I told her. "But I don't know how long it'll take for me to forgive him."

Gradually and slowly, though, I would forgive him. I had to. I would ask for his forgiveness as well, if I unknowingly did any injury to him. As for Fourth Sister, she would continue to love him, or perhaps forget him, one day. Hopefully, time would heal her wounds.

I thought back to the first moment I saw him, when I believed he would love me forever and that we'd be together till the end of our lives. Now all that seemed like a lifetime ago.

9

When I said good-bye to Auntie Wang, she pulled me into her arms. She was my mother's height, still taller than me in spite of her age. Her chest felt so soft and warm, making me wish I'd hugged my mother more. Then she pulled away and, with a sly smile, congratulated me on being pregnant—something I had tried to conceal from everybody.

As my train pulled out of the station, I leaned against the window and watched as trees and houses flew past. It dawned on me that my mother must also have been able to tell I was pregnant when I flew in from Italy a month earlier. She'd given me a red baby hat and sung me a lullaby. *"The little swallow, wearing a floral dress, comes here every spring. I asked the swallow why she comes here, and she said that spring is the most beautiful season."* I couldn't remember whether she sang me songs when I was little. She must have, but I was probably too small to remember. At the time, I'd thought it was just a sign of her senility, but now I understood. Before she passed away, Ma sang a lullaby once more, this time for the baby in my belly.

As it turned out, nothing got past her. But she respected me and didn't ask a thing—not how many months pregnant I was, nor who the baby's father was. Auntie Wang was the same. I didn't offer explanations, and she didn't ask.

Did Ma think I was a terrible daughter for not telling her about this huge event in my life? Could she possibly have guessed I hadn't yet realized I was pregnant? She knew I had an abortion when I was very young and another when I was older. I hadn't been pregnant for ten years, and I didn't expect to be ever again.

When I found out, I was shocked, terrified. But almost instantly, I decided that, this time, I would keep the baby. I threw myself wholeheartedly into preparation for motherhood. I bought books, read articles online, researched hospitals, and consulted numerous people about how to be a good mother. But I forgot to consult the best mother, my baby's grandmother. I didn't reach out, barely thought about her at all until four days earlier when I received the call about her imminent passing.

My mother always looked at me with an expression full of worry. How I wished she could be with me at this moment, letting me share this wonderful news. I would pull her hands toward me and place them on my belly, letting her feel the heartbeat of the life inside me.

"There it is! Oh, my youngest child! You have made me so happy!"

But no matter how hard I tried, I couldn't turn back time.

The train whistled loudly. The rhythmic *chugga-chugga* of the wheels' movement brought my thoughts back to January of that year.

January in Venice had been cold and windy, with hardly any tourists about. The Africans selling fake designer bags were nowhere to be found. I took a water taxi to the hotel. The Italian press had invited me to give a speech about my life at a publishers' conference. And because I had a little time before my meeting with a famous Italian journalist, they arranged for a photographer to follow me around.

At that moment in my life, I did not know how to mend my broken heart. I could practically smell the rotten odor of my own dead body. But I knew I had two choices. One was self-destruction: to numb myself in alcohol, to forget myself in sex, to treat life and relationships lightly, to become one of the walking dead. The other was to save myself, to find the old me, who couldn't be beaten down.

It was at that crucial juncture that I reunited with W, who was also in Italy working on a book.

We'd first met in 2004, at a birthday party for a British journalist stationed in Beijing. I had my husband with me. In his fifties, W was tall even for an Englishman and had a keen sense of humor. He had just published a period novel about a British family's life in China. He talked at me the whole night about how to get published in the UK, not aware of my multiple publications. We had a disagreement about Salman Rushdie's books. I liked them. He didn't.

After leaving the party, my husband and I stood outside to wait for a taxi. It was cold and drizzling. My husband told me that W was the CEO of one of the British trading companies responsible for bringing opium to China in the nineteenth century. His family had come to China as early as 1890, as missionaries, doctors, and railroad engineers. His father was once the head of the prestigious Hong Kong Jockey Club. His mother used to be a famous model. W himself was born in Hong Kong, lived in Japan before he was ten, and went to England for school. He'd been a sailor on a Norwegian boat and traveled throughout the Americas. He was awarded the Order of the British Empire by the Queen of England. *A fascinating character,* I thought. *A businessman who could write novels.*

"And," my husband added, "he's interested in you."

I didn't think so. But I was overawed by my husband and took whatever he said seriously.

Back when he'd first begun to sleep with Fourth Sister, we'd had a huge fight. He was driving, and I threatened to throw myself out of the car. He didn't respond. I tried to pull the hand brake. He just fended me off while continuing to drive. I opened the door and was about to jump when he brought the car to a screeching stop. He was as shaken as I was, yelling at me, "Do you really want to die?"

Yes, I had wanted to die then, and I wanted to again in Venice. In that city of canals, I was about to drown in my own sorrow. W appeared in the nick of time like a rescue boat. Most people in my situation would see nothing but endless water. But I saw that boat and swam to it desperately.

The conference in Venice, itself drowning, was the fourth time we'd run into each other. However, this time, it wasn't coincidence. I'd e-mailed W to tell him I'd be there.

After my speech, the conference organizers took me to dinner at the house of an Italian publishing tycoon. His house was one of the most famous buildings along the Grand Canal. Its walls and ceilings were decorated with historical frescoes. I had already drunk quite a bit when W called and said he had come to Venice to see me. I took a water taxi back to the historic Hotel Danieli. When I arrived, he was waiting in the lobby, wearing a heavy coat and looking worn. It wasn't just exhaustion. His eyes told me how unhappy he was.

When we stepped out of the hotel to find a café, I told him what I saw.

"How can you tell I'm unhappy?"

"You have been unhappy for a long time," I said.

He was quite taken aback.

We found a place and settled in to drink some wine. We talked about novels we'd recently read and our thoughts about writing. W had studied Chinese at the University of Hong Kong and had been a journalist for a time before getting into business. He was in Beijing in 1989. He'd witnessed firsthand the events I had lived through, and knowing that drew us suddenly close to each other. After the summer of 1989, he organized a camel caravan in the heart of the Taklimakan Desert, in hopes of finding a city that had disappeared seventeen hundred years before. In 2000, he drove an antique car from London to Beijing in forty days. After that, he started writing again during weekends and holidays. He asked me where I'd spent Christmas. I told him Munich. He wondered why, and I told him about my divorce. He revealed to me that his marriage too was coming to an end.

A new world of hope emerged from the abyss underneath me. So I was not suffering alone.

The high tide at Saint Mark's Square was knee-deep, and gondoliers rowed past. As the water receded, the stone columns were left with fresh watermarks and there were puddles everywhere on the stone sidewalk. We were the only ones out so late at night. Drizzle made my hair and clothes wet. Suddenly, I became anxious and wanted to find an excuse to run away. The more nervous I felt, the closer I leaned toward him. While we were standing on a bridge, he kissed me. I took him back to my hotel room.

The next morning, we left Venice by car. Although it had recently snowed, W drove fast. Our conversation distracted him, we got lost, and the hour-and-a-half trip ended up taking four hours. Around noon, we arrived in the beautiful, historic town of Asolo. We went to see the house where the English poets Robert and Elizabeth Browning had lived when they eloped. The house had several stories, its closed shutters covered in dried vines. Out front was an angel-shaped drinking fountain, and we stopped to quench our thirst. The story went that, after years of paralysis, Elizabeth Browning had regained the ability to stand through the magical power of love. Compared to these fabled poets, what W and I shared was just a one-night stand, or perhaps a brief affair.

I assumed he was thinking the same. In winter in Venice, a beautiful night together was merely that.

Shortly before going to Venice, I'd seen P again. It had been six years since we'd broken up. We met at Soho Square and went to a fusion Japanese restaurant for lunch. He had lost a lot of weight and aged quite a bit. He'd gotten his hair cut in the same style he had when we were together. He told me that he often googled me, trying to find photos of me online. His children had grown up, but his divorce was still dragging on. He was living with that girlfriend he'd written me about. Judging by the way he spoke about her, they weren't very happy.

Lunch was too short, and we still had a lot to talk about. Suddenly, we fell into each other's arms. We murmured to each other that we had to be together. He invited me over, saying his girlfriend was out of town, but then he changed his mind and told me we shouldn't rush things, but to wait for him to make proper arrangements so that we could start over. Since we were still in love, why not give ourselves a real chance?

I said I would wait.

But that was before I saw W in Venice.

It didn't change things with P—that was my thought. W would soon forget me. In the endless ocean, why would two boats come to the rescue of one drowning person? As it happened, they knew each other from boarding school—P was one class ahead of W. Both had graduated from Oxford. I told myself not to dream too much. I might have been swept off my feet by W, but P had always been there.

When I returned to London, W e-mailed me, telling me that when he drove to Venice through the southern mountains, he got a flat tire and would have had a terrible accident if another driver hadn't alerted him of that. God had given him one more chance, and he'd decided to spend it loving me. As soon as he got back to Beijing, he said, he would talk to his wife about a divorce.

On the day P and I had planned to meet, I brought my laptop and a day pack with me and went to Soho Square. I was early, so I walked around the area. My publisher's office was right across the way. Memories that had sunk to the bottom of the ocean were breaking through the surface, floating and churning. I shook my head. I watched from across the square as P arrived and stood by the statue waiting for me.

How could two people so deeply in love be together? The heavens would not allow that, and we must pay for our happiness. This thought grabbed hold of me. I wanted to walk over to him, but my feet were nailed to the ground. I needed a person who loved me completely, without any reservations, a person who loved me more than I loved him.

After all those years, I could not say for sure that P was that person. But maybe W was. He was like a new world—a real man, decisive and powerful, putting his feelings for me into action. I was no longer young, and I could not afford to start all over again. What's more, W had long been interested in Chinese culture and history and spoke fluent Chinese. P was only interested in China because of me, and he'd only been to Hong Kong. Like most Westerners, his knowledge of Chinese culture and history came from books.

I looked at P from afar. He took out his cell phone. I hurriedly turned off my phone. A half hour had passed since he'd arrived, and he began to look anxious.

My head was spinning. Which of these two men was to be my life partner? I couldn't make any more mistakes. I looked up. The London sky was gloomy as usual. The wind blew hard, stinging my face. I was torn, but I had to choose one of them. Stomping my feet, I turned and left, tears flowing down my face. Sorry, P, my dearest, I have let you down. I have let you down forever.

That night, I sent him an e-mail. "It's fate."

He must have been waiting in front of his computer. He responded immediately. "It is." I hoped that with the passing of time, he would eventually understand and forgive me.

Now, on the train, I was telling all these things to my mother in my heart. I believed her soul would accompany me on this journey. W was the father of the baby in my belly. After all the loss of lives and loves, I yearned to embrace a child. The notion could not have been more natural. I whispered to my mother, "This time I'm looking for a lover, not a father figure. After losing you, I have finally grown up. He wanted to come with me to Chongqing for the funeral, but he respected my need to bring things to a close myself. Every time I burned incense to you, it also came from him and our baby."

Taking from my bag the album my mother had made, I looked at the photos from the past, especially those with me and P. I looked so happy and so casual. I was glowing, and my eyes were so pretty, full of sweetness. At that time, everything I said was poetry, with amazing imagination and the most beautiful words. That was not me. It couldn't be me. I had no words to describe that kind of happiness, and I knew I would never have that again. The only word that came to mind was "unreal." Those people and places and events never existed. Who wouldn't love that version of me? Who wouldn't love the person responsible for drawing that out of me? I loved P with a passion that transcended everyday worries. But I knew that love would not survive the test of real life. Our love was like a beautiful flower that would eventually fade and die. The second time when we met, we caught a glimpse of that beauty again, and it was enough for me to be able to savor it for the rest of my life.

And my ex-husband? In my pictures with him, I rarely smile. My clothing is tight, showing off my curves. I have on sexy lipstick, deliberately presenting myself as a whore. He brought out another side of me, or magnified it. But with him, I was afraid, always worried about something.

Before I met W, I was melancholy, always ready to say good-bye to this world. After I met him, I became calm, and my eyes were lit up by an inner fire, rarely detectable by others.

I went on and on, spilling out everything to my mother. The train chugged toward my birth city, Chongqing, the city of hills. I spent the entire trip looking out the window. When I got on the airplane, I still hadn't finished talking to my mother. Those jumbled memories, those years and days broken by suffering, all surfaced in my conversation with my mother. They lined up in order, each supporting and connecting with the others.

10

At eleven o'clock that night, I arrived in Beijing.

Two days later, my mother's ashes were buried in the same tomb with my father. She could finally rest in peace.

The third day, a friend who knew both me and W's wife called to tell me that W's wife refused to divorce him. She wanted the case to drag on for years—three, maybe even ten. Even if she finally let W go, she would punish him by taking away everything he owned. The friend tried to convince me to give up W and not to keep the baby. I thanked her for calling me, but let her know that I would not change my mind no matter what. Though the path to true love was not easy, I believed in miracles.

Seven months after that, I gave birth to a daughter in a private hospital in Beijing. Her father was by my bedside, passing a crying newborn from the nurse to my arms. She stopped crying as soon as she touched me. Her body automatically curled toward mine. Her face was just like her grandmother's, with a high forehead and expressive lips. And yes, she was born in the Year of the Pig, just like my mother. They took her away for a bath, and tears ran down my cheeks.

I need to remain calm, I told myself. Everything will be all right.

After a while, they wheeled her back in, and my daughter was sleeping in an incubator next to me. Feeling that a long and painful journey was coming to an end, I finally relaxed and fell into a sweet sleep.

I dreamt that I was in the new apartment in Chongqing that I'd bought for my mother. It was two units combined, completely unfurnished. My mother was standing in front of a window. She waved at me. I said, "Our whole family can stay here." I looked again, and she was gone. I walked over to the window. I could see the river ceaselessly flowing east, the boats moving, their horns blowing, the mountains in the distance visible at all times.

A small fish was swimming in the water, followed by a big one. The small fish said to the big fish, "How perfect. In the previous life, you were my daughter, and in this life, you are my mother! Let's be together forever, never to be parted."

I woke up, my ears still ringing with that voice, which sounded exactly like my mother's. Her face? Of course, identical to my mother's.

ABOUT THE AUTHOR

Photo © 2012 Ling Daijun

Hong Ying was born in Chongqing, China, and began her writing career as a poet. In 1990, she relocated to London and authored over a dozen books, some of which have been adapted for television or film. She is best known in the English-speaking world for *Daughter of the River*, *Summer of Betrayal*, and *K: The Art of Love*. Her memoir *Daughter of the River* has been translated into thirty languages, and *K: The Art of Love* won the Premio Letterario Merck Award in 2005. Hong Ying currently resides in Beijing.

ABOUT THE TRANSLATORS

Gary Xu is a scholar, author, translator, and art curator. He is a professor of the Department of East Asian Languages and Cultures at the University of Illinois.

Shelly Bryant divides her year between Shanghai and Singapore, working as a poet, writer, and translator. She is the author of seven volumes of poetry, a pair of travel guides for the cities of Suzhou and Shanghai, and a book on classical Chinese gardens. Bryant's poetry has appeared in journals, magazines, and websites around the world, as well as in several art exhibitions. Her translation of Sheng Keyi's *Northern Girls* was long-listed for the Man Asian Literary Prize in 2012.

Nick Brown is a London-based musician and translator. Through his work in both fields, Brown has explored the languages and cultures of Europe, Asia, and North America.

Made in the USA
Middletown, DE
15 August 2020

14813697R00210